D1049688

The Non-Verbal Method in Working With Groups

The Non-Verbal

Method in Working With Groups

RUTH R. MIDDLEMAN

ASSOCIATION PRESS · NEW YORK

THE NON-VERBAL METHOD IN WORKING WITH GROUPS

Association Press, 291 Broadway, New York, N. Y. 10007

The quote from Frank Lloyd Wright appearing on page 269 is from a Sunday morning talk to the architectural apprentices of the Taliesin Fellowship, *House Beautiful*, November, 1955.

First Printing, 1968
Second Printing, 1969
Third Printing, 1970

Standard Book Number: 8096-1661-0
Library of Congress catalog card number: 68-11491

PRINTED IN THE UNITED STATES OF AMERICA

For Karl and Phil Middleman
who have shared their mother so much
with the typewriter

Foreword

Purpose, Form, Content, Process—these are the interrelated themes of this volume, providing a theoretical base for the use of non-verbal media in helping people to communicate with others and to develop social strengths. Although this book is addressed primarily to social group workers and educators, its content undoubtedly will be of interest to others concerned with non-verbal media as experienced in groups.

The uniqueness of the author's approach lies in her consistent emphasis on purpose, as it gives direction to the selection and development of program activities with groups. This particular book could have been written only by a social worker, for there is constant reference to social group work purpose as it must be reflected in the worker's use of non-verbal media. Does the activity enhance group relations? Does it help the participants to increase their sense of individual self-value and to feel more connected with others? Mrs. Middleman invites the reader to consider such questions in his use of program.

This is in no sense a "how-to-do-it" book; nor is it a text on how to teach courses in the use of program to social work students. Although both of these elements are present, they are given validity and depth by the substantial material of the first half of the book. A strong case is made for the use of non-verbal media as an integral part of the whole group work process, requiring all the qualities of social group work skill. The underlying theory presented here is *process* based, with its essential aspects of engagement and of time phases. Program is not separate from all this, but part of it, in the same way that courses in its use are integral to the social group worker's education. Education in the professional social worker's use of program, including actual introduction to a variety of activities, can be as scholarly and "graduate" in quality as any other course in the curriculum. The fact that this view is not generally held is discussed in the author's brief review of the historical development of social group work and education for it; in this review she focuses on the changing view of the place of program and its use in the curricula of schools of social work. An increasing number of schools are giving consideration to the introduction or re-introduction into the curriculum of courses in the use of program in social group work. For the educators in these schools, this book will be especially timely.

Ruth Middleman writes with authority from her experience in social work practice as group worker, supervisor, and consultant in a variety of social agencies—group-service, child-placing, and residential treatment centers; from her fourteen years of teaching the professional use of non-verbal media to group work students in the University of Pennsylvania School of Social Work; from her teaching of occupational therapy students in this University's School of Allied Medical Professions; and from her lively and developed interest in creative arts and aesthetics.

There is a strong hint throughout the book that in social group work practice is an art. Creative experience, Mrs. Middleman submits, does not spring up intuitively but must be developed in an ordered way if it is to give satisfaction to the creator and be accessible to others. The commentator on a recording of Schumann's Piano Quintet in E Flat (Opus 44) wrote: ". . . we must agree with Schumann that sequential patterns are perfectly suited to the nature of his material, and that he has brought about that perfect wedding of form and content that is among the highest aims of art." To this aim, Mrs. Middleman has added the achievement of social work purposes toward which group members are helped through engagement with others in non-verbal activities.

As the author's colleague in the education of many generations of group work students, I have seen the effect the approach to using non-verbal media presented here has had on their knowledge and their practice. As group work services rapidly expand, it is important that the professional use of program activities be understood conceptually and that it be valued. It is with profound satisfaction that I welcome the addition of this book at this time to the formulation of social group work theory, which group workers are now so actively pursuing, and its contribution toward increasingly helpful and skillful social group work practice.

HELEN U. PHILLIPS

Philadelphia

Contents

The Eternal Twins

Taking fun
   as simply fun
and earnestness
   in earnest
shows how thoroughly
   thou none
of the two
   discernest.

—Piet Hein

Introduction

> *. . . I stepped back from open-faced lyricism of uncontrolled expression (of my adolescent years) to a groping, self-conscious and thoughtful effort, creating according to the pull of intellect. In celebrating the purely intuitive, the intellectually involuntary, the unbridled, the freely formed, one celebrates a romance. For me, human accomplishment, its past, its future lies in the conscious apprehension of the universe, and in deliberate controlled acts of creation.*
>
> —Lorraine Hansberry *

This book is the outcome of a deep concern about all kinds of program activities that I have had for many years. I think I was thirteen years of age when I began to write down the words of all the camp and folk songs that I knew because I realized I would forget them otherwise. I still have and cherish that bulky, loose-leaf book that became my own personal songbook, and I have been a collector ever since—of songs, games, dances, craft ideas, and the whole range of program content.

Then after many years of camping and a more disciplined study of activities as a student at the University of Pittsburgh in health, physical education, and recreation, I was enchanted to find when I enrolled as a social group work student in the School of Applied Social Sciences, University of Pittsburgh, that these activities were considered an important necessity for a student of social work. Gladys Ryland, then preparing the manuscript with Gertrude Wilson of what was to be called *Social Group Work Practice*, had a masterful appreciation for, and knowledge about, all

* "Playwriting: Creative Constructiveness," *The Creative Use of the Unconscious by the Artist and by the Psychotherapist, Annals of Psychotherapy*, Vol. 5, No. 1 (1964).

kinds of program, and she stimulated her students to dance long hours up in the studio, to want to learn more about games, to work with clay, and to spend a good amount of time gaining experience in trying out a variety of non-verbal activities.

Naturally I was delighted when in 1950 I was asked to teach just such a program course at the University of Pennsylvania School of Social Work. And I have been at it ever since. While at the outset the title of this course was Program Skills and the exposure of the students to the various activity interests that their groups would probably have was patterned after what had been developed in Pittsburgh, gradually over the years we evolved our own emphasis and focus that parted company from the curriculum as offered at the University of Pittsburgh.

The title of the class became The Use of Program in Social Group Work Practice and the emphasis shifted from a concern about quantity of content and competence in execution to one about the special use the social group work student would need to make of the various program media *because he was a social worker.* Rather than aiming to develop "skills"—skill in music, skill in games, skill in dance, and all the rest—we unified the challenge to become the development of *one skill*—skill in the use of whatever medium was being utilized with any group at any particular time. This demand at once simplified and complicated matters. While less proficiency was demanded in every content field, more deliberate and responsible *use* was expected of all.

During the years since 1950 the interest in retaining and refining this course as an integral part of the curriculum for social group work students has not been just my own. Dr. Helen U. Phillips, Chairman of the Social Group Work Department, provided much support and stimulation of ideas in helping to relate this course to its place of deep connection with the Social Group Work Practice course. Dr. Ruth E. Smalley, Dean of the School of Social Work, has supported its necessity in the face of mounting pressure for more and more course content to properly equip the graduate for professional practice. Dr. Harold Lewis, Chairman of Research, has over the years stimulated my imagination, helped me conceptualize in broader terms my particular interests, and sparked my desire to pursue my hunches and intuitions in a more orderly and disciplined form; he is one who values the potential for adding to knowledge that further study of non-verbal and cultural achievements presents.

This book is an attempt to pull together and share with others my approach to the use of program with groups, which will now be termed *the use of the non-verbal method.* That I have included certain program forms which are in actuality quite verbal in their application—the use of drama, role playing, puppets, and the tape recorder, for example—must be allowed because of their deep symbolic and non-verbal implications as far as the choice of content is concerned. Actually "non-verbal" is used broadly in this book since there is no precise word to suit my purposes. The reader will note in the program excerpts included here a mixture of doing and talking. Perhaps it will be well to consider these content forms as "doing-oriented" or "acting-out media." At least, the emphasis on *action* as a point of departure in the program content rather than on verbalization is the unifying concept which "non-verbal method" is intended to convey.

The impetus toward this book has come from the requests of many of my colleagues who are teachers of social group work in other schools of social work. They have, over the years, expressed curiosity about our approach at the University of Pennsylvania School of Social Work. Two chief assumptions that underly this school's approach and lend uniqueness to its frame of reference as far as social work education is concerned are:

(1) Competence in the use of the non-verbal method of communication with groups and with individuals is so important to effective practice that an extra practice course in *the social work use* of such activities belongs in the graduate, professional curriculum. Some schools of social work have moved away from a concern with program content altogether, relying upon undergraduate education to supply the knowledge and experiences with concrete forms. Other schools have continued to focus a program course on providing the beginning worker with a range of experiences in various activities in order to develop some competence in them. We at the University of Pennsylvania place em-

phasis squarely on the application and relevance of such activities to social work's goals.

(2) The same teacher, rather than various specialists in the different content forms, is responsible for all the teaching in every content. Thus, the wholeness expected of the worker in practice is demonstrated in his training and experienced by him. It seems crucial to me that this class itself be both a doing kind of group experience and one that by the discussion method analyzes implications in the use of non-verbal content as well as that it possess a demonstrated unity in the person of the teacher.

This book is written primarily (a) to help group workers and others employed in group service agencies and in the special settings more recently making use of the social group work method—institutions, hospitals, and social agencies in which the social casework method had previously been the main avenue of service; and (b) to help "learners" in group work gain new insight and skill. "Learners" includes social group work students in graduate schools of social work and group workers involved in in-service training and staff development programs. This book may also be useful to caseworkers who have turned to the use of the group as a means of helping people. Also, I hope, practitioners from other professions who work with groups—teachers, recreation leaders, occupational therapists, psychiatrists, psychologists—may find something here that would be pertinent for their work.

I am speaking in this book, however, essentially to the social group worker, and draw all recorded excerpts of practice from the work of students or graduates of schools of social work with specialization in social group work. In contrast, I have tried to dip freely into the literature of other related professions as they have viewed non-verbal content for their own work in my development of some of the theoretical discussion. It is possible that with a base this broad as a point of departure group leaders, group workers, and group therapists of professions outside social work might make their own application of these concepts to their practice.

My approach in this book is primarily educative. It is strongly social-value oriented, that is, toward the thesis that it is desirable to learn to get along with others—to develop socially. This basic goal would hold true for all individuals—the ones who come to groups to pursue "normal" developmental needs and interests as well as those who come with special problems or handicaps and participate in the group for a rehabilitative purpose. *Growth of the self for all persons, whatever their particular situation in life might be,* is held out as the major challenge for the social group worker. The emphasis is not on the relation between non-verbal content and psychological goals per se, although pervasive implications exist along these lines. The psychological goals are viewed as important factors but not the only ones influencing group members and worker. To some practitioners who view their goals as strictly "treatment," this might be a disappointment. The broader focus here, on the individual coping with his social situation, is what I view as "social work." Nor does this book attempt to discuss the relationship between the goals of social group work as herein elaborated and the therapeutic goals of other professions in their work with individuals in groups (psychiatry, psychology, recreation).

Presented here are four major aspects of an approach to the use of non-verbal content with groups.

(1) A discussion of some key concepts and principles with a consideration of their historical development within the profession of social work as well as other professions—psychiatry, psychology, education, recreation. Out of these concepts some beginning theory of the use of non-verbal content is developed.

(2) A selection of anecdotal accounts—non-verbal vignettes—presented in a planned sequence. These case studies illustrate the concepts and principles and also serve as a source of ideas for program.

(3) A suggested guide to the reader for the analysis of non-verbal content as well as a chapter which focuses his attention upon exercises in learning to analyze his own non-verbal content according to certain proposed dimensions.

(4) A bibliography of books offering concrete non-verbal program collections with special emphasis on the writings of the last twenty years.

The case studies are a compilation primarily of the work of the students who, as students, look so critically at what they did and how they did it. It is assumed that the reader will get the message from the very imperfections of practice as well as from the moments of justifiable pride in a new insight well applied. I, in most instances, have added the *why*, that is, the purpose, to the discussions of the anecdotes since that is what the students are groping to understand.

These case studies are presented around certain major areas of focus. Three major categories spring from the point in time in a group's life when the content is introduced: (1) the beginning, (2) the developmental, and (3) the ending activities. Within each of these categories are illustrations that focus on the use both for the group as a whole and for the individuals—the dual focus that is characteristic of the group worker's methodology. The category of *developmental activities* is subdivided into several sub-purposes that have to do with such matters as these:

The use of rules
Competition and cooperation
Worker's role within the activity
Expressing feeling about one's self and others
Understanding the underlying purpose for the group experience
Accepting responsibility
Relating ordinary group chores to gamelike incentives
Aggression

I wish to gratefully acknowledge the contributions of the many workers within twenty-two agencies * whose material I have used. This compilation itself reflects the breadth of the contribution of the social group work method to all age groups in many diverse settings. The purpose of the agency and the worker will

* See Appendix C, page 275, for listing of agencies.

be either the fun and socializing experiences of those groups meeting in settlement houses, YM–YWHA's and Jewish Community Centers, housing projects, and camps or the rehabilitative purposes contributed by experiences with groups from physical rehabilitation centers, homes for the aged, residential care, a Department of Public Assistance, institutions for the delinquent, for the unmarried mother, meetings for the discharged psychiatric patient, and for children living in foster families.

Of the illustrations given in this book fifty-one are drawn from work with children, twenty-two with teen-agers, seven with young adults, five with older adults, and four with adults. As far as settings are concerned, forty-three are from work in settlements, housing projects, YM–YWHA's and Jewish Community Centers, thirty-four from institutions, six from foster children living in the community, two from groups of discharged psychiatric patients in the community, and one each from mothers receiving Aid to Families with Dependent Children and teen-agers in a summer camp. Five excerpts from class sessions with social group work students are also used.

The particular activities focused on in the records are as follows:

Activity	*Frequency*
Games	45
Arts or crafts	13
Drama, dress-up, puppets, stories	13
Groups tasks (e.g., clean-up)	11
Dancing	10
Gymnastics, races, stunts	9
Sports	8
Parties	8
Eating	8
Trips	5
Cooking	5
Singing, song-games	5
Doll play	1
Personal hygiene	1
	142

Considered from the standpoint of age range, setting, or variety of activity-form, this collection is varied and also representative of what is happening in the field of group experiences as a whole. No attempt was made to enumerate the quantities of verbal programming and it can be assumed that there was verbal interaction and discussion in all examples. It is hoped that the reader will develop a respect for the thoughtful search for the effective way of communicating—with diverse age groups through various program media—and for the meaning and value of the non-verbal in the lives of people as well as the complexity of professional skill demanded in its application by such a wide range of possible content choices.

Although the size of the group of workers whose records have been used makes the naming of each person impossible, their contribution in making this book possible and in keeping their observations closely related to the realities of present-day practice is deeply appreciated. I alone am responsible for the judgments and discussion of the examples and claim the burden of their imperfections.

Acknowledgment is also made to the help of the many students whose thoughtful and selective search of the literature of non-verbal content has contributed to the development of the resources bibliography.

That my thinking has been influenced by the writings of many others both within the profession of social work and within the several other professions similarly concerned with methods of non-verbal communication can best be acknowledged by urging the reader to note their names as they appear in the notes. My special thanks go to my friends and fellow social workers who were kind enough to read this book in manuscript form and make helpful suggestions, particularly Mrs. Renee Levine, my colleague at the University of Pennsylvania School of Social Work who also teaches courses in the use of program, and Frank Seever, with whom I have bandied ideas and hunches and experiences back and forth for many years. Special appreciation is expressed to Dr. Elizabeth A. Lawder, Executive Director of the Children's Aid Society of Pennsylvania, for reading and approving my use of the many record excerpts drawn from practice at this agency.

Dr. Arnulf M. Pins, Executive Director of the Council on Social Work Education, read the manuscript with an eye that reflected his own perceptive knowledge, understanding, skill, and experience, and offered suggestions that have immeasurably improved its contents. Finally, I wish to thank Robert A. Elfers of Association Press for his encouragement and suggestions that have helped me put my ideas into a more meaningful form.

My major hope for this book is to convey my belief that a creative use of non-verbal forms is less a matter of intuition applied by those special persons who are exceptionally gifted or interested in this aspect of group work and more a matter of a disciplined, learnable approach that can be mastered by any thoughtful, persistent learner who is willing to submit to the rigors of professional preparation demanded by this kind of activity.

RUTH R. MIDDLEMAN

1 The Evolution of Social Group Work—With Emphasis on the Increased Need for Competence With the Non-Verbal Method

> *Life must be lived as play, playing certain games, making sacrifices, singing and dancing, and then a man will be able to propitiate the gods, and defend himself against his enemies, and win the contest.*
>
> —Plato, *Laws,* 803–4

Early Roots

Social group work began as "group work" with its own unique history and heroes. It was not part of the mainstream of social work, which in the early days was synonymous with casework, as far as method was concerned. Social group work's ideological roots were in the self-help and informal recreational organizations, such as the YMCA, the YWCA, settlements, scouting, and Jewish Centers, and also in progressive education. The major thrust of the early group-serving agencies was toward the normal, rather than the maladjusted, person who would seek service primarily during his "leisure" hours. He came for recreation, education, enjoyment, and the development of special skills and interests. In the mid-thirties Grace Coyle distinguished group work from the rest of social work by its focus on the more nearly normally adjusted individual as well as by the fact that it was used by people of all strata of society rather than the lower economic classes alone.[1]

If the group work were at all problem-focused, then clearly the problem was of society's, and not of the individual's, making. The exponents of group work were imbued with the ideals of democracy and with the idea that all members of society should share in its benefits. And the small group was viewed as an ideal laboratory where individuals could learn the skills of getting along with each other and with the rest of the world. The origins of the various group-serving agencies reveal the intention of helping certain groups of people learn to cope with the particular problems of their situation.

For example, the settlements were concerned with the various immigrant groups who arrived in the "land of opportunity" and most frequently found themselves huddled together in the least desirable sections of the big cities. They needed to learn the ways of America. The settlements' services covered the gamut of the concrete needs that all individuals have—English classes, health clinics, legal and housing counseling, nurseries, credit unions, recreation, vacations, and the like. By the twenties and thirties the settlements modified their drive toward strict Americanization by deliberately adding programs to preserve the various ethnic identities of their members. The Jewish Centers were similarly set up to help the immigrant find his way, but from their inception also stressed the center as an institution for perpetuating Jewish identity among its members.

The YMCA and the YWCA, likewise, held as part of their goals the imparting of Christian values and a "good" way of life to the young men and women newly arrived in the big city. Often these newcomers came from the farms seeking economic betterment, and were as confounded as the immigrants by the morass of stimuli in the big city. As women began to find their way into industry and business after World War I, the YWCA was in the forefront of the struggle for the rights of women; voting rights, the eight-hour day, union participation, and the development of work skills were among the concerns.

The boys' clubs, scouting, and the recreation movements grew up around a concern for the rights of children, particularly children of the big city. These organizations expounded the need of children for play and recreational outlets. They stressed the development of character that accompanies the mastery of skills and the experience of playing with others under adult leadership. They were also concerned that city children have the opportunity to get back to nature and learn firsthand the lessons of life that come from direct experience with the natural environment. Camping and skill in the outdoors were stressed as a vital part of America's heritage for children.

That group work should be equally affected by and bound up with the reforms in education that were termed "progressive education" was historically inevitable. Like the leaders within recreation, the leaders of this movement—John Dewey, William H. Kilpatrick, and others—were concerned with the rights of children and how they can effectively learn skills for living. Dewey's efforts were aimed toward socializing the school systems, toward combating the ill effects of the school as a rigid institution. Again, the small group was stressed and self-determined and self-motivated learning—learning by doing—was stressed. Kilpatrick saw "group work" as a method to be used to advantage within the field of education.[2]

Perhaps the most significant contribution of the progressive education school of thought was to point its finger toward the teacher and cause him to look self-consciously at his teaching method. The old-line autocrat was held in disrepute. Instead, a more benign, encouraging teacher who looked harder at his group, as a group, was sponsored. Education for a democracy was seen as starting within a more democratically oriented classroom situation where children were encouraged to interact with each other, learn from each other, and discover solutions for themselves. If the class group were to function more democratically, then the teacher had to teach less controllingly.

The influence of progressive education concepts on the kindergarten movement and preschool education of the day was marked. The teachers of young children eagerly incorporated into their work the small interacting group as a valuable medium for the child to begin to learn to share with others, to give and take, and to give up his need to be the center of attention all the time. Less tied down to formalized curriculum demands, the kindergarten teacher was free to experiment and innovate in the area of learning—helping the child to get along with others and to experience a variety of activities through which he could express himself.

Thus in the 1930's a similar concern for the effective use of the group toward democratic ends characterized group work in the fields of informal education, recreation, and education. The group was seen as possessing deep educational potential: individuals would learn to cooperate and get along with others socially; individuals would enrich themselves through new knowledge, skills, and interests; and society itself would be bettered through the group's programs of responsible involvement in community problems. By learning to act more democratically in small groups and by pursuing social action programs that would bring to all members of society the deserved benefits of a democracy, the true heritage of America was to be available to all.

In these early days group work was not geared toward individuals with particular problems. All group members were helped toward normal growth needs and toward desirable social adjustment through experiences that were essentially educative. The person with severe emotional, social, or other problems who appeared in the group was incorporated as much as possible along with his peers or, when this was impossible, was referred for individual attention to a casework agency or psychiatric clinic. Most of the leadership of these groups was in the hands of teachers or of adult volunteers who had found their own niches in various life pursuits and felt they knew enough about certain recreational activities to offer their leadership to others.

Mid-Thirties to Mid-Forties

By 1935 Grace Coyle began more pointedly to separate group work from recreation and lodge it within the field of social work.[3] As the chairman of the new section of Social Group Work of the National Conference of Social Work she began to clarify in writing and in committee work the fact that group work was a method within social work and that recreation and education were other fields (professions) which might include group work as one method. By 1936 the American Association for the Study of Group Work was established, and distributed study outlines for groups in various cities to explore further what was meant by "group work."

Considering the close early identification of group work with the fields of education, recreation, and camping, it must be obvious to the reader that the stress on the *content* of the group experience was marked. In fact, the activities of the group were the most visible, identifiable entity of the group. They were easy for those possessing an interest in working with groups to latch on to. Perhaps the greatest concern of the person who considered doing group work was the problem "What do groups do?" The components of relationship, democratic functioning, and interaction, for example, were more elusive to the untrained eye than the interests, hobbies, talents, and skills in activities that brought people together. Hence, at the outset there was great preoccupation and focus on the activity and program of the group—a definitely mixed blessing which was to hold back in many subtle ways the full flowering of social group work as a theoretically sound method within social work. Even now the misunderstandings and negative connotations held by some of the "activity-centered" aspect of group work affect many practitioners—case workers, psychotherapists, and social group workers themselves.

In their self-conscious fear that the group might be seen as activity-centered rather than person-centered, group workers tended to play down the importance of the activity. It was, in addition, the least familiar aspect of group work to the rest of social work and so it was least appreciated and understood. The adverse effect that the emphasis on excellence in activity content had on a union of group work with the rest of social work can be illustrated by a look at the history of the Chicago community.

Although Chicago is forever distinguished historically by the early development of social services through Hull House and the pioneering work of Jane Addams, professional schools of social work in the city did not assume the responsibility for educating group workers for settlement house and other group work until relatively late, as compared with national developments. The University of Illinois graduated its first class of professionally educated social group workers in the late 1940's. The University of Chicago's School of Social Service Administration, one of the oldest of institutions for the training of social case workers, did not employ a social group work educator to develop a sequence in that field until 1958. This development came only after the faculty, having given careful consideration to social group work through consultation with Grace Coyle, decided that "there was an intellectual base and that theoretical underpinnings were identifiable and could be taught." [4]

This attitude is all the more understandable when one considers the influence of Neva L. Boyd in the 1930's.[5] She was actively interested in the play movement (her early training and experience being in kindergarten work). From 1911 to 1914 she and several associates conducted an experimental school, the first of its kind, for the training of professional play and recreation leaders. In 1927 the school was incorporated into the Sociology Department of Northwestern University and this later became the Group Work Division within the Sociology Department. It was Neva Boyd and her associates and students who provided staff for the Illinois settlements and state institutions—mental hospitals, educational, and correctional institutions.

The theoretical base for the training of these workers derived from the theories of play prominent at that time—the social values of spontaneous play of children and the continuing values of folk games and dances throughout the life span of individuals. A review of Neva Boyd's writings reflects this emphasis.[6] The reader can imagine how foreign this emphasis on play and folk customs must have seemed to the social work educators whose backgrounds stemmed from casework and whose concerns and experience were with the more serious life problems of troubled, inadequate clients. If this were group work, then it was something quite separate theoretically and philosophically from casework, and many years were needed before such a bedfellow could be seriously considered.

Many group workers in various large cities strove to emphasize the components of their methodology that were most closely akin to those of problem-based casework. The group worker did not like looking like a recreation worker or arts and crafts teacher, and so he deliberately put his attention elsewhere. The doing activities developed less status in the eyes of the social worker (and the psychotherapist) than the talking activities that were seen as leading more quickly toward self-understanding, insight, and behavioral change.

A similar development within the field of education can also be noted. Perhaps the greatest criticism of progressive education, which forty years' experience with it has exposed, is that the individuals subjected to it do not learn enough subject matter. Dewey's innovations have been attacked because they concerned themselves so much with the social and emotional adjustment of the learners, overstressing social and affective matters, that the individual did not develop his cognitive understanding sufficiently.[7] This attitude was brought dramatically to national attention in 1957 when the Russians launched their Sputnik.

Progressivism in education has borne to a great extent the brunt of enthusiasms and of criticisms according to the overall political-social climate of the times in which it strove to equip wide masses of students for effective living. Hence, it could hardly be expected to meet the diverse demands made by the vastly changing social conditions that characterized this country throughout its sweep of influence. In the year 1919, when the Progressive Education Association was founded, the social values of the times were ripe for idealism and for all kinds of progressive reform in diverse aspects of American life that was to affect the nation between the two wars. A swing of reaction to conservatism came after World War II, followed by the general alarm of the 1950's, when computers, mass media, automation in industry, and the harnessing of new sources of energy transformed the culture of the day and revealed that new quantities of information were being generated at an astonishing pace and that those preparing to enter this complex world needed to have new ways to assimilate all this.[8]

In fact, the very growth and proliferation of public and private social welfare agencies was one factor arming the opponents of the public schools who criticized their concern with matters other than education. Arthur Bestor was one of the most prolific and eloquent of the many critics of the professionals leading education. He claimed that the ultimate purpose of all education was intellectual training, the deliberate cultivation of the ability to think through training in the basic academic disciplines.[9]

One attempt to evaluate the effectiveness of the progressive approach during a period of progressivism's important influence was the Progressive Education Association's famous Eight-Year Study, 1932–40.[10] This was a minute follow-up study of 1,475 matched pairs of college graduates coming from progressive and from regular secondary school experiences. This study revealed that the balance in all areas studied was tipped in favor of those from the more experimental schools. The report concluded:

> It looks as if the stimulus and the initiative which the less conventional approach to secondary school education affords sends on to college better human materials than we have obtained in the past.[11]

Still, this five-volume report, *Adventure in American Education*, appearing as it did in the middle of a war, has never received the full attention and study it deserved, and its findings in support of a progressive approach were not sufficiently forceful to combat public opinion that was dissatisfied when Sputnik rocked the world. Sobering indeed was the 1958 attack by Admiral Hyman G. Rickover, previously an espouser of progressive education: that America's technical supremacy had been called into question and that the time for educational reform was upon us. Life-adjustment schools were simply not enough to satisfy the aroused parents of the day, and progressive education died a quick death.[12] Since that time, there has been a scurry toward curriculum reform, toward enlisting the help of university teachers—leaders in the forefront of advanced thinking in the sciences, mathematics, and the humanities—to find ways to introduce and make teachable new knowledge to the young.[13]

Although progressive education as a formal movement is gone, it has left an indelible imprint on modern pedagogy. There is still broad concern for "the whole child" and for the importance of a concern about motivating him creatively, despite a renewed curriculum content emphasis. In this whole experience with progressive education exists an important lesson for social group workers. Its success or failure relied to a major extent on the imagination and style of the particular teacher, for few concrete structures and specified content sequences existed for the teacher to follow. In periods when those imbued with the spirit of the movement were motivated by missionary zeal (as with those participating in the Eight-Year Study) it could produce quite exciting results. It could also, in times of less inspired teaching, be quite pallid. Its success in reaching its objectives called for a precision about content as well as methodology in the same way that social group work is learning that it must pay close attention to its methodology (the specific actions of the worker) so that lofty goals can begin to be approached.

But, to return to the early development of group work as a part of social work, it must now be stressed that strong as the education-recreation influence was, this was not the only thinking that influenced, then or now, its concepts. Clara Kaiser distinguishes eight significant thought systems which have given direction and content to the conceptual framework of social group work:

1. The ethical, social and theistic beliefs embodied in the Judeo-Christian religions.
2. The humanitarian movement of the late 19th century which found expression in the social settlement movement in England and later in the United States.
3. The educational philosophy of John Dewey and his followers who formulated the theories of progressive education.
4. The theories of certain early sociologists who saw in the small group the key to studying the relation of the individual to society, especially Durkheim, Simmel, Cooley, Mead.
5. Recent basic research in small group theory by social scientists, such as Kurt Lewin, Moreno, Elton, May and Merton.
6. The democratic ethic not only as it applies to a political system, but as it permeates all forms of social relationships, and as expressed in the writings of such authors as Mary Follett and Edward C. Lindeman.
7. The psychoanalytic school of psychiatry.
8. The values, principles, and methods of social work as the profession within which social group work has developed.[14]

Mid-Forties to Mid-Fifties

By 1946, due to the efforts of many persons such as Grace Coyle, Clara Kaiser, Wilber Newstetter, Gertrude Wilson, and Helen Phillips, group work was more fully rooted within the profession of social work. Some of the group work faculty of Western Reserve University, which had offered the first course in group work in 1923, had moved to Columbia University (then the New York School of Social Work) and to the University of Pittsburgh to establish group work sequences. Similar sequences had begun to be developed in many other schools such as University of Minnesota, University of Pennsylvania, and University of Denver.

Grace Coyle produced two important statements in 1946: The first clearly separated group work from recreation once and for all while the second, with equal sureness, placed it within social work. In the group work section meetings of the 1946 National Conference of Social Work, G. Ott Romney delivered a paper, "The Field of Recreation," which was followed by a companion statement from Coyle, "Social Group Work in Recreation."[15] Romney spoke movingly and clearly of recreation:

> Recreation as an end in its own right—as a definable, distinguishable, identifiable something—suffers from inaccurate and fragmentary interpretation. It is frequently confused with its dividends (as in health, education, therapy, democracy, character-building, and physical conditioning) and with its methods (as in social group work). . . . Recreation includes everything the individual chooses to do in his own time for the gratification of the doing . . .[16]

Grace Coyle continued this distinction in her presentation, beginning with the following one statement:

> Recreation is a function to be performed; social group work is one method of fulfilling that function. . . .
>
> Social group work arose out of an increasing awareness that in the recreation-education activities which went on in groups there were obviously two dimensions—activity, including games, discussions, hikes, or artistic enterprise, on the one hand, and, on the other, the

> interplay of personalities that creates the group process. To concentrate on one without recognizing and dealing with the other is like playing the piano with one hand only. Program and relationships are inextricably intertwined. Social group work method developed as we began to see that the understanding and the use of the human relations involved were as important as the understanding and use of various types of program.[17]

The second piece of major importance in 1946 was Grace Coyle's "On Becoming Professional." In her discussion of developing a professional consciousness, she referred to a then-current baffling problem that plagued practitioners: "We must, it seems, be either educators or social workers." She continued with the further vital message:

> While group work as a method developed in the recreation and informal-education agencies, it should be used in, and in fact is spreading into, agencies with other functions, such as children's institutions, hospitals, or churches. . . . A large part of our difficulty in knowing what we are has come out of the words "social work." To many people, they connote relief, or dealing with the poor, or uplift, or some other unpleasant facet of life. . . . My own hope is that the emerging definition of social work may define it as involving the conscious use of social relations in performing certain community functions, such as child welfare, family welfare or health services, recreation, and informal education.[18]

According to Coyle casework, group work, and community organization were all based on understanding human relationships, and shared a similar underlying philosophy and approach—respect for personality, and belief in democracy.

Through such efforts at clarification group work practitioners were urged to seek an identity with the rest of social work, unfamiliar as some of its concerns seemed, rather than with education. The American Association for the Study of Group Work had become in 1946 the American Association of Group Workers with some twenty-three hundred members. In 1949 this association published a report entitled "Definition of the Function of the Group Worker." The beginning sentence of this statement now placed in first order the group process; activities had moved into second place. The current attention of the leaders of the profession was expressed as follows and has remained in this sequence ever since:

> The group worker enables various types of groups to function in such a way that both group interaction and program activities contribute to the growth of the individual and the achievement of desirable goals.[19]

This first attempt at definition was primarily descriptive of the conditions conducive to the practice of group work and the values and knowledge underpinning this practice. It was not the time yet for discrete attention to how this would be done, i.e., what comprised the *skill* that was uniquely the social group worker's.[20] The methodological aspects were handled by such vague references as "groups function *in such a way that* . . ." or "*Through experience he* (the group worker) *aims to produce* these relationships. . . ."

To pursue this book's concern with the role of non-verbal content, certain other references from this definition that pertain especially to this area are now lifted out of the total statement and restated here:

> He [the group worker] is aware of both program activities and of the interplay of personalities within the group and between the group and its surrounding community. . . .
>
> According to the interests and needs of each, he assists them to get from the group experience the satisfactions provided by the program activities, the enjoyment and personal growth available through the social relations, and the opportunity to participate as a responsible citizen. . . .
>
> The group worker makes conscious use of his relation to the group, his knowledge of program as a tool, and his understanding of the individual and of the group process. . . .[21]

The value placed on the conscious use of program activities is unmistakable. It is also significant, however, that when this same statement discussed the knowledge base that undergirds the practice of group work, the need for knowledge about program content and activities was ignored. Reference was made to the importance of knowledge of individual and group behavior, of social conditions and community relations, which is based on "the modern social sciences." How the group worker was to get his knowledge about program content that would become a necessary condition for his thoughtful use of it remains a mystery.

Clara Kaiser acknowledged this omission in her discussion of the 1949 definition of the function of the group worker in the following way:

> In spite of this affirmation of the indivisibility of the significance of the quality of the social processes engendered in group life and the intrinsic values of the group's activities, there has been some tendency to subordinate the latter to the former ingredient in pursuing the objectives of the social group work process. Perhaps it is necessary to rethink the concept of program activities as *tools* or *media* rather than ends in the process of developing the intellectual, social, and emotional potentials of the individual and the effectiveness of the group in accomplishing a progressively more meaningful and significant task.[22]

This backward look and wistful glance at the previously emphasized program content, this acknowledgment of its importance to effective social group work practice, this wonder about the more hidden depths of its potential, has continued right up to the present time to reappear in the thoughtful speculations of those concerned with the contribution of the social group work method.

By the end of the 1940's social group work had its "Definition of the Function of the Group Worker"; regularly appearing definitions of "social group work" in the *Social Work Yearbook;* a professional organization with chapters in various cities, The American Association of Group Workers; a professional publication, *The Group;* and a regular established place within the National Conference of Social Work, where practitioners and educators could get together to present papers for mutual stimulation, clarification, and enrichment. Several new textbooks had been published that served to formalize the thinking of the day and enrich the conceptual base and the practice of social group work practitioners and students.[23]

Social Group Work Practice by Gertrude Wilson and Gladys Ryland contained the most thorough exposition on the area of program content of any of the early texts and of any text that has been published since 1949. Part II of this book is entitled "Analysis of Program Media" and the ensuing chapters deal with such topics as the values of play, the values of games, and the values of rhythms. This volume was most important historically, for it was the first to make available to social group workers in one source the accumulated thinking about the underlying values of non-verbal content as viewed and developed by professions other than social work—psychiatry, psychology, education, and recreation primarily—using such content as well as those understandings which had been developed within social work itself. The recorded excerpts highlighted the potential and the values of each medium. The book served as an excellent beginning charge to the social group work student and practitioner to consider carefully what he introduced into his group and to value its helpfulness as an agent of growth and change for the group and its members. Its most serious lack, which was inevitable considering the date of its appearance, was of an analysis of its *use* by a social group worker with particular emphasis upon relating the content to the particular purposes of social work.

Reexamining the recorded excerpts, one can find the omission of such things as just what the worker did and why. The documentation is there for the *value* part, but the next step had yet to be taken, i.e., asking the question, How is the content purposefully applied, given these values? Perhaps such a connection between social work purpose and the use of program had to await another decade's emphasis on clarification of the unique purposes of the social group worker in his engagement with groups. Since the appearance of *Social Group Work Practice* the number of books and articles which have extended the theoretical and conceptual base of the social group work method has increased substantially,[24] making possible additional contributions of a more definitive nature within the area of the use of program content.[25]

During the 1950's social group work further clarified its own distinctiveness and moved into many more schools of social work throughout the United States and Canada as a method to be taught to students who wished to specialize in this practice as well as to students of casework. It moved as a method of practice into many "specialized" settings previously reserved for the practice of casework, and united with other professional groups within the social work profession to form the National Association of Social Workers in 1955. As a helping method that used the group as its unique medium for offering service, social group work now wrested itself from the growing field of social psychology termed group dynamics and also distinguished its methodology from the similarly developing specialization of group psychotherapy.[26] The process toward a definite identity was not unlike what had happened earlier with respect to the field of recreation.

By now social group work was being tested as a method for reaching persons with a variety of developmental problems in a wide range of settings. The responsiveness of certain individuals to the medium of the group in contrast to their resistance to more individualized service was exciting, both to the group work practitioner and to the other social workers in the host setting to which he brought his skills.[27] Social-group-work-educated graduates were attracted into the so-called "special settings," e.g., medical and psychiatric hospitals, institutions, programs for the handicapped, and child guidance centers, in ever-increasing numbers for a variety of reasons. For some it was the opportunity to remain in direct group work practice rather than move into supervision and administration and to sharpen the basic skills of direct service. For still others, it seemed to be more important or more nearly like "social work." For others matters of prestige, working conditions, and salaries made such a move important. A study by Gladys Ryland of employment responsibilities of social group work graduates of 1953 and 1954,[28] found more than one third of the graduates in their first job employed in the special settings. Statistics on the decade of the 1950's show in the total national picture a trend similar to the Ryland survey. A report of the U.S. Department of Labor indicates:

> In 1960 about 116,000 persons were employed in social welfare positions. Three-fourths of the 62% doing direct-service were specialized in casework, 9% were specialized in group work, and 7%

in community organization. Of those who specialized in group work (15,404), 10,456 were employed in programs termed "group work" and 4,888 (almost one-third) in other programs—public assistance, family service, child welfare, etc. Of the 76,464 workers whose special training was casework, none reported engaging in a basic program called "group work." This would suggest a primary job identification of casework even when the worker might also be doing some work with groups.[28]

The movement into the new settings was cause for alarm in some quarters and still persists to the present day. Some professionals call for a return to the social action commitment and heritage of the early group work practice and others proclaim that the present shortage of professionally educated social group workers demands that priorities be set so that the limited expertise can be most effectively used, and that the priorities should be within the treatment, corrective, and rehabilitative functions of group work.[30]

Mid-Fifties to Mid-Sixties

By the end of 1956 the Commission on Social Work Practice of the newly created National Association of Social Workers developed a "Working Definition of Social Work Practice" which attempted to set encompassing criteria that pertained to casework, group work, and community organization. The following points drawn from this definition are pertinent to the focus of this book:

> Under the discussion of necessary *Knowledge*, the practice of the social worker is guided by:
>
> Ways in which people communicate with one another and give outer expression to inner feelings, such as words, gestures, and activities.
>
> Group process and the effects of groups upon individuals and the reciprocal influence of the individual upon the group.
>
> Self-knowledge, which enables the individual practitioner to be aware of and to take responsibility for his own emotions and attitudes as they affect his professional function.

Under the discussion of *Method* (an orderly systematic mode of procedure) a list of *Techniques* (instruments or tools used as a part of the method) is developed:

Use of activities and projects

Provision of positive experiences.[31]

The "Working Definition of Social Work Practice," in contrast to the 1949 "Definition of the Function of the Group Worker," acknowledged that the worker needs *knowledge* about ways in which people communicate and about activities. However, when *techniques* are discussed as a part of *method,* the two techniques mentioned above—the use of activities and projects, and the provision of positive experiences—are in fact ways of actualizing the rest of the techniques, which will now be elaborated:

1. Support
2. Clarification
3. Information-giving
4. Interpretation
5. Development of insight
6. Differentiation of the social worker from the individual or group
7. Identification with agency function
8. Creation and use of structure
9. Teaching
10. Stimulation of group interaction
11. Limit-setting
12. Utilization of available social resources
13. Effecting change in immediate environmental forces operating on the group
14. Synthesis

As the central thesis this book will attempt to show in subsequent chapters, activities and projects and positive experiences are primarily a means of communication and use, most frequently, the non-verbal method of communication. As such, they belong along with *talking* as a means for effecting these other *techniques.*

Another statement was developed in 1956, *The Practice of Social Group Work,*[32] which attempted to distinguish between social group work and work with groups. This source defined social group work as:

> A service to groups where the primary purpose is to help members improve their social adjustment, and the secondary purpose is to help the group achieve objectives approved by society . . . the definition assumes that the members of groups receiving social group work services *have* adjustmental problems . . . and that the programming in the group is determined by the findings of the diagnoses (of the problems of the members).

This statement and its accompanying questionnaire were circulated to all members of the Group Work Section. Less than one fifth of the membership agreed with its narrowness, its focus on the adjustment of the individual and its emphasis on correction and treatment. An emphatic plea to the field in response to this statement and subsequent trends within the thinking of the Group Work Section Practice Committee was developed and circulated by the University of Pittsburgh Graduate School of Social Work.[33] This paper called on the field "to review current trends, to reexamine practice goals and to reaffirm our dedication to enhancing the social realities which shape individual lives." Replying to the emphasis on the individual's social functioning, this position stated, "We are *abandoning our social goals* and making a fetish of method."

A second document of the 1950's that contained implications for the development of social group work was Volume XI of *The Curriculum Study,* conducted by the Council on Social Work Education, entitled *The Social Group Work Method in Social Work Education.*[34] This study attempted a systematic examination of group work concepts and practice through analysis of selected documents, published writings that comprised the new body of group work literature, and certain materials from individual schools; in addition ten schools with group work sequences were visited and four position papers were developed by leading group work educators and appended to the study. This volume serves as a bench mark for assessing the status of group work in the present day, as it pulls together into the one source current thinking, trends, and implications for further clarification.

A small segment of this report deals with non-verbal content. In Chapter III the "Essential Characteristics of Social Group Method on Which to Base Curriculum Objectives" are discussed. The following reference is the third of nine "propositions further identifying the method":

> The group worker is concerned simultaneously with program content, and with the ways in which persons relate to each other. Achievement, however, cannot be measured in content and process themselves, but in relation to the social work goal, enhancement of members' social functioning, as far as this can be observed in changes in thinking and behavior.[35]

This statement parts company with the past in two essential respects: (1) The use of program content is now clearly tied up with the special purpose of social work—enhancement of social functioning. It is not enough that program be "good" or that its process be meaningful. It must contain a social work focus. (2) Further, the actual test of the effectiveness is change in thinking and behavior on the part of the group member.

Chapter IV, which deals with "Learning Experiences and Curriculum Organization," contains a section which attempts to pull together "Common Concepts and Common Components in Social Work Methods." The following paragraph is part of the thread of this book's concern:

> Although the communication skills intensively used in social work, such as interviewing, recording, non-verbal communication, interpretation, role playing, are widely recognized as being needed by both group workers and caseworkers, if not by all social workers, these content items appeared to be distributed fragmentarily between class and field instruction, often without clear assignment of their place in the curriculum. . . . The impression remains that, while these skills are recognized as significant to use of group work method and requiring provision of learning opportunity for students, more development is needed in ways of teaching them.[36]

This reference reveals an interesting trend in social group work's development which grew from its movement into a close relationship to social casework and became increasingly apparent as social workers of both methods compared their concepts and practice and attempted to evolve broad, encompassing generalities that could unite both methods. That is, both methods have a verbal and non-verbal content flow and for group work, this non-verbal communication might include what was termed program activities in the past.

But because the non-verbal or the program activities can be such a huge amount of the interaction experience in social group work, especially in work with children, the drawing of a parallel with social casework presented many problems to be further explored. The *Curriculum Study* found so much diversity of opinion and unresolved question around the area of "Program Media and Program Skills" that it then appended in its report two and a half pages of discussion on the differences expressed around this subject—the largest amount of space allotted to any part of the method in its review! This discussion is reproduced in full in Appendix B.

It would be premature now to try to discuss fully the questions raised in this statement. This whole book, in fact, is an attempt to provide some direction to the many confusions expressed. The *Curriculum Study* reported a consistent view among the schools that they had responsibility to teach a specific theoretical approach to use of program media. But how much actual trying out and evaluation of media is essential to learning theoretical understanding of them is questioned as well as where this learning should take place—in the field or in the school? Again the sensitivity of group workers about emphasis on activities was expressed. Some felt knowledge about various media is more properly derived from the "life-learning" experience of the student.[37] By way of brief argument to such a point of view, this author suggests that a knowledge about childhood or adolescence, for example, sufficiently comprehensive and disciplined to be useful for a social worker's professional practice has never been deemed to be sufficiently obtained through the learner's own life-learning! Furthermore, without a more orderly and professionally oriented approach to this subject area the very objectives of the social group work curriculum [38] which this volume proposes cannot be met. The *Curriculum Study* includes the following statement in its "Suggestions About Unsolved Problems":

> More substantive evaluation is needed of the program media and skills component of group work curriculum, based on results achieved in practice and on growing theoretical knowledge as it becomes available in social work and in allied disciplines.[39]

Clearly, then, there is a charge for necessary further investigation in the future. One final and more encouraging reference from the *Curriculum Study* should be cited as evidence of movement in this direction. In Clara A. Kaiser's position paper, "The Social Group Work Process," attention is drawn to "concepts pertinent to the methodology of the social group work process" as developed in an earlier work of Gisela Konopka [40] in which she describes "guidelines and essential parts of the generic group work method" and which is later again emphasized in Konopka's book, *Social Group Work: a Helping Process:*

> The understanding and conscious use of non-verbal as well as verbal material: I especially put non-verbal material first, since the group worker deals to a large extent with this, especially in work with children. His capacity to use program materials which do not demand verbal expression and yet are helpful should be very wide.[41]

Why is this encouraging? Because this clear statement about the importance of the *conscious* use of non-verbal material is put forth without the earlier sensitivities, without self-consciousness, without an after-thought quality. It is ranked as an entity of major importance at last. That the clarity of the importance of precision in using non-verbal content should be so certain in Konopka's viewpoint is probably due to her years of preoccupation with group work in clinical and rehabilitative settings. Where the bulk of the practice of direct group leadership has been in the hands of the professionally educated worker, the necessity of the group worker's collaboration and scrutiny of the meaning and value of his own work in the treatment process has been insistent due to the simultaneous work of other professional disciplines as part of the team. And the accountability for the quality of the group experience in terms of change in attitude, feeling, and behavior has been emphatic. Furthermore, the very problems of communicating with the emotionally disturbed—the withdrawn, the acting-outers, the regressed, and so on—demanded the use of a non-verbal approach.

The Sixties

During the 1960's the problems of achieving clarity and some degree of consensus among the practitioners of social group work continued to beset the field. Group workers continued to stream toward the therapeutic settings to pursue a direct-service intent.[42] The focus on individual social development, growth, or adjustment consumed a larger part of the attention. In addition, the group workers practicing in the traditional group service agencies, whose focus was more on normal growth and development, were largely performing administrative, supervisory, and planning functions rather than the basic service of group work. With the scarcity of available professionally educated workers in the group work method, coupled with the increase of national awareness of the potential helpfulness of the group method of serving people and the new settings seeking to fill job openings, the controversy still rages. Discussions of setting priorities for the attention of the professional group workers, restructuring community services to further clarify their utilization more effectively, and settling for less than the professionally educated social group worker were frequent.

But although there was broad interest at this time in serving individuals through the group, in the rehabilitative and restorative purposes of group experience, and in the extension of social group work into different settings and fields of practice, this was by no means the total concern of those involved in the development of the method. Reference has already been made to Alan Klein's plea to the field that the traditional concern of group work for social goals not be abandoned.[43] Dorothea Spellman, in a brief but thought-provoking response to the current dilemmas, viewed social work as a continuum of services addressed to a range of needs and group work's competence reserved neither for dysfunctioning individuals alone nor for the range of services to maximize potentials.[44] Rather, she stated, "All social services can use this competence [group work], but with stated criteria for which [ones shall be the various] categories of groups and with defined expectations of the role of the worker." Calling for social group work to concern itself both with the enhancement of social functioning and with major dysfunctioning, Spellman proposed that the extremes of the continuum of needs be the first areas of focus (the range of dysfunctioning and the range of maximizing potentials), while at the same time efforts also be addressed through extended application of movement and measurement scales to "that misty middle" range of situations so that eventually some means of preventing deterioration and of discovering leadership potential could be more discretely initiated here. In short, she called for "a more definitive, non-expedient determination of the use of competence" and placed such matters as the lack of professionally educated manpower to staff the burgeoning needs of vast expansion in all social welfare services as separate issues to be dealt with by measures appropriate to this problem.

The writings of William Schwartz that appeared during these same years called for an increase of attention to that aspect of service uniquely characteristic of group work, that is, the entity of the group itself, as well as a more minute and precise view of the methodological aspects of practice.[45] Speaking historically about the alliance of group work with social work (i.e., casework), Schwartz cited group workers' loss of a certain "spirit of inquiry that had marked their early association with many sources of knowledge and insight" and the substitution, "in many quarters, of the prevailing uncritical acceptance of a single explanation of human behavior . . . the Freudian system—part science, part doctrine—with characteristic missionary enthusiasm, weakening its essential contribution by holding it up as a theory that excluded all other theories. . . .[46] Schwartz further urged that group work stop following the path of casework development and move to identify and elaborate its own unique contribution to social work theory and practice. Speaking of the impossibility of philosophical foundations that emphasized choices between false dualisms—the "psychiatric" and the "social," means and ends, "process" and "content," Schwartz urged the abandonment of such grandiose visions of outcomes and a concentration on hard, step-by-step methods of achieving them.

A recurring theme which occupied Schwartz's central attention was the need for more specificity with *method.* The qualities needed by the group worker—what he knows, believes, is, and hopes to achieve—do not lead to an understanding of what he does, but only give clues to what he needs in order to carry out his function. Schwartz further stated that in describing the nature of the helping process, the description should begin with an assignment of function within the group process, made in terms of concrete and immediate action rather than ultimate, hoped-for outcomes. Schwartz called for a minute examination of method and added, "Method, properly understood, is neither mystical nor mechanical."

In a further attempt to separate professional skill from worker's goals, knowledge, feeling for the client, value commitments, and personal attributes, Schwartz cited the gap between the worker's intent and his effect. To him the very language of the literature illustrated this confusion. "Terms like 'enables,' 'provides for,' 'functions in such a way that,' 'aims to,' and other phrases produced closure without coming to grips with the theoretical problems involved in designing a strategy of professional practice." [47] Schwartz, in short, asked for and offered a functional definition of group work skill through a statement made "in terms of action rather than intent, or function rather than purpose." He attempted to break down the method into its component activities or "tasks" around which the various actions of the worker in any given client-worker system are organized. Schwartz's chief aim was to view the social worker *in action* as a clue toward further understanding of his method.

In his concern for theory building and, more specifically, for closer scrutiny of the group worker in action, Schwartz has very little to say about the use of non-verbal means of communication. In his discussion of "Structural Ordering—The Circumstances Under Which the Group Establishes and Maintains Its Position Within the Agency," Schwartz stated:

> Another important structural aspect lies in the complex of prepared events, activities, and ethnical commitments which agency administrations perceive as integral to their function and as substantial elements in their contributions to group life. Under what conditions do these prepared events and prestructured experiences become functional or dysfunctional for the groups for which they are intended?[48]

No wonder the place of program is left as a confusing, unanswered question in the midst of an elaborated, assuredly presented point of view previously discussed. It seems that the very fixedness and mechanical quality ascribed by Schwartz to program content in this statement would, of necessity, leave it out of his otherwise dynamic view of worker action.

Returning to other developments of the 1960's, with the increased availability of funds, national and state, to further meet the vast problems of unmet human needs, ways to train the "social work associate" or "aid" to offer services to groups and individuals is increasingly popular, most frequently under the direction of the caseworker or psychiatrist. The caseworker has also moved into the area of serving groups of people, but with less self-consciousness about possible gaps in his training and skill in group process than the group worker has felt in turning his attention, when necessary, to serving individuals in the one-to-one situation more intensively.[49] Neither caseworkers nor psychiatrists have drawn to much extent upon the special knowledge and skill of social group work in forming and developing their programs of group services. In one study of 350 psychiatric social workers leading groups, 24 per cent had no training for group leadership.[50] Another study of the backgrounds and professional activities of psychotherapists engaged in group therapy revealed that 59 per cent of the respondents reported that they were self-trained in group psychotherapy.[51]

To meet the mental health needs of large segments of the population, psychiatrists are training non-medical professionals—often college students of psychology, anthropology, and sociology—to become "therapists." The following significant statement was made in the introduction to an issue of *Social Service Review* devoted to "Community Psychiatry and Social Work":

> Of especial interest is the fact that all the discussion groups pointed out the importance of the use of groups in providing services in social agencies. While skilled casework is in no sense outmoded, the caseworker also needs to be able to work with groups.[52]

Clearly then, the rapid proliferation of services to groups among the various fields of social welfare and the direction of these groups by many people not trained in social group work present serious problems in further development and refinement of the method. A recent article which deals in detail with these many problems states:

> The actual array [of various kinds of groups in diverse settings] is testimony to the fact that in social work the use of the group as a medium of service has assumed the proportions of a movement. Indeed the impression is that today, for example, more groups are being led by caseworkers than by group workers.[53]

The authors of this article, Louise Frey and Ralph Kolodny, deal extensively with the problems arising from differences in opinion, orientation, training, special skill, and the like. They made a broad plea that the present state of social work practice with groups, with its many internal contradictions, gives cause for concern and demands much further self-analysis. A further statement of these writers pertains directly to the focus of this book:

> If practitioners only know how to work with members who are prepared to sit down and talk through their intrapsychic problems in the presence of other group members and a leader-therapist, they may be excluding themselves from helping people who could also benefit from a group—but not the kind of group familiar to the worker. There is also the possibility that the client may be forced into a mode of interaction that is not helpful or appropriate for him simply because the worker knows no other way of working or assumes that this is *the* method of social work with groups. . . . There is much to be done by social workers in developing knowledge of, and skill in, practice with groups differentially formed and with technique and objectives related to client need. Such an approach requires additional dimensions in understanding and changes in attitudes about the significance of a variety of forms of group treatment by both group worker and caseworker.[54]

By 1964 a further attempt at distinguishing the practice of social group work appeared, "Working Papers Toward a Frame of Reference for Social Group Work."[55] These "working papers" represented a further attempt to extend the work of professional definition begun by the overall Practice Commission of the NASW with a statement clarifying concepts, ideas, and principles of method for social group work. This statement, the composite work and thinking of many practitioners and educators, is aimed at broad generalizations and abstractions that might bring together the widely divergent thinking characterizing social group work today. The final mimeographed statement was presented as no ultimate, final, or official statement on the nature of social group work, but rather as a working document of a process (the fourth draft!) of an effort to incorporate thoughts and ideas of a wide segment of group workers. The statement accurately portrays the controversies around focus, emphasis, and content between those who would limit social group work to services for normal individuals and groups, and those who would reserve it for corrective services for social dysfunction. The issue now included not only the question of whether these two should be grouped together coordinately, but also of whether those advocating either emphasis could permit in their definition the inclusion of the other focus! This serious ideological conflict is still presently unresolved.

The statement presents in its "Focus" the social group worker as giving simultaneous attention to the group processes and to the functioning of the individual members and as drawing upon knowledge and skill in understanding and acting in each area.[56] However, if the ranking of the five purposes for the method is any guide to an evaluation of current overall emphasis, the balance has been definitely tipped toward therapeutic group work. The corrective and preventive purposes are dealt with first, and the areas of "normal social growth, personal enhancement, and citizenship responsibility and participation" come next.

William Schwartz, in an attempted analysis of the papers,[57] pointed out that as far as purpose and value were concerned the group work definitions were generally assimilable into the framework of the social work definition that was taken as a starting point. In reaching toward greater precision in the purpose area, concepts such as "enhancement of social functioning" seemed more satisfactory than the Practice Commission's reference to "equilibrium" and "disequilibrium." The stress within group work was seen as being strongly on the necessity to conceive of social work purpose in general developmental terms, rather than solely as a therapeutic agent—as a righter of wrongs, curer of illness, strengthener of weakness, and so forth.[58] Schwartz further saw that the "sub-professional" aspects of group work tradition had practically disappeared in the various statements, and the primary effort was definition of an entity that was an integral part of the social welfare field and the social work profession.

Within this massive attempt to delineate the characteristics of social group work within social work, only passing interest and attention was accorded the sub-category within the method followed by this book—the activities and non-verbal content. Each statement differed with respect to its concern with this entity. However, among the questions posed by Ruby Pernell at the 1962 Annual Meeting of the Group Work Section at the National Conference of Social Welfare, "Implications of the Frame of Reference," were these:

> What of the increasing use of groups with a fixed program of discussion which focus on the individual member and his problem, depending on verbal stimulus and support of other group members rather than on aspects of groups process per se? . . . ("group casework"!) . . . How important is program? And what will be its future in the thinking and doing of social group work.[59]

One final point within William Schwartz's analysis must be considered. Commenting on the *knowledge* component, he states that the group work definitions include much the same basic ingredients as the overall social work statement of the working definition. However, he adds that Helen Phillips's statement is useful in that "it is almost unique in its stress on the importance of knowledge about *processes* (the meaning of 'experience' the 'nature of process,' etc.) rather than an exclusive concern with entities (the individual, the group, the community, etc.)." [60] Actually, Helen Phillips also discusses process as an integral part of the method: "The practitioner engages the group members in a process of relating to each other, to the agency, and to the worker." Talking further about process she states:

> The social group worker's major responsibility is to engage the members of the group in interaction with each other and with him (as a representative of the agency), in the development of their group life. He consciously brings to bear his knowledge of the universal time phases of process—beginning, sustaining and ending—both within the time span of each meeting and in the duration of the group's existence. He affects, but does not determine or control the group process.[61]

The focus of this book grows directly out of Helen Phillips's emphasis on the central importance of the worker's responsibility for affecting the group process. If the group process is seen as the conveyor of the group work method, the means of communicating between worker and group members and among the group members themselves, then it can be more clearly seen that part of the process is verbal interaction and part is non-verbal. This book explores the complexities of the non-verbal.

For the Future

The decade of the 1960's then, finds social group work reexamining itself amid the stress of many influences. Some of these can be listed as follows:

1. Further emphasis on clarification of purposes, key concepts, and boundaries within the profession of social work. At the present time several schools of social work have developed a generic approach to teaching casework, group work, and community organization method. Through a variety of different models of curriculum organization they are endeavoring to teach what is felt to be the core knowledge and skills needed by each method and by all methods.
2. Similar strivings for clarification, effectiveness, and innova-

tion within the fields of education, psychiatry, and the behavioral sciences.

3. The insistent need of the field of social welfare to expand services and meet human need more aggressively through extension of group services as well as through innovations in the means of intervention into areas of human problems by the casework, group work, and community work methods.
4. The direct example and influence of community involvement on the part of college students, laymen of all backgrounds, religious leaders in such movements as civil rights, poverty programs, the Peace Corps, and VISTA.
5. The development within all three basic social work methods of a so-called "sub-professional" category of worker with the accompanying demands for broad-scale in-service and staff development training programs. The rising importance of utilizing "indigenous leadership" in various programs as a key means of involving the client directly in the outcome of a program.
6. The infusion into all social work methodology of new concepts of the social sciences concerning such things as reference groups, role theory, transactional and communication systems.

Helen Harris Perlman was asked to sum up the changes within the first decade of the National Association of Social Workers, 1955–65, as far as all three methods of work are concerned.[62] She said the very changing vocabulary of social work indicates a shift in emphasis toward a more aggressive, innovative, and reaching-out mode of action. Social workers are no longer simply "enablers" who help the client adjust, but rather "change agents" who help the client cope with his situation and change it as well as himself.

In discussing changes in group work, Perlman speaks dramatically:

> It has burst the too narrow seams of its basketball uniforms and arts-and-crafts smocks; increasingly it appears in the contrasting

> symbolic garments that bespeak the poles of its present scope—the authority-cool white coats of hospital and clinical personnel and the play-it-cool windbreaker of the street corner gang-worker. . . . At one of its surging edges group work is increasingly involved with the persons, places, problems and even some of the processes that not too long ago were assumed to "belong" to casework.[63]

Earlier in her discussion, Perlman made similar references to changes in caseworkers' practice when she stated that "the caseworker who does not carry at least one group is just plainly out of style." [64] Just where such meanderings into each other's method and setting will carry the field of social welfare is hard to predict. Certainly, it can be safely said, as was emphasized in "A Critique of the Working Definition," [65] that attention to *practice* has shifted toward concern with the "social worker-in-action" as an idea more concrete and more dynamic than the abstraction "social work."

As Perlman discusses "the problems of self-definition" confronting social group work practice today, the confusions and stresses with which it is presently struggling, she makes the following fervent plea to her sister method:

> It would be a service to all social work methods if group work did not too immediately and slavishly imitate the casework model; if, rather, it asked and answered some questions of its own. . . . What is suggested is that group work's present thinking on its problems of method development and practice theory might serve all three social work methods if it did not too quickly surrender its uniqueness for the comfort of prefabricated action principles of another method.[66]

Such sound advice must now be taken seriously! Social group work is now quite well established within the profession of social work as one of its three basic methods. Self-consciousness about its uniqueness and its difference from its elder sister can only hold back the sounder formulation of its theory base, which it has relentlessly searched for throughout the past three decades.

One final event that portends much for the development of the social work profession as a whole is the appearance of Ruth Smalley's new textbook, *Theory for Social Work Practice.* Its uniqueness rests in the fact that it is the first book to present a unified theory applicable to casework, group work, and community organization. From now on, students and practitioners of each basic method will be led more directly to an understanding of the generic base of all methods as well as of the specificity within their own (if their professional education still teaches the methods separately). Smalley attempts to show a unifying process, a social and a psychological basis for all methods, as well as certain generic principles for practice. She is quite clear, however, in her belief that "what is generic to all social work method can be learned and can *best* be learned in a single method, mastered in some depth, rather than through exposure to, or a more superficial experience in, several." [67] She states further:

> . . . [It is] the thesis of this book that, as generic principles of practice are developed, as has been here attempted, it is increasingly possible for a student whose concentration has been in one method to learn to use another in the course of his practice. But it should also be clear that sufficient difference has been identified for each of the methods to suggest a two-year process concentration in one method . . . to produce even a beginning practice skill.[68]

In speaking of the uniqueness of social casework, Smalley sounds a bit like Perlman in her exhortation to group workers quoted earlier that they should not emulate too closely the casework model:

> It seems important to continue to identify and develop that uniqueness in order that the wealth of what is known of one-to-one helping may not be lost through too quick and easy an embracing of a single social work method. Such a move, in practice and education, could detract from the continued development of casework as a process in its own right and from the enrichment its understanding can bring to each and to all of the other social work methods.[69]

Thus, leading social work educators have advised both group workers and caseworkers to value their differences even as they explore their commonalities. Just what the future developments within the profession will be is impossible to predict. The demands of practice as well as the innovations in the methods courses within schools of social work of varying emphases point in the direction of a greater coming-together of the present three methods into one central social work method. And yet, there is caution enough when viewing the uniquenesses of each method, to make unattractive an oversimplified reduction of all methods to one set of basic practice skills. At least it can be said now that much further development still remains in the hands of the future leaders of the profession who may be just now only beginning to learn that there is a profession called "social work."

* * *

The movement of group work from its early identification with the fields of education and recreation to its present firm entrenchment within the profession of social work has carried with it profound changes in ideology, methodology, goals, priorities, and emphases. The change and development must go on! In place of the "group leader," who benevolently or authoritatively *led* his group, is the "group worker," who affects the interactional process and, according to some viewpoints, actively intervenes and instigates change.

A distinction has emerged in the group worker's use of authority. Authoritarian control and determination on the part of the worker has shifted to be more inclusive of the group member's participation in the process. In social work, as in other helping professions, the client is seen to have some authority about his own life situation and some responsibility for control of it.

In this writer's view the main task in reaching out to the hard-to-reach, in involving families as dynamic interacting units, in enhancing the effectiveness of therapeutic milieus, or in communicating with hitherto uninvolved segments of the community, is to help each individual through his encounter with a social worker to know and appreciate more fully his own potential and his own essential freedom as a human being to affect the world about him.

The individual, in knowing more fully his self-responsibility for his actions and his role in the process of changing the social conditions that surround him, has an enhanced awareness of his own personal freedom of choice and its attendant responsibility, which can come to influence not only how he responds to the social worker, but how he responds within the myriad social interactions which are simultaneously confronting him in the rest of his life.

Notes to Chapter 1

1. Margaret E. Hartford, "The Search for a Definition, Historical Review," *Working Papers Toward a Frame of Reference for Social Group Work*, NASW, 1964. Additional references of a historical nature are as follows: Grace L. Coyle, "On Becoming Professional," in Harleigh B. Trecker, ed., *Group Work—Foundations and Frontiers* (New York: Whiteside and Morrow, 1953), pp. 328-42; Clara A. Kaiser, "Group Work Education in the Last Decade," in Trecker, op. cit., pp. 353-69; Charles S. Levy, "From Education to Practice in Social Group Work," unpublished doctoral dissertation, N. Y. School of Social Work, Columbia Univ.; Grace L. Coyle, "Group Work in Psychiatric Settings: Its Roots and Branches," *Social Work* (January 1959); Gisela Konopka, *Social Group Work: A Helping Process* (Englewood Cliffs, N. J.: Prentice-Hall, 1963), Ch. I and II; Konopka, "Group Work: A Heritage and a Challenge," *Social Work with Groups, 1960;* papers from the National Conference of Social Welfare, NASW, N. Y.
2. William Heard Kilpatrick, *Group Education for a Democracy* (New York: Association Press, 1940), p. vii, as quoted by Konopka, *Social Group Work*, p. 11.
3. Grace L. Coyle, "What Is This Social Group Work?" *Survey* (May 1935), and "Group Work as a Method in Recreation," *The Group*, IX (April 1947).
4. Personal communication by Dr. Mary Louise Somers, Professor of Social Group Work, Univ. of Chicago, The School of Social Service Administration.
5. The author is indebted to Mary Louise Somers for her valuable research in seeking out early information surrounding the work of Neva L. Boyd.
6. Neva L. Boyd and Dayny Pederson, *Folk Games and Gymnastic Play* (Chicago: Saul Brothers, 1914) and *Folk Games of Denmark and Sweden* (Chicago: H. T. Fitz Simons Co., 1915); Boyd and Florence W. Brown, *Old English and American Games for School and Playground* (Chicago: Fitz Simons, 1915); Boyd, *Hospital and Bedside Games* (Chicago: Fitz Simons, 1919) and *Home Games* (Chicago: Fitz Simons, 1942). Important early articles of Neva Boyd include "Group Work Experiments in State Institutions in Illinois," *Proceedings*, National Conference of Social Work, 1935, and "Play as a Means of Social Adjustment," *New Trends*

in Group Work, ed. Joshua L. Lieberman (New York: Association Press, 1938).

7. J. McV. Hunt, "Introduction" to *The Montessori Method* by Maria Montessori (New York: Shocken Books, 1964).
8. Lawrence A. Cremin, *The Transformation of the School* (New York: Knopf, 1961), pp. 345-53.
9. Arthur Bestor, *Educational Wastelands* (Urbana: Univ. of Illinois Press, 1953).
10. Cf. Wilford M. Aiken, *The Story of the Eight-Year Study* (New York: McGraw Hill, 1942) for a summarization of the experience of 30 secondary schools and 300 colleges that waived their formal admission requirements to accommodate recommended graduates of the participating progressive schools.
11. *Ibid.*, p. 150.
12. H. G. Rickover, *Education and Freedom* (New York: E. P. Dutton, 1959), pp. 189-90.
13. For example, 1959 Woods Hole Conference of thirty-five scientists, scholars, and educators to discuss the improvement of education in science in primary and secondary schools; Education Committee, National Academy of Sciences; curriculum projects of the School of Mathematics Study Group; the Biological Sciences Study Committee as reported in Jerome S. Bruner, *The Process of Education* (New York: Vintage Books, 1960), preface.
14. Clara A. Kaiser, "The Social Group Work Process," *Social Work* (April 1958), pp. 68-9.
15. *Proceedings of the National Conference of Social Work, 1946* (New York: Columbia Univ. Press, 1947), pp. 195-208.
16. *Ibid.*, pp. 195-6.
17. *Ibid.*, pp. 202-3.
18. Grace L. Coyle, "On Becoming Professional," *Toward Professional Standards* (New York: American Association of Group Workers, 1947).
19. Coyle, "Definition of the Function of the Group Worker," *The Group*, XI (May 1949).
20. Helen U. Phillips, *The Essentials of Social Group Work Skill* (New York: Association Press, 1957).
21. Konopka, *Social Group Work: A Helping Process*, pp. 14 and 15.
22. Kaiser, "The Social Group Work Process," *Social Work* (April 1958).
23. Coyle, *Group Work with American Youth* (New York: Harper and Brothers, 1949); Gertrude Wilson and Gladys Ryland, *Social Group Work Practice* (Boston: Houghton Mifflin Co., 1949); Trecker, *Social Group Work–Principles and Practice* (New York: Whiteside, 1948); and Konopka, *Therapeutic Group Work with Children* (Minneapolis: Univ. of Minnesota Press, 1949).

24. Some selected examples of such writing include Trecker, *Social Group Work—Principles and Practice,* rev. (New York: Whiteside, 1955); Phillips, *The Essentials of Social Group Work Skill;* Konopka, *Group Work in the Institution* (New York: Whiteside and Morrow, 1954); Marjorie Murphy, *The Social Group Work Method in Social Work Education,* Vol. XI (New York: Curriculum Study, 1959, Council on Social Work Education); Konopka, *Social Group Work: A Helping Process; Social Work With Groups,* NASW, 1957-61 (selected papers on group work from National Conferences on Social Welfare).
25. Cf. Sallie Churchill, "Pre-Structuring Group Content," *Social Work* (July 1959), "Program Variations to Meet Group Needs," NASW (mimeod), and "The Therapeutic Advantage of a Summer Day Camp Associated with a Child Guidance Clinic," Univ. of Michigan, School of Social Work (mimeod); Jack Simos, *Social Growth Through Play Production* (New York: Association Press, 1957); Fritz Redl and David Wineman, "Programming for Ego Support," in *Controls from Within* (Glencoe, Ill.: The Free Press, 1952); Ruth R. Middleman, "Arts and Crafts as a Group Centered Program," *The Group* (December 1954) and "Teaching the Use of Program," *Methods of Teaching Social Group Work,* 1959 Proceedings, Workshop Report, Council of Social Work Education; Paul Gump, "The Ingredients of Games and Their Impact on Players" (Detroit: Wayne State Univ. Press, 1955, mimeod); Robert D. Vinter, "Program Activities: An Analysis of Their Effects on Participant Behavior" (Ann Arbor: Univ. of Michigan Press, 1960, mimeod); Gump, "Observation Study of Activities for Disturbed Children," *Group Work and Community Organization,* 1953-54, National Conference of Social Work (New York: Columbia Univ. Press, 1954); Gump et al., "Activity Setting and Social Interaction: A Field Study," *American Journal of Orthopsychiatry,* XXV, 4 (July 1955); Gump and Brian Sutton-Smith, "The 'It' Role in Children's Games," *The Group,* XVII, 3 (February 1955); Fritz Redl, "The Impact of Game Ingredients on Children's Play Behavior," ed. Bertram Schaffner, *Group Processes* (New York: Josiah Macy, Jr., Foundation, 1959).
26. Konopka, "Similarities and Differences Between Group Work and Group Therapy," *Proceedings, National Conference of Social Work,* 1951 (New York: Columbia Univ. Press); Philip Zlatchin, Clara A. Kaiser, and Saul Scheidlinger, "The Group in Education, Group Work, and Psychotherapy," Round Table, 1953, *American Journal of Orthopsychiatry,* XXIV, 1 (January 1954).
27. A full list of the articles dealing with the application of social group work to the different settings and problems would be impossible. The following examples are merely suggestive of the trend:

Marian Sloan, "The Special Contribution of Therapeutic Group Work in a Psychiatric Setting," *The Group* (April 1953); Constance Impallaria Albee, "Group Work with Hospitalized Children," *Children* (November–December 1955); Raymond Fisher, "Contributions of Group Work in Psychiatric Hospitals," *The Group* (November 1949); Ralph Kolodny, "Therapeutic Group Work with Handicapped Children," *Children* (May–June 1957); Konopka, "The Social Group Work Method: Its Use in the Correctional Field," *Federal Probation* (March 1956); Ruth R. Middleman, "Social Group Work in a Maternity Home," *Child Welfare* (February 1959).

28. Gladys Ryland, *Employment Responsibilities of Social Group Work Graduates,* Council on Social Work Education, 1958, p. 6.
29. U.S. Department of Labor, Bureau of Labor Statistics, *Salaries and Working Conditions of Social Welfare Manpower in 1960,* National Social Welfare Assembly and U.S. Department of Health, Education and Welfare, New York, pp. 11 and 27.
30. Robert D. Vinter, "Group Work: Perspectives and Prospects," *Social Work with Groups 1959,* Selected Papers from the National Conference on Social Welfare, NASW, New York.
31. Harriett M. Bartlett, "Toward Clarification and Improvement of Social Work Practice," *Social Work* (April 1958).
32. Gertrude Wilson, *The Practice of Social Group Work,* Summary of the Report, The Committee on Practice, Group Work Section, New York, NASW, 1956.
33. Alan F. Klein et al., *Social Group Work Revisited: 1964, A Statement of Position,* Univ. of Pittsburgh, March, 1964.
34. Marjorie Murphy, *The Social Group Work Method in Social Work Education, A Project Report of the Curriculum Study,* XI, Werner W. Boehm, Director and Coordinator (New York: Council on Social Work Education, 1959).
35. *Ibid.,* p. 39.
36. *Ibid.,* pp. 48-9.
37. *Ibid.,* p. 50.
38. See Appendix B.
39. Murphy, *op. cit.,* p. 70.
40. Konopka, "The Generic and Specific in Group Work Practice in the Psychiatric Setting," *Group Work in the Psychiatric Setting* (New York: Whiteside and Morrow, 1956), pp. 21-2.
41. Konopka, *Social Group Work: A Helping Process,* pp. 166-7.
42. The following incomplete listing of recent publications bears out the trend toward a broader use of group methods: Marjorie Montelius, *Working with Groups: A Guide for Administration of Group Services in Public Welfare,* Bureau of Family Services, Welfare Administration, U.S. Dept. of HEW, 1966: Trecker, *Group*

Services in Public Welfare, U.S. Dept. of HEW, 1964; *Helping People in Groups,* U.S. Dept. of HEW, 1965; Norman Fenton and Kermit T. Wiltse, ed., *Group Methods in the Public Welfare Program* (Palo Alto, Calif.: Pacific Books, 1963); *Group Method and Services in Child Welfare* (New York: Child Welfare League of America, 1963); *Group Treatment in Family Service Agencies* (New York: Family Service Association of America, 1964); *Guide for Use of Group Methods in County Welfare Departments* (Calif. State Dept. of Social Welfare, September 1962); *Potentials for Service Through Group Work in Public Welfare* (Chicago: American Public Welfare Association, 1962); June Jackson Christmas, "Group Methods in Training and Practice: Non-Professional Mental Health Personnel in a Deprived Community," *American Journal of Orthopsychiatry* (April 1966); Lloyd Conklin et al., "Use of Groups During the Adoptive Postplacement Period," *Social Work* (April 1962).

43. Klein, *op. cit.*
44. Dorothea Spellman, "Nucleus and Boundaries in Social Group Work," *Social Work,* VI, 4 (October 1961), 90-5.
45. Three important sources for William Schwartz's thinking are Alfred J. Kahn, ed., "Group Work and the Social Scene," *Issues in American Social Work* (New York: Columbia Univ. Press, 1959); "The Social Worker in the Group," *New Perspectives on Services to Groups, Social Work with Groups, 1961* (New York: NASW, 1961); and "Toward a Strategy of Group Work Practice," *The Social Service Review,* XXXVI, 3 (September 1962).
46. Schwartz, "Group Work and the Social Scene," p. 124.
47. Schwartz, "Toward a Strategy of Group Work Practice," p. 268.
48. *Ibid.,* pp. 274-5.
49. Helen H. Perlman, "Social Work Method: A Review of the Past Decade," *Social Work,* X, 4 (October 1965), p. 168.
50. Committee on Practice, Subcommittee on the Psychiatric Social Worker as Leader of a Group, *Report on the Psychiatric Social Worker as Leader of a Group* (New York: NASW), p. 33.
51. C. Winick, A. Kadis, and J. Krasner, "The Training and Practice of American Group Psychotherapists," *International Journal of Group Psychotherapy,* XI, 4 (October 1961), p. 422.
52. "Community Psychiatry and Social Work," *Social Service Review,* XL, 3 (September 1966), 245.
53. Louise A. Frey and Ralph L. Kolodny, "Illusions and Realities in Current Social Work with Groups," *Social Work,* IX, 2 (April 1964).
54. *Ibid.,* pp. 88-9.
55. Margaret E. Hartford, ed., *Working Papers Toward a Frame of Reference for Social Group Work,* Committee on Practice of the

National Group Work Section of the NASW, 1959-63 (New York: NASW, 1964).
56. *Ibid.*, p. 5.
57. William Schwartz, *Analysis of Papers Presented on Working Definitions of Group Work Practice*, excerpted from minutes of Practice Committee and Group Work Section, March 1960, pp. 53-61.
58. *Ibid.*, p. 56.
59. *Ibid.*, p. 92.
60. *Ibid.*, p. 57.
61. *Ibid.*, p. 50.
62. Perlman, *op. cit.*, pp. 166-7.
63. *Ibid.*, p. 169.
64. *Ibid.*, pp. 169-70.
65. William Gordon, ed., "A Critique of the Working Definition," *Social Work* (October 1962), p. 4.
66. Perlman, *op. cit.*, p. 171.
67. Ruth E. Smalley, *Theory for Social Work Practice* (New York: Columbia Univ. Press, 1967), pp. 294-5.
68. *Ibid.*, p. 294.
69. *Ibid.*, p. 29.

2 Non-Verbal and Verbal Content—The Components of Program Content

From my mother I also inherited a terribly passionate temper, which she again had inherited from her father, who was a very good man but very quick-tempered. My disposition showed itself in games; I played every game with terrible earnestness, and got angry if anyone else did not enter into it with all his might. When I was nine or ten years old, I struck my sister Adela, because she was a very slack opponent in a game, and through her indifference let me win a very easy victory. From that time onwards I began to feel anxious about my passion for play, and gradually gave up all games.

—Albert Schweitzer*

What Is Non-Verbal Content?

Non-verbal content often refers to such things as a blush, a gesture, a glance, a frown, or even deliberate silence—as indicators that communicate attitude and feeling without words. Psychiatry and psychology have devoted much attention to "kinesics," a study of bodily movements as they convey what the patient does not verbalize. Certain writings in those fields have shown this aspect of communication as being crucial for a full understanding of the patient.[1] Psychiatrists are also concerned with the meaning and usefulness of expression through non-verbal activities as a part of the dynamics in treatment.[2]

The meaning of *non-verbal* as used in this book is more nearly "the *doing activities,*" but *non-verbal* is used because of its mean-

* *Memoirs of Childhood and Youth* (New York: The Macmillan Co., 1955), p. 23.

ing to others and because of the place of this term in a larger frame of reference previously studied by others. Actually, as this discussion will reveal, our concept of the use of program or "doing experiences" includes verbalization as a vital part of the experience. The distinction is that *the primary method of communicating begins with and is related to some kind of action.*

The concept of program employed here is a dynamic one demanding much creativity, flexibility, and adaptation of the given activity to the particular needs of the group and its individual members at any given moment in time. This implies a view of program as an active, changing entity—never quite the same twice, like an amoeba—taking its shape from the demands of the situation in which it is used. It is similar in this sense to John Dewey's thought:

> It is no linguistic accident that "building," "construction," "work," designate both a process and its finished product. Without the meaning of the verb that of the noun remains blank.[3]

One can add *program* to these other words. It, too, is both a verb and a noun. Too often "program" has been viewed in the noun sense—a static entity introduced to do some special thing or express some particular outcome of a group's endeavors. Generally workers have moved over the years to see program as a means and not an end—a tool to effect some particular end.

But seeing this means—this tool—as something that itself changes while it is being applied has been less clear. One could liken program to putty, or at least to a movable tool, such as a pair of pliers, which adjusts to the size demanded by the bolt to be twisted. Most often *tool* brings to mind something like a hammer, which does not change. Of course, one can apply it in different ways, hitting with more force or less, depending on the density of the wood into which the nail is being driven. In this sense, it is the person who applies the hammer (tool) differentially to suit the occasion.[4]

But putty changes its very form; it is thick or thin, it goes into a long line or a round hole with a dab here and a dab there, and its very amorphous quality is what makes it the proper tool for a particular job. *The user changes his use, and the tool also changes in the process of doing a job.* Thus, in this sense, the tool (program) cannot be prescriptive in a definite way as some of the writings in the literature emphasize.[5] It is not even itself the same thing every time it is applied, but has to change because of its dependence on the unique style and skill of the particular worker and, at the same time, the different states of the group. Thus, further study and research to improve the quality of program would be better centered upon the *particular use of the content by a certain worker at a specific point in the group's life* rather than upon the precise content itself as containing definite and predictable characteristics that can be applied by the knowing worker with a cause-and-effect expectation. Increased knowledge about the characteristics and qualities of program media is all to the good, but the ever-changing and changeable program itself, as it is *used* and adapted by the worker, ought to be the main focus for inquiry and study.

What Is Program Content?

This writer's view of just what comprises the program content of a group experience is a broad one. It is the accumulated totality of all the group does—both verbal and non-verbal—inclusive also of horseplay, clean-up, setting up a projector, and such. It consists of both the constructive and the distracting activities that comprise the group's experience and the individual's tangential or related experiences within the overall group session. It may be initiated by the worker or by the group members themselves, arising spontaneously or as the outcome of the deliberate planning. In time duration, program may range from a brief episode to an experience of several hours or to a continuing recurrent or developmental part of several meetings—perhaps ritualized into every meeting.

Program is *what* is being done and *how* it is done, and, viewing it from the worker's point of view as he helps set it in motion, it includes the *why* of what is done. The program content, the worker's use of his relationship with the group members, and his effect upon their interactional process combine to become the social group work process itself—that precious entity through which the aims of the individual members, the group, the worker, and the sponsoring agency come to life.

To put it another way, *progam is the vehicle through which relationships are made and the needs and interests of the group and its individual members are fulfilled.* The goals for the use of program should be identical with the goals motivating the worker who is employing it, depending upon his purpose as a professional, whether he be a social group worker, a psychiatrist, an occupational therapist, a recreation leader, or a teacher. A social group worker would use program, then, to help the individuals grow in self value and to help the group become able to act on increasingly responsible and social goals.

Program Content as Communication

The form of program content as it leads in this overall direction can be either verbal or non-verbal, or both. What would determine the most appropriate form—verbal or non-verbal—should be the freedom of the group to express itself, i.e., to communicate. Factors affecting the capacity to communicate would include the ages of the group members; their life experiences to date in expressing themselves with words and in the doing activities; their comfort in the various forms of their culture, i.e., in knowing something about games, dance, or drama; their health and physical capabilities; their intellectual capacity; their emotional stability; their own likes and dislikes; norms for acceptable behavior; and, finally, group mores and values.

Taking all these factors into consideration, the worker moves with his group in either verbal or non-verbal content forms. Since the goals from the worker's point of view would often transcend the group's goals in behalf of itself, it would be safe to assume that program should not only be interesting, pleasurable (or fun), and fulfilling to the group members, but it should also lead one to increased awareness of himself as an effective person, to greater self-esteem, and to group pride, group awareness, and responsible group behavior. Because of goals such as these, it would be important to see program as developmental, leading somewhere, and often including the group's increased concious awareness of such development. Thus, throughout the experiences—whether verbal or non-verbal—there would need to be periods of evaluation, of looking at what has been accomplished and looking to the future. Within the non-verbal activities particularly would be points of verbalization deliberately injected by the worker so that some assessment, however brief and primitive, were made conscious to the group and to the individuals in it that they were doing thus and so. Naturally, when the content is of a verbal kind this type of taking stock periodically happens all the more easily.

Growth Through Program

Non-verbal content to be most effective has intermittent periods of verbal exchange and interpretation running throughout the experience. In this way the full impact of the accomplishment (or lack of accomplishment) is made known to the group members and some insight is obtained. But there is much to the non-verbal experience itself that might never be anything more than an overall reaction to a combined, felt experience. On the most elementary level, it might be expressed as "We had a good day," or "We had fun." The group can move on to have even more demanding kinds of good days and fun because they have felt the experience, even if they do not always know why it was so good. How much self-assessment the group is capable of with the worker again depends on age, sociocultural background, and many other things. But growth toward increasingly responsible behavior can proceed, with or without the group members' conscious awareness of the total process. It is up to the worker to make known to a group and its individuals, as much as he can, the full measure of their movement and to help them move in desired directions whether or not he shares his insights verbally.

The ideal program experience for any group would include both the verbal and the non-verbal means of expression, primarily because this is the true order of living itself. People express themselves through words and actions and the group experience should reflect this same balance. Oftentimes, one gets a truer picture of just what the needs, interests, potentialities and problems of individuals and groups are through a combination of both the asserted interests and the performance level. The gap between how persons present themselves verbally and how they act is particularly noticeable in teen-agers. The following brief excerpts from three consecutive weekly meetings of a small group of teen-aged girls who are in foster care in a large children's agency illustrate this point.

Peggy and Rita are sixteen years old and Dorothy is thirteen. These girls have been in the care of the agency since they were eight years, thirteen months, and one year respectively. It has been their habit since childhood to await many of their appointments with their caseworkers in the agency playroom. In this room are dolls—Negro and white, a playhouse, trucks, and other toys, as well as a stove, an eating area, and a phonograph. Now they come to a discussion and activity group as teen-agers, and for lack of other space they meet in this same playroom. After a few meetings where the ice was was broken for them and the group worker, the following happened:

> 7/13/66
> Dorothy spoke rather immaturely and idealistically romantic about her views of marriage. We also discussed favorites in clothing and the girls compared notes on likes and dislikes and also asked me my point of view on clothing. The remainder of the session continued as it started: Dorothy talking rapidly and with much giggling often. Peggy talked a fair amount and at times acted fairly childishly as she liked to play with some of the dolls in the playroom. She recalled her earlier life coming to the agency and playing with the dolls. She liked to hold one of the dolls and seemed to enjoy this kind of behavior. . . . The girls continued to dance and chat. At one time, Dorothy came to me and said, "Gee, I certainly like coming here; we can do anything we want to do."
>
> 7/20/66
> Dorothy eventually brought up the topic of pregnancy and said that she had heard that pregnancy was the most painful thing that a person could go through in her life and that she didn't want her "guts all torn out." We talked about this for a while and I explained . . .

Further discussion was initiated about movie magazines. Peggy, as usual, played with the Negro doll that she had played with during the other two meetings and soon Rita and Dorothy followed by picking up a doll. All sat around, continuing to talk, and held their dolls and reminisced about childhood days. A few jokes were told and the girls appeared to be having a good time . . .

8/1/66

Following our meal, we very smoothly began playing the drawing charades which I had introduced at the last meeting. Overall, the game did not seem to catch on as well as it had during the previous week and we played the game for a short time and very naturally ended it when Peggy decided she was more interested in playing with one of the dolls she usually plays with. She began cuddling one of the dolls and taking it for a stroll around the room in one of the big doll carriages.

. . . As the meeting continued, Peggy at one point asked Dorothy how she felt when she was first kissed . . .

One advantage for this group is the opportunity to talk out the fears and problems in growing up so that their attitudes toward life's dangers and rewards can be modified. The talk is pretty typical of the interests of all teen-aged girls: clothes (self-image), movie magazines, sex, love, and marriage. The interest in dancing, too, is an important action within this same area of interest. But the desire, here in the comfort of a room which symbolizes childhood to them, to play with dolls reveals the other side of the teen-age dilemma, which these particular girls were free enough to act out; others might feel this way but do not usually have the circumstances so conducive to really express their backward yearnings. It could be supposed that the brief moments in which these girls were able to regress to the experiences of earlier days, joke, and talk about their years of connection with the agency (the main continuity in their lives at this point) helped them considerably as they tried to cope with the more complex problems of living that they were presently encountering.

Thus, the non-verbal experience of this group presents an important clue to the group worker as she attempts through their discussions to help the girls talk out their adolescent concerns.

Sometimes the full impact of the growth potential in a program experience is focused on the individual. In the illustration that follows, a group of boys who knew each other very well dared to confront two individuals with their perception of them through the guise of playing a game. As the illustration shows, this perception differs markedly from one group member's anticipation of how his peers would describe him.

> The next game that I had on the score sheet was *What Am I?* Garey was anxious to be the first to leave the room and I allowed him to do so. The game requires that one person leave the room while the group thinks of something which this person is. For example, the boys used such things as a boxer, a car racer, and a gorilla. After using those, the group moved to using parts of the body such as kidneys, blood, lips. Up till this part of the game, it went very smoothly and all enjoyed their participation in it.
>
> Finally, the movement of the group turned into using adjectives to describe the person who left the room. I was hesitant at first when they began to use more negative adjectives rather than positive. For example, the adjective they used for Bob was "stingy." This is an adjective which they have used to describe him in the past. I did not know what the reaction would be but I was curious to see how the group and the boys would handle it. There was some feeling in the group that perhaps they should not use it once Bob had come into the room. When I asked them if they would like to choose another word they, however, said they would like to continue. Bob was quite amusing as he listed things trying to think of the adjective. He used such adjectives as "the greatest" or "terrific." He never did guess, and the group told him. There was no noticeable reaction on his part and he accepted it willingly. They also used an adjective for Kevin. They called him "a teaser." Kevin finally did get this as the group was very active in giving hints and helping him to reach the answer. The boys had a lot of fun even with these adjectives since it was given in fun. I sensed no hard feelings in using the adjectives or in telling the boys who were in the "It" position what was chosen.

This "game" turned, indeed, to serious life business for this group. An important early learning for all individuals is that others may view them differently than they view themselves.

Though the game was not exactly "fun" for the two individuals so singled out, it was a beginning for them to take in by means of an acceptable, rather than derisive, way some opinions held by others about themselves that they might wish to modify in the future.

The Development of the Self Through Interaction With Others

One of the earlier philosophers of this century, George Herbert Mead, expressed in the mid-twenties ideas about the importance of actions which were destined to have considerable influence within the field of social psychology and, subsequently, the behavioral sciences. His central thesis was that action ("the act") determines the relationship between the individual and the environment. Action toward the self or self-awareness grows out of acting toward the non-self. According to Mead, the self arises through a series of communications through the "conversation of gestures between animals involving some sort of cooperative activity,"[6] through gestures and language of individuals, and through children's activities of play and the game.[7]

Child play, i.e., playing *at* this or that role, precedes playing at a game in which a child must be able not only to take one role but also the attitude of everyone else involved in the game, understanding the relationship each role has towards every other role. Thus, the child becomes interested in the rules of the game. The game represents the passage in the life of the child from *taking the role of others* in play to the organized part that is essential to self-consciousness in the full sense of the term.[8]

According to Mead, in order to define one's self, to become a self, one must simultaneously be his own subject and object. A person must be able to step outside himself, so to speak, and look back at himself. Such multiple visions vis-à-vis one's self are learned through childhood games through which one experiences the "generalized other"—society's representative, beginning as the small game group, or any social group, and progressing to the whole organized community eventually. The *generalized other* (Mead's best-known term) is society's representative in the individual, linked closely with both self-control and social control. Hence, according to Mead, through gesture, language, and play and games (the actions), communication is established between the self and others, and through these elementary interactions one's whole sense of being and perception of the world about him develops.

More recently, Jerome Bruner speaks of play also as an important prerequisite for effective cognitive learning in school.

> With respect to play and playfulness, it is first of all an attitude in which the child learns that the outcomes of various activities are not as extreme as he either hoped or feared—it involves learning to place limits on the anticipated consequences of activity. We have been struck by the difference in parents in respect to their encouragement of playfulness in their children—the children whose learning blocks we have studied and normal schoolchildren. In some instances, among normal children, we are told of "breast play" in which the very consequential act of nursing at the breast is altered into an occasion for playing—nipple in and out in a kind of loving tease. And throughout growth, it is as in the famous remark of Niels Bohr to one of his graduate students who complained of the seeming unseriousness, the amount of horseplay and joking, around Bohr's laboratory: "But there are some things so important that one can only joke about them." In time, the attitude of play is converted into what may best be called a game attitude in which the child gets the sense not only that consequences are limited but that the limitation comes by virtue of a set of rules that govern a procedure, whether it be checkers or arithmetic or baseball. . . . play serves the function of reducing the pressures of impulse and incentive and making it possible thereby for intrinsic learning to begin; for if ever there is self-reward in process it is in the sphere of "doing things for merriment." [9]

The Balance in Communication Between Verbal and Non-Verbal

Returning to the theme of the group's program content then, it seems essential, based upon the naturalness of the *doing* and the *talking* activities as means of communicating with others and of knowing one's self, that both form the fabric of the group experience. Sometimes, however, a group needs to be helped to express itself in either the verbal or the action area; the balance between both kinds of expression may not exist for reasons which we shall discuss.

All group workers are familiar enough with the many adults in society who need help before they can feel right about having fun, either as an individual or in their group life. And they are equally familiar with the group of children who seem only capable of "letting off steam," who race madly from one thing to another and can only with great difficulty be encouraged to catch their breath, sit down, and talk for a minute. Between these two extremes lies some balance for both the doing and the talking, and this would hold true no matter what the purpose of the group. Even formal classes and discussion meetings often do better at their main purpose when there is a coffee break injected and some opportunity to socialize and ramble on seemingly inconsequential topics informally over the coffee. The deeply verbal adult psychotherapy sessions, it is found, change significantly with the inclusion of the simple activity of eating.

The non-verbal is being given primary attention in this book, not because it is thought to be the more important of the two basic forms, but rather because it has received relatively little attention. The worker needs to be comfortable enough to reach out liberally and use the wide variety of non-verbal forms available, instead of simply sticking with the particular ones he likes and feels comfortable with.

In this writer's experience, one of the most difficult aspects of teaching the group worker to use non-verbal program content rests in helping him to be fully there for the needs and interests of the group and to move with it within any non-verbal content form, according to the group's needs rather than the worker's own special skill or comfort. For alas, the worker too is a product of his own particular development in a culture and is prone to biases, blindspots, and inferiorities just as the group members are. The worker is too often immobilized from free engagement unless he is given deliberate help to work in all content forms; to risk exposing himself with all his own lacks and imperfections; to see himself as able to introduce and guide an experience in, say, art or singing if this is what is called for, without reaching to an outside specialist. Somehow the worker must learn that his helping potential resides in his heightened skill in the use of whatever form he employs and that this skill is constant and available even if he does not have mastery of the medium. Only through such deliberate acceptance of responsibility for all content will the involvement with program become anything more than intuitive and related to the worker's special gifts and interests—a heretofore serious and unnecessarily personal coloration of the group experience. The groping and courageous testing of one's self in a variety of non-verbal media can be seen in the remarks of one student as he discussed his development in using program:

> . . . since I have started school my knowledge of various programs has expanded greatly and there seems to be a greater ease in working with activities that I once felt I knew little about or was unskilled in. The use of program as a means of communication for me and the group members is a vital link in the establishing of relationships necessary in carrying out social work goals. . . . I have also been given a sense of wanting to explore and find out and try activities that are new and untried by me. Program as the group worker's means and vehicle of communication to his groups and for his groups was a new concept for me when I started school. The importance of program and the planning and forethought that go into it has been something that has been growing on me as the school year has progressed. I realized that the more time and thought I put into the planning and the types of program that I used, the better the program would go even though not always successful. I have grown to see more and more that it is not only the program per se that makes a session a success but the way in which I plan the program, taking into account the needs and desires of the group, and the way I use and handle myself in regard to the activities for the day. The more that we talk about program the more I believe that it is a bottomless pit. A pit that is rewarding and helpful and something that there never seems an end to. I'm stimulated but sometimes scared that there is so much to know.

It is obvious in this statement that learning to move with some freedom in hitherto unknown content is not easy and would demand, in the words of Lady Macbeth,

We fail? But screw your courage to the sticking place and we'll not fail.

Notes to Chapter 2

1. Cf., for example, Ray L. Birdwhistell, "Body Behavior and Communication," *International Encyclopaedia of the Social Sciences* (December 1964).
2. A few illustrative references are suggested: Frederick H. Allen, *Psychotherapy with Children* (New York: Norton, 1942), Ch. V; Erick H. Erickson, *Childhood and Society* (New York: Norton, 1963), Ch. 6; Hertha Riese, *Heal the Hurt Child* (Chicago: Univ. of Chicago Press, 1962), Ch. 7 and 12; "The Creative Use of the Unconscious by the Artist and by the Psychotherapist," *Annals of Psychotherapy,* V, 1 (1964); Earl A. Loomis, Jr., "The Use of Checkers in Handling Certain Resistances in Child Therapy and Child Analysis," *Journal of the American Psychoanalytic Association* (1957); Carl Whitaker *et al.*, "Experiential Psychotherapy: Evaluation of Relatedness," *Journal of Existential Psychiatry* (winter, 1963); Newell Fisher, "Ping Pong?" *Voices, the Art and Science of Psychotherapy, Journal of American Academy of Psychotherapists,* II, 2 (summer, 1966). The current annual meeting of the American Orthopsychiatric Association (44th annual meeting), 1967, Washington, D. C., lists two workshops of interest to this subject: "Creative Arts Programs in Various Settings: Realistic Expectations of Use of Art, Drama and Music with the Economically Deprived" and "Rules and Freedom: Games as a Mechanism for Ego Development in Children and Adolescents."
3. John Dewey, *Art as Experience* (New York: Capricorn Books, 1958), p. 51.
4. For a discussion of the importance of the way the tool is used in program terms, i.e., the nature of the intervention, cf. Alan Klein, "Program Utilization in Social Group Work," Implementation of Diagnosis Proceedings of Educational Institute, NASW, New York City Chapter, 1961.
5. Robert Vinter, "Program Activities: An Analysis of Their Effects on Participant Behavior" (Univ. of Michigan School of Social Work, mimeod); Paul Gump and Brian Sutton-Smith, "The 'It' Role in Children's Games," *The Group* (February 1955); Paul Gump, "The Ingredients of Games and Their Impact on Players" (Wayne Univ. School of Social Work, 1955, mimeod).
6. Cf. George Herbert Mead, "The Genesis of the Self and Social Control," *International Journal of Ethics,* XXXV (1924-5), 251-77.

Also, *George Herbert Mead on Social Psychology,* ed. Anselm Strauss (Chicago: Univ. of Chicago, 1964).

7. *Ibid.,* pp. 210-14.
8. *Ibid.,* p. 216.
9. Jerome S. Bruner, *Toward A Theory of Instruction* (Cambridge, Mass.: The Belknap Press of Harvard Univ. Press, 1966), pp. 134-5.

3 Non-Verbal Content as an Avenue for Learning

> *The art form which has been most successful at capturing the essence of contemporary America is jazz. Here, if anywhere, we can sense the meaning of process. Musicians grope for a line, follow it, explore it, soar with it. They are as our children claim, "way-out"—as much in space in their own particular way as our astronauts. . . . Speaking of World War II, the German pianist Jutta Hipp wrote: "I remember nights when we didn't go down to the bomb shelter because we listened to jazz records. We just had the feeling that you are not our enemies, and even though the bombs crashed around us . . . we felt safe.*
>
> —Marshall Fishwick *

First Experiences of One's Self Are Through Action

The primary reason for emphasizing non-verbal content in individual and group expression is a psychological one. There is increased evidence that through the doing kinds of activities the individual first learns and experiences a sense of himself with all his innate potentialities as a creative and expressive person. Such insights spring mainly from the study of childhood—a period of life when the mastery of language, which is perhaps the most powerful socializing and self-affirming tool of every culture, is developed. The immense difficulties involved in communicating, learning acceptable behavior, developing feelings of adequacy, overcoming fears, and in all ways gaining a feeling of comfortable

* From *Saturday Review,* March 3, 1962. Marshall Fishwick is Professor of American Studies at Washington and Lee University.

equilibrium with the environment are observed in work with babies and nursery-aged children.[1]

In the writings of Lois Barclay Murphy, and associates, one can follow the minute recorded observations of early life and first socializing experiences with family and school. These investigators recorded an important point they noticed as follows:

> Over and over again we saw how the impact of a new challenge intensified the child's awareness of himself: his capacity to meet such a challenge enhances his pleasure, his sense of adequacy, and his pride. Through the successive experiences of spontaneous mastery of new demands and utilizing new opportunities for gratification the child extends and verifies his identity as one who can manage certain aspects of the environment. Through his coping experience the child discovers and measures himself, and develops his own perception of who and what he is and in time may become. We can say that the child creates his identity through his efforts in coming to terms with the environment in his own personal way.[2]

One little girl's awareness of her own developing power as an individual is summarized quite simply by her own statement: "I can jump!" Throughout this book is an important theme that in the psychological development of the child "'I do' *precedes* 'I am.'" The doing, for the most part, represents the developing of skills through individual coping efforts and through beginning interactional activities. These were observed at the Menninger Foundation in preschool children at a situation termed "a party," where the children were introduced into group activities of an unknown nature for the first time. The primary skills the child attempts to master are (1) the handling of himself, i.e., his body, through physical activity, and (2) the handling and manipulation of objects, through activities which lead toward drawing, painting, and eventually toward arts and crafts, playing musical instruments, cooking, and the range of related activities.

From observation of the stimulation and encouragement of babies by mothers, one can also see the great value placed upon action and activity—a value which becomes deeply rooted in the individual as he develops toward adulthood. The mother responds with a smile and with love to early sitting-up on the part of the infant, to standing, to the first steps. And she responds with fear and doubt when her infant does not achieve such activity as early as do other babies. Such pleasure and approval thus become deeply embedded in the young child's awareness of successful and valued activity. It is small wonder that physical skills and ability are so important to the school-aged child as he sees himself in relation to his peers. Awkwardness, lack of coordination, and lack of physical strength are all powerful liabilities, not only to his success and popularity with others as he sees himself, but equally as determinants of acceptance by peers and family. Perhaps one of the deepest values of both our culture and our individual psychology in the United States is this emphasis on action and success. The great preoccupation with competition in games, which all group leaders notice in their groups, springs from just such early childhood interactions with those whose approval and response sets the tone for one's own drives.

People Learn Through Their Muscles—Through Action and Behavior

Within the past ten years psychologists have increasingly brought new insights into the field of education, stemming in large part from their awareness of the enormous importance of Jean Piaget's work in minutely documenting early childhood development; the psychologists have consequently made an impact on the conceptual thinking that underlies curriculum building, educational objectives, and the stance of the school as a major institution in our society. Much of this thinking has grown out of the attempts of psychologists and educators to become more effective with the underachievers who are not grasping the necessary skills for life-needs for either intellectual lacks or sociocultural limitations. In such inquiry there is renewed interest in the place of the non-verbal and its relationship to the development of verbal skills and abstract thinking.

"Present teaching methods," according to Professor Jerome Bruner of Harvard, "place too much emphasis on the verbal. The result is that youngsters too often display great skill in using words that describe words that describe words, with no real feel for, or image of, the concrete phenomenon itself."[3] Bruner states that while language more than anything else distinguishes human from animal learning, verbalization is not the only way people learn or know. We know things "enactively," which is to say in our muscles. Children can be very skillful on a seesaw without having any concept of what it is and without being able to represent it by drawing a balance beam (the use of imagery) or by writing Newton's law of moments (symbolic representation).

Also significant in present-day educational psychological research is the work of Professor B. F. Skinner, also of Harvard, and his followers. Skinner defined learning as "a change in behavior." The essence of his approach is that any behavior can be produced in any person by "reinforcing," i.e., rewarding it. The desired behavior or close approximations to it must be rewarded appropriately and right away, so that with frequent small steps one can shape a student's behavior toward any predetermined goal.[4]

The emphasis on action and behavior as being more vital than mere verbalization in the learning process can be found increasingly in present-day psychological research. In discussing learning, Jerome Bruner describes the findings of investigators from centers all over the world with respect to mental growth: Knowing is principally knowing how to do, and there is minimum reflection. Following this action stage, which Bruner sees as the first phase of mental growth and terms the "enactive stage"—characteristic of the child from about ages five to seven years, comes a period of more reflective functioning. During this second stage, the iconic, the child can make internal representation by representative images of greater chunks of the environment. Finally, something very special happens around adolescence, when language becomes increasingly important as a medium of thought. At this stage, the symbolic, there is the ability to consider propositions rather than objects.[5] Dr. Bruner proposes a view of human beings who develop three parallel systems for processing information and for representing it—one through manipulation and action, one through perceptual organization and imagery, and one through symbolic apparatus. These three are not stages of development but are emphases progressing from the central core of the person to the less egocentric levels.

According to Bruner, these three systems of skills correspond to the three major tool systems to which the mature individual must link himself for the full expression of his capacities—tools for the hand, for the distance receptors, and for the process of reflection. Emphasizing the importance of early life experiences in achieving full development, Dr. Bruner cites results of animal studies as indications that virtually irreversible deficits can be produced in mammals by depriving them of opportunities that challenge their nascent capacities. In the last few years there have been reports showing the crippling effect of deprived human environments as well as indications that "replacement therapies" can be of considerable success even at an age on the edge of adolescence. Unless the basic skills are mastered, later, more elaborate ones become increasingly out of reach.[6]

There is now some growing realization that the reading-readiness concept that used to guide curriculum building is only a half-truth, since one *teaches* readiness or provides opportunities for its nurture. One does not simply sit back and wait for this to occur. Psychologists now find that most subjects can be translated into forms that place emphasis upon *doing*, or upon the development of appropriate *imagery*, or upon *symbolic-verbal* encoding. That is, if one wants to teach calculus in the eighth grade, he must begin it in the first grade by teaching the kinds of ideas and skills necessary for its mastery later.

Folk Models Transmit the Behaviors of the Culture

The work of Dr. Omar Khayyam Moore, of the University of Pittsburgh, to name but one other psychologist, is presently concerned with the problems of learning and the efforts of the behavioral scientists to develop theory to guide inquiry into how man learns to cope with his environment. Moore makes the following observations:

> Early in human history, man created models of the most important features of his environment. These were abstract models, which col-

lectively covered relations holding between (1) man and nature—insofar as nature is not random, (2) man and the random or chancey elements in experience, (3) man in his interactional relations with others like himself, and finally (4) man and the normative aspects of group living. Structures falling within these four classes of models were created by unsung Newtons, so that there does not exist a society, however primitive, that does not have cultural objects falling in these four categories of models.

Every society, as far back as we have any evidence, has *puzzles* which stand in an abstract way for man–man relations. Every society has some *games of chance*. Every society has *games of strategy*. These games capture some of the peculiar features of interactional relations among men, relations in which no party to an encounter controls all of the relevant variables upon which the final outcome depends, though each controls some of these variables and each participant can take account of the potential actions of others involved in the same situation. Every society has *aesthetic* entities: art forms, which we claim give people the opportunity to learn to make normative judgments about their experiences. All societies make use of these cultural objects in the socialization of the young and for the re-creation or recreational enjoyment of those who are older. Simple forms of these models are internalized in childhood, and more complex versions of them sustain us in adulthood.

The ordinary man in any society should be thought of as having in his mind at least four classes of models which he can use in a highly abstract way to guide his behavior. From this standpoint, it probably would not have been possible for mankind to develop complex civilizations without these abstract folk models . . . man not only developed these fascinating conceptual structures; he also devised suitable techniques for seeing to it that they were mastered. For the most part, one learns, but is not necessarily taught, to play with folk models. What is taught are the "rules of the game." Once the rules are understood, each participant is largely on his own except when the models are perverted by professionalism.

In every society there are social norms which distinguish between serious matters, on the one hand, and fun and games on the other. Generally, specific times and places are set aside for the enjoyment of these folk models. Also, the stakes for winning or losing are kept at some nominal value insofar as profit and loss enter in. In addition, there are norms which regulate expressions of feeling and

> emotion with reference to using these folk models. During the course of playing with a model, one is permitted to experience a fairly wide range of feelings and emotions, but extremes are excluded. These models, as it were, serve as a school for emotional expressions. . . . All in all, the set of norms governing the use of the models and the models themselves have proved so successful that people have to be prohibited from playing too much, despite the conceptual depth of the materials with which they deal.[7]

It is Dr. Moore's belief that through the use of these four kinds of folk models the child learns ways of getting along with his environment—both nature and other persons. He learns the behaviors appropriate to his culture. He learns how to behave in the face of challenges. It is of great interest that the kind of experiences he details as basic to the evolution of a civilized way of living—for whatever culture—are essentially the same kinds of activities which the group worker is concerned with—the "doing things" through which child and adult test themselves out in relation to the self, to others, and to things.

Cognitive Learning Follows the Awakening of All the Senses Through Stimulating Experiences

Professors in the schools of education and psychologists alike have, of late, revised their theories of education. Motivation and the importance of developing cognitive learning are major challenges facing the public schools in our present world. Some impetus, as cited earlier, has come from the attack leveled against the progressive education of the early part of the twentieth century. There has been enough time to realize that "in recent years, emphasis on social and emotional adjustment has tended to overstress social and affective matters at the expense of cognitive development."[8] The pendulum is swinging back again. This is due in part to the developments in technology which put a new premium on the ability to solve problems in linguistic and mathematical terms. The computer age has demanded different skills with respect both to our domestic affairs and to our place in the international arena of space and military power.

Those children lacking these skills are finding less and less opportunity to participate in the culture, even to the degree that they can earn a living. Children born to parents without these skills suffer that cultural deprivation associated with poverty and slums which makes them retarded in the underlying capacities required to succeed in the public schools.

The newest trend in education to meet the problems of the culturally deprived of our ever-growing inner cities is the government-supported programs like Operation Headstart which aim to enrich the early-life experiences of preschoolers. Such nurseries which focus broadly on a rich variety of living skills are really not new at all. Maria Montessori established similar "Children's Houses" in the slums of Rome in the early 1900's. In rereading her descriptions of the social conditions she aimed to reform, the close comparison in situation to our present-day problems is striking.[9]

After having been virtually ignored since World War I, the Montessori Method in education is returning to a place of prominence, modified by the new insights of psychology. But much of her method is seriously considered in light of its present-day applications. Her stress on muscular education and education of the senses as a prerequisite to the development of reading and writing skills, an approach appropriate to children coming from all strata of society, is important. Likewise, her mixing of several age groups (three through seven years of age) into single classes with the child free to progress at his own particular rate in using the various "didactic materials" presented to all is impressive to modern educators. Also to be cherished is her stress upon invention and on-the-spot modifications of the learning situation by the teacher to foster the child's psychological development.

Although modern educators do not exactly agree with all of Montessori's theories, they tend to value her techniques and practices. J. McV. Hunt states:

> The belief that it is the motor response that is all-important in learning is less tenable than it was half a century ago. Although the issue is still far from settled, recent evidence appears to indicate that the role of the eyes and the ears, and perhaps the tactile organs, may be much more important in the organism's on-going informational interaction with the environment than are the motor outlets.[10]

In speaking thus about the necessary life experiences of individuals from birth through their preschool years, Hunt lends emphasis to this book's thesis that children who are exposed early to a variety of stimuli are more open to the more complex kinds of learnings demanded of their school years. Psychological and educational theory has moved away from such concepts as the fixed IQ, predetermined psychological development and behavior inherited through the genes, the unimportance of formal school training in ages as early as three years, the theory of inborn instincts, and all behavior being a response to certain motivations.

The foregoing thinking emphasizes the value of non-verbal content as a means through which the individual both learns and perceives himself in relationship to others and his environment. His developing skills enable him to incorporate from the culture that surrounds him the learnings and experiences that become his way of expressing himself in action, in attitude, and in thinking.

Non-Verbal Communication Is the Most Effective for Some People

A second important reason for using non-verbal content is one of technical necessity. Most probably the group worker himself is primarily a verbal human being as he interacts with others in the normal course of his life demands. As a person who is college educated and often post-graduate educated, he is probably proficient verbally. Many a social work student is jolted by the realization that communication with the people he intends to help often requires a marked simplification of his very language. He must very often develop as well an appreciation for interests not his own and at times contrary to his own preferences. It is not helpful, for example, if the group worker summarily rules out the dance that is currently the rage simply because he considers it objectionable; he accomplishes nothing by being willing to engage with his group members only in the kind of dancing that is acceptable to him. The same reasoning would hold true for personal preferences in classical music as against rock and roll, or folk singing, or opera, or abstract art, or what have you. Group workers have known for a long time that one must "start where the group is." To this valid concept should be added and emphasized, "but you need not leave them there!"

In addition, the group worker must often turn to the non-verbal forms because it is often through such expression that the group member is most comfortable—and most expressive. Certainly children are often at a disadvantage in verbal exchange because of their very age. To equalize the opportunity for exchange and for meaningful interaction in the child's world, the worker must possess appreciation for the meaning various activities have to the child and must also possess some skill in joining with the child in such expression.

The same kind of rationale is offered for work with the socially and culturally disadvantaged group member. It is increasingly clear that *communication* is the essential ingredient for any work with this group and that it is the group worker who must reach to the world of ideas, actions, and interests that have meaning to the individuals. His own value system and social skills must not get in the way of his communication.[11] The same kind of thinking would apply to the emotionally disturbed, the physically handicapped, and persons with other kinds of social problems that social workers encounter through the very nature of their services.

Thus, proficiency in a range of non-verbal program forms becomes a technical necessity—a means of getting across to the group member and group the essential purpose for the worker's being with the group altogether. It demands of the worker that he know clearly his objectives with the group and individuals and be able to connect these overall goals with each concrete program entity used. This subtle connection of means and ends is difficult to grasp and to use skillfully. Sometimes program is seen as busy work or is introduced with emphases that inadvertently work against the very underlying purposes the worker is trying to promote. How is it possible, for example, to lead the group toward more tolerant and cooperative concern about its members if in all the games played the emphasis is fiercely competitive? In the program examples included in this book there will be a deliberate attempt to show concretely the non-verbal method used by the worker in terms of its content (the choice of activity) and its structure (the conditions surrounding its use) as well as its relationship in time in the process of a single meeting or within the year's experience so that the underlying purposes which direct the worker's engagement with the group are supported. Some attempt will also be made to illustrate situations where a confusion in form and/or structure will actually work against the basic purposes of social work.

Notes to Chapter 3

1. Pioneering efforts in studying the child's relation to his world can be found in the works of psychologist Jean Piaget. Cf., for example, his *The Moral Judgment of the Child* (Glencoe, Ill.: The Free Press) for a consideration of the "rules of the game" and the child's sense of morality; also *Play, Dreams, and Imitation in Childhood* (New York: Norton, 1951); *The Child's Conception of Number* (New York: Humanities Press, 1952); *The Construction of Reality in the Child* (New York: Basic Books, Inc., 1954); and with Barbel Inhelder, *The Child's Conception of Space* (London: Routledge and Kegen Paul, 1956).
2. Lois Barclay Murphy, *The Widening World of Childhood* (New York: Basic Books, Inc., 1962), p. 374.
3. Charles E. Silberman, "Technology is Knocking at the Schoolhouse Door," *Fortune,* August 1966.
4. *Ibid.,* p. 125.
5. Jerome S. Bruner, *Toward A Theory of Instruction* (Cambridge, Mass.: The Belknap Press of Harvard Univ. Press, 1966), pp. 10-14, 22-38.
6. *Ibid.*
7. Omar Khayyam Moore, "Technology and Behavior," *Proceedings of the 1964 Invitational Conference on Testing Problems* (Princeton: N. J.: Educational Testing Service, 1965), 62-64.
8. J. McV. Hunt, "Introduction" to Maria Montessori, *The Montessori Method* (New York: Shocken Books, 1964), p. xxxiii.
9. Montessori, *The Montessori Method,* Ch. III.
10. Hunt, *op. cit.,* p. xxix.
11. Cf. Frank Reisman, *The Culturally Deprived Child* (New York: Harper & Row, 1962), Ch. IX.

4 Non-Verbal Content and Professional Purpose

In an archery contest no special emphasis is laid upon piercing the target, for the strength of the contestants varies. It is style that is important; such was the way of the ancients.

—Confucius

It has been mentioned earlier that non-verbal content is not solely the tool of the social work profession. It is, in fact, safe to state that more direction to date in the purposeful use and in the understanding of the value of non-verbal content, as far as the general public is concerned, has stemmed from the conceptualizations of practitioners in professions other than social work. Notable among the professionals who have contributed to the general understanding of play, of leisure, of learning through doing, and of creative experiences are the educators, recreation leaders, psychiatrists, psychologists, therapists (occupational, music, etc.), and persons concerned with camping.

Two Purposes of Social Group Work

Within the field of social work, and in group work in particular, the purposeful use of non-verbal content would follow two main directions, determined primarily by the underlying purpose for which the sponsoring agency has placed the group worker into a communicating relationship with the group. One broad purpose would include those activities which aim at encouraging *socialization, fun and relaxation, pleasurable group experiences, creative use of leisure, democratic group processes, increased social re-*

sponsibility, and actions geared toward the overall social good. A second broad purpose that would give direction to the non-verbal activities is aimed at the *growth and development of the individual, the rehabilitation of those who suffer from social, emotional, and physical ills as well as intellectual lacks.* In this second focus, the development of the group as a group may be absent or, more often, may take a secondary place in the worker's focus. His primary set is toward serving individuals through their participation in a group under his direction so that their social, emotional, or physical functioning as individuals is enhanced. It is most important that the worker is eminently clear in his overall objectives and that his program choices are, in fact, conductive to the goals he is pursuing.

Importance of Fun and Socialization

The first set of goals can be termed roughly the "fun and socialization" ones. Many adults have to be taught how to enjoy themselves; for our present society, with its pressures to work, get ahead, and succeed, makes them feel tired and overwrought, as well as guilty about any attempts to have fun. And particularly these days, in which the amount of national time available for leisure pursuits has increased rapidly (from an average of one fourth in 1900 to one third in the present day, with an anticipated two fifths by the year 2000), the need to help adults find rewards through pleasurable activities becomes an insistent challenge.[1]

According to Dr. Karl Menninger, study of the backgrounds of mental patients has produced evidence that those who have suffered breakdowns have in their histories less ability to pursue pleasurable activities and less hobby outlets than comparable groups who function adequately.

> One might say that patients become mentally ill when all their sublimations fail them, when they can no longer work or play. Consequently, they must be taught again to work and play, and it is often easier to teach them to play than to work. This is a principle of psychiatric treatment which is more and more recognized to be fundamental.[2]

Play

Menninger said that play is anything but aimless and unnecessary, despite the long history of public attitude to the contrary. He distinguished play from work, in that it is pleasurable activity in which the means is more important than the ostensible end.[3] Play is an end in itself, an opportunity for the discharge of aggressive energy in forms that are not only painless but actually pleasurable; this energy would otherwise be repressed at a definite psychological expense or else expressed in harmful ways. He continued:

> Life is hard; reality is stern; civilization has added heavy burdens to the already great difficulties of living and loving. For this reason we can assume that the more complicated civilization becomes, and the more intense and elaborate the machinery of living is made, the more necessary it will be to create that temporary retreat from reality which we call play.[4]

Work and play make it possible for us to live and love because they help absorb the aggressive energy which would otherwise overwhelm us. And, if play is good for sick people, it is even better for well people, for it is one of the best antidotes against disturbed morale—demoralization—to which we are all at times subject. "People who do not play are potentially dangerous!" [5]

The confusions and multitude of connotations surrounding the word *play* can be suggested by a casual review of its meaning in any unabridged dictionary. The recently published *Random House Dictionary of the English Language* [6] lists seventy-four interpretations of this one word! One can play the piano or play quarterback or play cards or play house or cowboys. One can also "play the fool" (act stupid), or "play possum" (pretend), or "play both ends against the middle" (maneuver for personal gain), or "play down" (belittle), or "play it by ear" (improvise), or "play up" (magnify), or "play with fire" (act dangerously), or "make a play for" (attract sexually). One can "play God" (act omnipotent), "play the game" (be fair), and "play Hamlet" (take the role of Hamlet onstage). One can play the radio or play on a word (pun). Fountains and lights can play. "A play" refers to a specific thing—a dramatic production. And yet, one can "play the horses" or "play the stock market"—serious business! And one can refer to going to the gym for physical improvement (which ought to be considered fun and sport) as going for a "workout." Clearly, these few examples convey the shadings between the serious, the fun, the aesthetic, the action, and the intellect. The present-day concept of play contains a mass of historical usage and attitude that is chameleon-like in quality.

Johan Huizinga provided a fascinating study of a history of culture entitled *Homo Ludens* ("Man the Player").[7] His emphasis was not on defining the place of play within culture but rather on showing how far culture itself bears the character of play. He approached play historically in order to understand it as a cultural phenomenon. In Huizinga's view, play is older than culture, for culture presupposes human society; animals play! Play goes beyond the purely biological, physiological, physical, or psychological. It is a *significant* function of living in and of itself, i.e., there is some sense to it, it has meaning. "In play there is something at play which transcends the immediate needs of life and imparts meaning to the action." [8]

Huizinga's evaluation of play is encapsuled as follows:

> Culture arises in the form of play; it is played from the very beginning. . . . As a culture proceeds, either progressing or regressing, the original relationship between play and non-play does not remain static. As a rule the play-element gradually recedes into the background, being absorbed for the most part in the sacred sphere. The remainder crystallizes as knowledge, folklore, poetry, philosophy, or in the various forms of judicial and social life. The original play-element is then almost completely hidden behind cultural phenomena. But at any moment, even in a highly developed civilization, the play-"instinct" may reassert itself in full force, drowning the individual and the mass in the intoxication of an immense game.
>
> A certain play-factor was extremely active all through the cultural process and produced many of the fundamental forms of social life. The spirit of playful competition is, as a social impulse, older than culture itself and pervades all life like a veritable ferment. Wisdom and philosophy found expression in words and forms derived from religious contests. The rules of warfare, the conventions of noble

living were built up on play-patterns. Civilization is, in its earliest phases, played. It does not come *from* play like a babe detaching itself from the womb; it arises *in* and *as* play, and never leaves it.

Real civilization cannot exist in the absence of a certain play-element, for civilization presupposes limitation and mastery of the self, the ability not to confuse its own tendencies with the ultimate and highest goal, but to understand that it is enclosed within certain bounds freely accepted. Civilization will, in a sense, always be played according to certain rules, and true civilization will always demand fair play. Fair play is nothing less than good faith expressed in play terms. Hence the cheat or the spoil-sport shatters civilization itself.[9]

This view of culture as arising out of play elements that develop and lend themselves to various forms of human achievement, knowledge, and social life can now be considered alongside the formulations of Omar Khayyam Moore, cited in the preceding chapter, concerning how children learn the various vital aspects of their culture. There is, in a sense, the need for each new generation to repeat through their play, beginning in childhood, a direct encounter with their culture as they have received it so that they can know it.

Two main forces keep the adult from being able to readily take part in play and hobby activities. The first springs from the pleasure principle, so operative in early childhood and controlled with such difficulty by the disciplined adult personality. Within the developmental process itself the maturing individual is taught that such pleasures are somehow wrong and he thus is inhibited by his own inner sense of guilt for wanting such expression. Secondly, the Puritan tradition, with its attending moralistic prohibitions against such pleasures as dancing, wasting time, and other nonproductive pursuits, has been a deterrent to the frank enjoyment of recreation. Coupled with these two powerful shapers of adult attitudes toward having fun are the vast range of individual life experiences with economic factors that have weighed against an early childhood experience with recreation and play. Many people who come as adults into a group worker's group have simply never known the experience of leisure, of fun and play, of expression through creative experiences. All too often they are experts in work, work, work! No wonder that the initial reaction to a game or a song by many adults is withdrawal, or a "That's for children!"

It is the experience of this writer that the group leader also is all too often a product of these same forces. He too has been subtly affected by these psychological and cultural restraints, and has to learn to feel right about working in such a medium—that fun and game experiences can be serious business in his hands. Unless the group worker reaches out and faces his own biases against helping through media in this lighter side of living, he tends to agree with the initial rejecting response encountered in his adult groups. He then tends to fail to move ahead in the face of this resistance and help the group toward what often they most need but can't accept—the opportunity to pursue goals of fun and socialization or of individual growth and development, through games, dancing, singing, and the rest.

The Difference Between Play and Work

One definition of a game which this writer likes to use to urge students toward understanding the subjective importance of what they do is that "a game is an attitude of mind in which fun and enjoyment is important." In other words the *style* of the participation, as Confucius said, is what determines the value of the activity.

For Willie Mays baseball would be *work*, not a *game*, because it is his serious business. But perhaps one who knew Willie intimately would say that he has such grace and style in his work that he has actually made of his major life occupation, *play*. Huizinga laments the increasing systematization and regimentation of sport in present-day culture. He believes something of the pure play quality has been lost:

> The spirit of the professional is no longer the true play-spirit; it is lacking in spontaneity and carelessness. . . . In modern social life sport occupies a place alongside and apart from the cultural process. The great competitions in archaic cultures had always formed part of the sacred festivals and were indispensable as health and hap-

> piness-bringing activities. This ritual tie has now been severed; sport has become profane, "unholy" in every way and has no organic connection whatever with the structure of society.[10]

It could be added here that the performance of Willie Mays is neither free nor possessing the end-in-itself quality. He is definitely set upon winning for the sake of the eventual win of the pennant and the resultant salary increase.

One could go on citing examples of other successful individuals who perform their work with such sensitivity, feeling, and pleasure that the joys usually associated with play come to them through work. The particular, subjective meaning of each activity to the individual in the long run distinguishes *how the participant feels about what he is doing*. If this is so, then as the case studies will illustrate, many of the complex problems of group life can be met through improvised gamelike activities that meet a situation in a light vein but meet it meaningfully.

Likewise, in all other activities one's subjective attitude toward what he does makes of it either work or play. In the excerpt that follows, two girls preparing for their group meeting meal dived into the food preparation with a gusto as soon as they arrived. To them, is this work or play?

> The preparations for the spaghetti sauce and the spaghetti, the setting of the table, the making of the salad, were all handled very neatly by Dorothy and Phyllis. Although at times I suggested ways of doing things, the girls were very insistent that I not help them. However, they were both very willing to accept suggestions from me and did not seem to resent this interruption. Rather significant during the preparations of the meal was Dorothy's reaction to me while she was mixing up the meatballs. As she was mixing the hamburger, onion and egg together she commented to me that I probably would not want to eat the meatballs because she was mixing them up. I questioned Dorothy and she just said that maybe because I thought her hands were dirty. I said that I saw that she had washed her hands earlier and that I did not feel her hands were dirty and that most certainly I would want to eat the meatballs.
>
> Later while Dorothy was browning the meatballs, she took her fork and took part of the meat from one of the meatballs and ate it. She

then looked at me and asked if I would like part of the hamburger which I accepted. Although she did not say anything, I felt this was a test to see if I would eat the meat she had prepared. I was also interested to note that while Dorothy and Phyllis were preparing the meal they were able to work together very well. I directed the sequence of events, but both girls were able to accept their own particular responsibility and carry through on this. I commented to the girls when we were almost ready to eat how impressed I was about the way they worked together. I said that it is always easier for a person to do things alone because there is no one there to be different in his approach to something, but I said it is good that they are learning to work together as a team.

Most probably, if these girls were asked how they felt about what they did this day, they would respond that they had fun or that they had a good time. Surely, they would not say that they slaved over a hot stove during their meeting.

And yet, on a deeper level they were truly hard at work! The episode reveals that in the hands of this group worker, these girls were helped to cope with two crucial problems of living: (1) Dorothy and Phyllis are Negro and the worker is white. Through Dorothy's self-deprecatory comment about her dirty hands and through the worker's response to this as well as to the eating of a piece of Dorothy's hamburger *both girls* could perceive on a very human level this worker's value of them. (2) The life task of learning to get along with others was experienced in working closely together and affirmed verbally by the worker as a success experience so that the girls could learn to value also the times when they could cooperate, could give and take. Their pride in a successful joint accomplishment was directly enhanced by the worker's acknowledgment of it. Both of these very serious underlying aspects of the worker's attention bring into action one of her underlying purposes in working with these young adolescents: *to help them gain in their own sense of self-esteem.* The avenue toward feeling this way about themselves is through what was to them a fun activity and what was to the worker good, hard work.

It is of greatest significance, furthermore, that the most meaningful level of the worker's help to Dorothy and to Phyllis occurred through non-verbal means—through an acceptance of Dorothy's mixing of the meat and through actually eating some of her hamburger. In these simple gestures the full force of the worker's valuing of Dorothy got across to her! This attitude-in-action can be felt and be real for Dorothy—more than a thousand protestations in words!

It is sometimes asked, "Is it right to make work into play—to make a game of things rather than help the group learn to accept responsibility as the serious part of group living that it is?" Actually, only a thin line separates work from play and games; the whole distinction rests in its meaning to the person, particularly the essential freedom of choice in involvement in play and games. The attitude of the individual determines whether a game or any activity is more work than fun or whether necessary obligations of living can be accepted with a spirit of enjoyment. Those who have found some way to add the light touch to living are able to live more fully and gain a richer enjoyment from their living. Tom Sawyer enticed his friends into whitewashing his aunt's fence for him and paying him in precious trinkets for the privilege by suggesting what fun it was—not something that just anyone could do well! Twain concludes this famous anecdote with a bit of philosophical musing:

> Work consists of whatever a body is obliged to do, and
> Play consists of whatever a body is not obliged to do.[11]

The close relationship between work and play is also recognized by Paul Goodman in his discussion "Making Sense of Adult Leisure." [12] He states that enjoyment is not a goal in and of itself. It is a feeling that accompanies important ongoing activity; pleasure is always dependent on function. "Thus the important question is: If there is little interest, honor, or manliness in the working part of our way of life, can we hope for much in the leisure part?" [13]

In thinking back of the definition of *recreation* by G. Ott Romney, "Recreation is an end in its own right and includes everything the individual chooses to do in his own time for the gratification of the doing," and of the discussion of *play* by Johan

Huizinga, "Play is a significant function of living in and of itself . . . it is unrelated to wisdom or folly, good or evil, truth or falsehood," then one must disagree with Paul Goodman's thought that enjoyment is not a valid goal but rather a by-product of an action. Enjoyment is a goal for leisure (play) as for work, but because of the freedom attending the use of leisure, the enjoyment might be a more primary purpose. However, Goodman's connection of the ways of being in the working part of life, "interest, honor, manliness," with the leisure part of life is entirely to the point. It is obvious, by now, that both leisure and work are components of the culture itself and man's attitude toward both endeavors springs from a unitary frame of reference.

Play Acting as a Therapeutic Experience

Dr. J. L. Moreno, one of the founders of group psychotherapy, of the psychodrama, of the sociodrama, and of sociometry, developed a therapeutic method which centered on bringing people together in groups and involving them in acting out in the "here and now" the same problems and ways of meeting problems that characterize their way of living. "Dr. Moreno emphasized the fact that he differs with the psychoanalytic approach in another very significant way, namely, that the analyst works backward to an explanation for the individual's conduct while he takes the individual's conduct as the starting point and works forward." [14] Stressing a doctrine of "Spontaneity-Creativity," Moreno felt that creativity without spontaneity becomes lifeless, and spontaneity without creativity is empty and runs abortive. "Spontaneity and creativity are thus categories of a different order; creativity belongs to the categories of substance—it is the arch substance—spontaneity to the categories of catalyzer—it is the arch catalyzer." [15] Speaking of spontaneity, Moreno continues:

> Spontaneity operates in the present, now and here; it propels the individual towards an adequate response to a new situation or a new response to an old situation . . . a great deal of man's psycho and socio-pathology can be ascribed to the insufficient development of spontaneity. Spontaneity "training" is therefore the most auspi-

cious skill to be taught to therapists in all our institutions of learning and it is his task to teach his clients how to be more spontaneous without becoming excessive.[16]

As early as 1921, Moreno developed his spontaneity-creativity theory in his Stegreiftheater, counting and measuring interpersonal relations among actors, measuring the adequacy or inadequacy of their performances in terms of their spontaneity. He soon discovered that the less fictitious these interactions were for the actors, the more personally and privately they were involved in these roles and interactions, and the more meaningful also became the counting of seconds, inches, words, and choices in the spontaneity research.

Moreno emphasized action rather than analysis in his therapeutic method. Rather than use free association stemming from the position of reclining on a therapist's couch, he preferred spontaneous acting out among people (therapist included) as an expression of a universal function of human behavior. He further stated, "The greatest asset of psychodrama and the psychodramatic arts (spontaneous dance, music, and painting) is the rise of form and beauty from the ashes of spontaneous production." [17]

The group worker of the present day, seeking to evaluate the importance of his use of non-verbal forms, owes much to the pioneering work of Moreno. Although his work was exclusively in the area of the drama, the same insights with respect to spontaneity and creativity apply to games, rhythms, dance, singing, and the rest. To the extent that the method of interacting within any medium is not plotted out by a script or score or definite rule, the participant is freed to make his own use of the medium *in situ*, as Moreno would say, and in the very using of this experience he will bring into the situation all of his private, personal world.

Games Analysis in Group Therapy

More recently another psychiatrist has built a system to unify individual and social psychiatry by using group therapy as the basic method and the analysis of games as a major element in the treatment.[18] Dr. Eric Berne believes people can achieve a new self-awareness by analyzing their behavior in terms of games and so learn to live more constructive lives. Investigating what he terms "social transactions," Berne states, "The most gratifying forms of social contact, whether or not they are embedded in a matrix of activity, are games and intimacy. Prolonged intimacy is rare, and even then it is primarily a private matter; significant social intercourse most commonly takes the form of games." [19]

By "games" Berne is referring to verbal exchanges among adults, the patterns of which are laid down in childhood through the subtle observation of the parents' interactions. The "game" is an ongoing series of complementary *ulterior* (emphasis mine) transactions progressing to a well-defined, predictable outcome. Games have an ulterior quality and a payoff. The ulterior quality is the seeking of advantage which comes to the winner in the payoff—emotional gratification. The "game" should not be misleading because of its name . . . it does not imply fun or even enjoyment, but is a very serious transaction of interpersonal relationships.[20]

Berne believes that games form the basic structure for the emotional dynamics of each family and are learned by children from their earliest months through significant experiences in everyday living. In his opinion, theories of internal individual psychodynamics have so far not been able to solve satisfactorily the problem of human relationships. These are transactional situations which call for a theory of social dynamics that cannot be derived solely from consideration of individual motivations.[21]

The kinds of games categorized by Berne include life games, marriage games, sexual games, party games, underworld games, consulting room games, and good games. Berne's novel approach suggests that therapists are presently only at the brink of truly assessing the meaning and emotional value of interpersonal relationships in their psychodynamic meanings. "Games" have the social function of structuring time satisfactorily, i.e., giving people known patterns of ways to relate in their social intercourse, as well as being urgently necessary for the maintenance of health in certain individuals. The psychic stability of these persons is so precarious, and their positions are so tenuously maintained, that to deprive them of their games may plunge them into irreversible despair and even psychosis.[22]

Fun Activities Should Be Fun

So far, this discussion of content and professional purpose reveals that both the professions of psychiatry and of social work can pursue their particular purposes through their own distinctive use of the content of the experience. And while each profession might borrow certain theory, techniques, and insights from the other, there must be a basic difference in approach simply because the aims of the professions are different.

In social work, program activities must be consistent with the two broad directions that the group worker aims to pursue with his group: the goal toward fun and socialization and the goal toward individual rehabilitation. It is of crucial importance that the group worker and the group understand clearly the underlying purpose for the use of content material that might appear on the surface to have some other purpose.

If the purpose is pleasure, fun, and socialization, the content should emphasize "togetherness," comfort, easy accomplishment, and the like. How often a so-called "fun" activity puts someone on the spot! Consider the many mystery games, for example, in which one person or a part of the group is left dangling a long time. They are the butt of the group as the mysterious trick—like passing the scissors crossed or uncrossed when actually the legs of the person determine the trick—drags on and on. Of course the person has to feel stupid! Or think of the many elimination games during which most of the group is unoccupied for most of the action. No wonder additional confusion is the end result. And some of the mental games, e.g., when you have to remember in turn what each person took along with him on a trip, are anything but fun. Under the guise of stimulating healthy competition much too much downright sadism is allowed to operate.

And what group worker has not observed the cardinal signal of the group's only self-defense in such unpleasant circumstances—to lose interest and refuse to play? The massacre of the pleasurable experiences inhering in art, drama, and music activities is so common that many people protect themselves by refusing to get involved in the first place. The group worker often uses the same media as the school teacher and sometimes must deliberately work to develop new connotations for activities whose pleasure content has been eliminated by unfortunate school experiences. With smaller groups and different goals from those of the school teacher, the group worker should use his content with his fortunate freedom in mind and not copy the more formal approach in his teaching. It ought to be quite different in many ways from the school experience since the underlying purposes are not the same.

Fun Activities for Rehabilitative Purposes

When working with groups which have been formed around certain problems, the content of the experience should be obviously for fun when this is the goal and just as obviously for individual growth when this is the purpose. A confusion in members' interpretation of a fun game is illustrated in Chapter 9, Case Study 47 of the anecdotes. Once, in this writer's experience, she gave a simple puzzle toy to one little boy in a residence for foster children. Her motive was simply to give him something interesting to do. Billy took the puzzle—it was better than nothing—and worked for a while. Then he commented, "This is just like what the psychologist had me do when I was being tested." It was clear that there was no fun in this challenge because of its meaning to Billy.

Likewise, when non-verbal media are used to help people work on their problems, some interpretation of the goal must be added frequently within the seemingly funlike media. The individuals and groups must not be left with the impression that "we are just here to mess around." Dramatics has frequently been used to help individuals and groups work on social or psychological problems. As mentioned earlier, the whole therapeutic technique of J. L. Moreno rests with the use of the drama to recreate the experience of a personal problem situation and through direction to develop insight into the problem.[23] If the group worker wishes to use the drama form to get into problem areas rather than for purely aesthetic, socialization, and recreation purposes, the group must also understand and want to use the drama in this way. The illustration below shows how an interpretation by the worker can clarify for the group—in this case in the midst of the action—the unique purpose for which this group in this agency (a child guidance center) is to use an activity:

> Frequently a boy is seduced into a fight, needing to defend his honor against the insult "He's afraid." In such a case the group worker stops the fight and points out that the boy is afraid. Boxing is for fun, and a boy does not have to box in the group room when it is not fun. The worker points out that every boy is afraid of something, though not necessarily of boxing. By universalizing fears, the worker involves all the children. The group worker tells the child that the worker is sorry he is afraid and that the clinic will try to help him. As the worker speaks, not only one child but the whole group hears. Fears are established as legitimate in the group. Children are enabled to accept the no-boxing rule for one child, since the interpretation assures them of like understanding in relation to their own fears.[24]

Workers sometimes get confused by their concept of "fairness," i.e., rules have to be applied equally to all group members. The above example illustrates that the force of group pressure can be constructively used to create special rules applying differentially to individuals according to their particular needs. In this case, the overall ground rule is that all people have fears, although of different things, and they should not be forced to participate in something they are too much afraid of. How different this is from evolving either a *boxing* or *no-boxing* rule for the group!

Thus it can be seen that such an activity as boxing could be used by groups whose main purpose is fun and socialization and also by groups whose main purpose is individual rehabilitation. The rules and conditions (the structures) surrounding the activity would be profoundly affected by the purpose of the group as well as by the purpose of the professional person working with the group. In the following chapter the significant effects of varying the structure of an activity, depending upon the underlying purpose behind its use, will be further explored.

Play and Games as Life

> As extensions of the popular response to the workaday stress, games become faithful models of a culture. They incorporate both the action and the reaction of whole populations in a single dynamic image . . . Games are dramatic models of our psychological lives providing release of particular tensions. They are collective and popular art forms with strict conventions. Ancient and nonliterate societies naturally regarded games as live dramatic models of the universe or of the outer cosmic drama . . . All games are media of interpersonal communication, and they could have neither existence nor meaning except as extensions of our immediate inner lives . . . In games we devise means of nonspecialized participation in the larger drama of our time.[25]

Thus, games and living itself are closely interrelated. Both are serious business with wins and losses. Both can be fun. Both can be frustrating. To some people life is a game and their same patterns of meeting the unknown, learned in early childhood interactions, serve them well as adults.

It seems fitting to conclude this discussion of games, content, and professional purpose with a reference to the thinking of George Herbert Mead, whose pioneering ideas have served as a beacon light to those of us who came after.

> The game has a logic, so that such an organization of the self is rendered possible. There is a definite end to be obtained; the actions of the different individuals are all related to each other with reference to that end so that they do not conflict. . . . The game is then an illustration of the situation out of which an organized personality arises. Insofar as the child does take the attitude of the other and allows that attitude of the other to determine the thing he is going to do with reference to a common end, he is becoming an organic member of society. . . . The importance of the game is that it lies entirely inside of the child's own experience, and the importance of our modern type of education is that it is brought as far as possible within this realm.

> What goes on in a game goes on in the life of the child all the time. He is continually taking the attitudes of those about him, especially the roles of those who in some sense control him and on whom

> he depends. He gets the function of the process in an abstract sort of way at first. It goes over from the play into the game in a real sense. He has to play the game. The morale of the game takes hold of the child more than the larger morale of the whole community. The child passes into the game, and the game expresses a social situation in which he can completely enter; its morale may have a greater hold on him than that of the family to which he belongs or the community in which he lives . . . Such is the process by which a personality arises.[26]

Games fulfill a vitally important function in the development of the child. In addition, as this discussion has emphasized repeatedly, they (along with all the other doing activities) continue to contribute important pieces of life itself to the individual of any age.

Notes to Chapter 4

1. Stewart Case, "The Potentials for Camping in the Growing Leisure Society," *Bulletin of American Camping Association of Philadelphia* (February 1966).
2. Karl Menninger, *Love Against Hate* (New York: Harcourt, Brace and World, 1942), p. 183.
3. *Ibid.*, p. 169.
4. *Ibid.*, p. 172.
5. *Ibid.*, p. 179.
6. *The Random House Dictionary of the English Language,* ed. Jess Stein (New York: Random House, 1966), p. 1104.
7. Johan Huizinga, *Homo Ludens: A Study of the Play-Element in Culture* (Boston: The Beacon Press, 1955), paperback ed.
8. *Ibid.*, p. 1. For a fuller view of Huizinga's thinking regarding play as a function of culture and the essential characteristics of play (It is voluntary and free; it is not ordinary or "real" life, but rather in time and place containing its own course and meaning; it creates order and is related to aesthetics; it is unrelated to wisdom or folly, truth or falsehood, good or evil, but contains internal ethics of its own) the reader is referred to Ch. 1.
9. *Ibid.*, pp. 46-7, and p. 211.
10. *Ibid.*, pp. 197-8.
11. Mark Twain, *The Adventures of Tom Sawyer* (New York: Harcourt, Brace and World, 1963), Ch. 11.
12. Paul Goodman, *Growing Up Absurd, Problems of Youth in the Organized Society* (New York: Vintage Books, 1956), pp. 234-6.

13. *Ibid.*, p. 236.
14. William Alanson White in Forward to J. L. Moreno, *Who Shall Survive* (New York: Beacon House, 1953), p. xciv.
15. J. L. Moreno, *Who Shall Survive*, p. 40.
16. *Ibid.*, p. 42.
17. *Ibid.*, p. lxxvi.
18. Cf. Eric Berne, *Transactional Analysis in Psychotherapy* (New York: Grove Press, 1961); *Games People Play* (New York: Grove Press, 1964); and *The Structure and Dynamics of Organizations and Groups* (New York: Grove Press, 1963).
19. Berne, *Games People Play*, pp. 19-20.
20. *Ibid.*, pp. 49-50.
21. *Ibid.*, p. 59.
22. Edward Albee treats the subject of games as adult verbal interactions aimed at certain outcomes in a "payoff" dramatically in *Who's Afraid of Virginia Woolf?* (New York: Atheneum, 1962). The inexorable playing out of the games among his four unhappy characters is one dominant theme of his drama.
23. Moreno, *op. cit.*
24. Sallie Churchill, "Pre-Structuring Group Content," *Social Work*, IV, 3 (July 1959), 57-8.
25. Marshall McLuhan, *Understanding Media: The Extensions of Man* (New York: McGraw-Hill, 1965), pp. 235, 237-8.
26. *George Herbert Mead on Social Psychology*, ed. Anselm Strauss (Chicago: Univ. of Chicago, 1964), pp. 223-4. Copyright © 1934, 1936, 1938, 1956 and 1964 by the Univ. of Chicago. Rev. ed., 1964. First Phoenix ed., 1964.

5 Structuring Non-Verbal Content

The performance of the acrobat appears easy and relaxed but let us not lose sight of the long preliminary ordeal which enables him to give this effect. It is the same with painting. With hard work, the mastery of one's medium should pass from the conscious to the subconscious; only then can one successfully give an impression of spontaneity . . . An artist is an explorer. He has to begin by self-discovery and by observation of his own procedure. After that he must not feel under any constraint. But, above all, he must never be too easily satisfied with what he has done.

—Henri Matisse *

With every piece of non-verbal content that is introduced into a group experience, there are two interacting entities that combine to condition the quality of the experience: the precise form of the medium selected, the *content;* and the incentives, limitations, procedures, materials, and all conditions attending its use, the *structures.* That both the content and the structuring of the content bear important relevance to the tone and the outcome of each experience is all too little understood. The content may be just right for the purpose and yet be undermined by a lack of attention to how it is structured. Likewise, inappropriate content can be turned to good use because of a restructuring of it by the worker. Examples of both such situations will be found in the case studies in Chapter 9. (See Number 68 for an example of poor structuring of acceptable content and Number 33 for an example of restructuring inappropriate content.)

* Quoted by Monroe Wheeler in *The Last Works of Henri Mattise* (New York: The Museum of Modern Art, 1961), p. 5.

Choosing Appropriate Non-Verbal Content

There is much writing, stemming primarily from the fields of education and recreation, to guide the worker in making an appropriate choice of content. The activity must contain the possibility of successful accomplishment. It must be safe and interesting, as well as appropriate in terms of age, sex, cultural background, intellectual endowment, etc. It must be appropriate for the size of the group, size of the room, physical setting (indoor or outdoor, for example), and encompassable without alienating other groups meeting in the next room, the neighbors, or the community. A brief review of the games books, to take but one example, will clearly show how these determinants are recognized by the specialists who write recreation books. There is much known in the present day that can guide the worker in the selection of content. In addition, there is ample writing, as mentioned before, that illuminates for the worker the values inherent in various non-verbal forms.

Structuring Non-Verbal Content Appropriately

Less attention has been given to the matter of structuring the content. Inserted here are two outlines for possible structuring of activities, in art and in singing, that have been developed by this writer as an aid to guide workers in the way they offer their content choices. These outlines merely suggest the possibilities of developing a two-dimensional way of viewing every program content.

PROVIDING STRUCTURE IN ART ACTIVITIES

Structure the activity and apply limitations by means of:

1. Content and purpose
   a. Doodle picture—extreme freedom of form
   b. Design—imaginative flower
   c. Rhythmic writing—draw to music, then color part of scribble

   d. Crazy letters in sign making
   e. Cutouts and paste-ups to make desired effect without drawing
   f. Use of a theme, e.g., seasonal ideas, city sights
2. Materials used
   a. Big brushes, huge paper, magic markers
   b. Metals, woods, or natural objects
   c. "Blow Pictures"—apply drops of color to paper (no tools) and blow here and there; also jiggle paper about to make colors run into patterns
3. Time
   a. Short time contains less risk
   b. Several different experiences, all limited in length, developing one after another
4. Responsibility for whole
   a. Group project—each individual having a role but not responsible for the total product
   b. Working in pairs or in three's—develops relatedness but not full responsibility or risk for outcome (can be frustrating to those more competent in the activity itself to have to share idea and execution of it)
   c. Size of group—relates to kind and quality of experience

PROVIDING STRUCTURE IN SINGING ACTIVITIES
(Especially useful in introducing new songs)

1. Content
   a. Motion songs—"Let Everyone Clap Hands with Me," "Under the Spreading Chestnut Tree"
   b. Nonsense songs—"99 Bottles of Beer," "Put Your Finger in the Air"
   c. Repetitive songs—"Old MacDonald Had a Farm," "Drunken Sailor," "Bring A Little Water, Silvie"
   d. Additive songs—"Green Grass Grows All Around," "Twelve Days of Christmas"
2. Materials used
   a. Waxed paper held lightly over lips

   b. Clapping—"Deep in the Heart of Texas," spirituals
   c. Instrument—ukelele, etc.

3. Time—short as possible (Avoid long narratives such as "Barbara Allen" and "Grandfather's Clock"; these are for groups that love to sing.)
4. Responsibility for the whole
   a. Two different parts—"Zum Gali Gali" (often one simple part merely keeps the tempo)
   b. Leader/follower—"Little Sir Echo," "I am a Musician," "Snitzel Bank," "Hand me Down My Silver Trumpet" (Any song can be introduced as a leader/follower song by simply singing one line and having group repeat the sung line after.)
   c. Simple new verses created by one group member spontaneously during the song—"Hey Lolli," "Cindy," "Aiken Drum"
   d. Rounds
5. Purpose
   a. Make game—Sing Down (categories: old favorites, folk, popular), nursery rhyme singing contest
   b. Keep step while hiking
   c. Help coordination while skating
   d. Campfire songs
   e. Work songs

The Interrelatedness of Content and Structure

From the examples cited it can be noted that many ways are available in structuring art and singing activities to relate what is offered to the precise needs of the group at a given moment. This writer believes that the degree of sensitivity demanded of the group worker so that non-verbal content can be tailor-made to fit a situation is tremendous. Even with group work students who minutely watch and analyze all that they introduce, an incident such as happened during the seventeenth week of the school year can highlight in a flash just how difficult it is to be sufficiently aware of every aspect of each activity introduced.

Each student introduced the puppet he had made which might be used in one of his groups and discussed what was involved in constructing it. Mr. K showed his puppet made from a real potato. The class and he were full of positive responses to the possibilities of such a puppet for his settlement house work in a Negro neighborhood. It was quick and easy, inexpensive, of readily available materials, creative, etc. At length, I tried a direct approach to one neglected aspect of the puppet, in my view its most important and useful value, i.e., its brown skin. I asked what pertinence this puppet had for his work with Negroes. There were a few comments about being inexpensive, and Negroes using potatoes and possibly formerly having grown them in the South. But not one of the eighteen students was aware that the puppet had a brown skin! When I mentioned this, they were shocked that they had missed the point and then proceeded to have a lively discussion on the aspect of race, how they might use puppets to lead toward such discussion, and what their position ought to be.

Just after this episode Mr. P proudly showed his puppet, stating that he had made one that was entirely glued rather than sewn since he didn't know how to sew. He accepted his lack of sewing skill quite matter-of-factly until I directed the class's attention to this as a cultural lack. Should men be able to pass off so lightly their lack of proficiency in sewing or cooking? Might they not be depriving their group of some valuable learning experience because of their cultural bias? Later Mr. E showed his puppet whose dress was stapled rather than sewn. He was thoughtful as he added that in his work with postpsychiatric patients he thought he would prefer to staple the puppets with his men because he was concerned with helping them get settled on their true sexual identification.

In response to Mr. E's thoughts about not sewing with his men, the teacher said that it was not of great importance *per se* whether the puppet was sewn or stapled, just so the method of construction was selected with some deliberateness with respect to the needs of the group rather than through a casual, half-thought-out approach of the worker. The subtleties residing within the making of a simple puppet as they affect members' attitudes toward race, sex, and cultural expectations are all contained in this little example. It is clearly seen here how the content (the puppet) is vastly affected by its attending structures (the material used and the method of construction). The value of the experience to the group can be enhanced or undermined by the worker's sensitivity to the totality.

This type of double sensitivity is also illustrated by the following example. An experienced group worker who was calling a square dance for unmarried mothers almost broke up the group that was dancing with great gusto by a simple slip of the tongue, an inappropriate content "Lady go right, Gent go left." The group stopped and was flustered when the word "gent" was mentioned. The worker recovered with a "Lady go right, Lady go left" and action proceeded despite what might have appeared to be a more ambiguous call.

On another occasion when the worker with these same unmarried mothers in residence attempted to involve them in folk singing, again a content blunder suggested how very carefully a group worker must always be with the precise material introduced. In this instance, the worker was effective with familiar, slow, repetitive ballad-type songs (structures) that were easy to follow and possibly known to the group. However, she didn't think ahead to recall in advance all the lyrics. When in the course of "On Top of Old Smokey" they got to the "false-hearted lover," the worker could see looks of self-consciousness and sad embarrassment come over the faces of many of the girls. These examples show clearly just how responsible the group worker must be on every possible level—content and structure—with all that is introduced. In all cases, there is a subjective reaction to every nonverbal content, the meaning of the experience to each individual, which becomes the heart of the service.

6 Non-Verbal Content and Process

Step by step we go into the night—the movement itself is the only truth. It is not the outcome of actions that is crucial but rather the style of the behavior itself—how one chooses.

—Ingmar Bergman *

Non-Verbal Content as Means Rather than End

In Chapters 4 and 5 the program content of a group experience was seen as a means through which the purposes of the sponsoring agency, the group worker, and the members themselves could be effected. Further, to insure that such goals were consistent with the actual demands of any given experience, close attention needed to be given to the precise demands of the content as well as the stipulations created by the worker for its use. Thus, content itself and the structures affecting it and deliberately supplied by the group worker combine to make the activity carry out the underlying intention in its use—the purpose.

Connecting purpose and concrete experience and making them consistent is one of the most difficult parts of the group worker's task. Specific illustrations of activities selected to further particular purposes will be detailed in Chapter 8. One overall guiding principle to achieve an organically sound program experience is to take the focus off the actual success or failure of the program experience *per se* and to put it squarely on its usefulness as part of the *process.* Of course, while the group worker might place less emphasis on ends and more on means, it must be admitted that the group, too, has its own expectations and standards for

* From *The Magician,* as quoted by Donald F. Krill, in "Existentialism: A Philosophy for Our Current Revolutions," *The Social Service Review,* September, 1966.

itself in terms of outcome. The program as an end must always be interesting enough to engage the group in the first place, and successful and rewarding enough on its manifest level to develop satisfaction and group pride.

Although growth for the group and its members can spring from the experience of failure as well as success, the reason for the failure has meaning to the members if it is due to their own misjudgment, lack of responsibility, inconsistency, or whatever, rather than the worker's ineptitude. The worker, by and large, should let the group profit from his experience and judgment, guiding them away from pitfalls and never deliberately planning for the group to experience failure so that they will prepare and involve themselves differently the next time. He holds a responsibility for pointing out to the group in advance possible flaws in planning and possible failures in program if he sees them; the decision to follow his caution rests with the group.

Non-Verbal Content as Process

It must now be clear that a large amount of the group process of many groups emanates from non-verbal content of various forms. The group worker affects the quality of this process by his selection of content or his help to the group in their choosing, as well as the way in which he interacts with individuals and group throughout the experience. While the worker does not control the group's process or their use of the program content, he also does not sit passively by and observe the interaction. His participation in the process should be significant and meaningful, stemming from his professional objectives (and his agency's) and made effective by his level of skill as a helper.

The group members must also understand the intention behind the group worker's engagement with them. They should know why they are in the group, not only from their point of view but also from the worker's and the agency's. There should be no mystery to the process. One should not "group work a group" without their knowing it. The goals, whether they be fun and socialization or remedial individual growth experiences, should be shared consciously by both worker and group members.

In using program content dynamically to support the complicated process of interaction between worker and group and among the group members, a helpful way of viewing program content is to see (1) beginning activities, (2) developmental activities, and (3) ending activities. This conceptualization would hold true for any form of content, from archery to zither playing. Thus, program content to be effective must be appropriate according to the particular time phase in the group's process.

Beginning Forms

There has been some awareness of the *beginning* aspect of game activities in writings in the field of recreation, especially in what has been known as "social recreation." The names "icebreakers" or "mixers" are used to describe particular games or dances which help the group members get to know each other or help the group get started in spite of itself. There has been less attention to date in applying the icebreaker concept broadly to all activities in the same way that it has been applied to games and dances. All too often when a worker does realize that he ought to do something through program to help "break the ice" in his group, he will rely on a game when the game form, itself, is thoroughly inappropriate for his particular group. Perhaps they come with the attitude that games are for children. Or maybe they regard their group as too serious in purpose to indulge in games, particularly at the outset. Many factors may make a game, despite its built-in opportunity for mixing the group, inappropriate.

Practically every program medium can be geared through its content and structure to possess the same potential as the game to be a *beginning* activity. The group can be helped to begin through a particular kind of craft activity, for example, if the mixer aspects are added to it by the deliberate intention of the worker. To illustrate the principle of adapting various content forms to beginning activities for a group, several examples follow of the work of social group work students from class sessions where the focus was on beginning activities.

BEGINNING THROUGH CRAFTS

Mr. K divided the class into four groups of five students each and gave each a copy of an old *Photography* magazine, some scissors, paste, and a large piece of cardboard. Each group was to go through the magazine and select pictures according to one covering theme which they would select. Then they would cut out appropriate pictures and paste them on a small poster. No time limit or other competitive aspects were added. Immediately there followed a hub-bub of busyness and planning. In short order each group produced its product—"Children Around the World," "Leisure Pursuits," "Emotions," "Approaches to Photography." Some were montages with overlays and irregular cuttings. Others were simply mounted in symmetrical fashion. Each was quite different and each group seemed proud of its result.

BEGINNING THROUGH DRAMA

Mr. P divided the class into four groups, making certain to mix the sexes. He asked that each group pantomime "an embarrassing situation." There was much laughter in the various groups as they settled on the incident. One group showed a man inadvertently entering a ladies' washroom. A second showed a person slipping in the street as she ran for a bus and simultaneously waved at a friend. Others were in similar spirit objects of laughter and appreciation as the "audience" attempted to guess the situation. In analyzing what made these good beginning activities, the class recognized that the structuring of the incidents around the theme of embarrassment (which immediately provided a farce atmosphere) and the pantomime form (which reduced the dramas to the simplest, least demanding skill) as two prime conditions.

BEGINNING THROUGH SINGING

Mrs. G distributed little pieces of paper to all. Each contained one of four well-known, simple songs. Before distribution she told all to start singing the song aloud, thereby finding the others who had their song, and when they all collected to sing their song together and loud. For the next few minutes the room sounded like the Tower of Babel, but quickly all had accomplished the directives. Mrs. G was active throughout in helping any who had difficulty sing their way to the others.

BEGINNING THROUGH CRAFTS

Miss L distributed a thin sheet of notebook paper and a crayon to all. She explained that the meeting room contained many interesting textures in its various surfaces, e.g., the rough brick walls, the metal spirals of the notebooks, the grids on the stove. Each person was asked to fill the paper as he wished by carefully tracing over various surfaces. The class was at first astonished by such an activity but became quickly involved. They got up and moved individually, but were soon exchanging their colored crayons with each other and making suggestions to others as they spied and used something which gave an unusual effect. At the end the various pages were held up for all to see. In analyzing how the activity progressed, they saw the wide range of individual or collaborative activity this contained. There was much mutual help involved, rather than competition and secretiveness. This was attributed to the fact that this activity had come after many other beginning activities and that the group already knew one another quite well. They recognized that this same activity could be either a *beginning* or a *developmental* activity according to how experienced the group was with one another.

Through the above examples of beginning activities certain general components can be extracted and applied to any activity to enhance its beginningness. Some of the obvious elements in all of these beginners include (1) simplicity of skill demand, (2) simultaneous involvement of all, (3) lack of structures that increase the competitive aspects, e.g., no time expectation, no instruction to make it "good" or "most original." A further element that often goes along with such simultaneous activity is slight confusion and humor. All of this adds up to helping the group get going in spite of itself.

Within the category of beginning activities there are actually three different kinds of beginners. First, there are the deliberately peppy and engaging kinds of activities—the mixers and icebreakers—that *impel a group* into doing something despite itself. The three examples cited in the list below under games as well as most of the other examples given are of this order. They are calculated to help the group begin as a group—perhaps a new group which needs to learn one another's names or to determine what they expect to accomplish.

Secondly, there are beginning activities that specially *help an individual* find a place in an ongoing group. In the case studies in Chapter 9, Number 4 is illustrative. Often at a party, for example, the worker must plan the beginning activities of the session to be able to accommodate people who might enter one by one. It is hard to have the group wait for all to be present in order to start, and yet the situation the late comer encounters ought to be flexible and fluid enough so that he can find his place within the fabric of the experience without waiting. Often decentralized, short-term experiences are a help so that the total group experience does not jell too early.

A few specific illustrations of beginning activities in various non-verbal contents are listed below. This list includes the two kinds of beginners mentioned above, those that help the group as a whole and those that help the individual. Other specific examples and discussion of beginning activities can be found in the case studies, Numbers 1 through 17.

BEGINNING ACTIVITIES

Games: Zip, Zap; Human Tic-Tac-Toe; Chinese Walking Game.

Crafts: Draw a name tag; draw a caricature of your neighbor to your right; draw anyone in the room and then introduce him.

Songs: "Hello"; "Hey Lolli Lolli" (inserting own name); "Green Grow the Rushes O" (using members' names); "I Been Working on the Railroad" or any other well known, bouncy song a group might already know.

Dances: Singing game; Train (What's your name?); Hokey Pokey or other circle or line dances where members start as individuals without partners; Follow the Leader to music which can evolve into Grand March figures; Paul Jones; Balloon Dance; Multiplication Dance.

Dramatics: Pantomime something you did on the way to the meeting; pantomime your favorite ambition.

The third aspect of beginning activities differs considerably from helping either the group or individuals to begin. It has to do more closely with motivation toward risking an experience in a new, possibly frightening medium. The *beginning* for the group, and/or individual, is *within activity content itself*. It is helpful for the worker, when he is trying to motivate a group to try something new and to overcome their natural resistance to the unknown, to deliberately relate the frightening to what is more comfortable and known. One of the best ways known to this writer of doing this is to make the new into a game, i.e., to add gamelike incentives to the fearsome experience. Thus, in crafts, dramatics, singing, and dancing much resistance is dissipated if the group uses a fun form or gamelike form of the activity. For such simple beginners a progression can be plotted toward a more valid use and enjoyment of the activity stemming from its own qualities. Examples of gamelike beginning activities are listed below.

GAMELIKE BEGINNING ACTIVITIES

Crafts: Draw a Charade; Newspaper Scramble (teams cut out of a newspaper and paste up on a sheet words to form any given sentence in a race against time); Newspaper Tableaux (teams must dress everybody around a stipulated theme in a certain amount of time using a supply of old newspapers).

Songs: Sing-Down Contest with nursery rhymes (group is split in half and each side must come up with a new song at the conclusion of the other side's last line until one side runs out of ideas); motion songs (attention from singing is diverted by the actions); clapping songs (the beat keeps people focused on the rhythm as they sing); leader-follower songs (the group doesn't have to memorize words and tune but simply follows the leader's direction and comes in as a group); song-games—Pass The Shoe; Dollar Dollar; Wonder Ball.

Dances: Lucky Spot Elimination Dance; Cinderella Dance (one shoe is put in pile in center and boys choose); Broom Dance; I've Been to Harlem; Paw Paw Patch.

Dramatics: Charades; Lemonade (or Trades); paper bag dramatics (relay race in which individuals have to get dressed with contents in their bags, run to goal, make short speech and return).

Nature Items: Scavenger hunt or treasure hunt; guess contents in small cloth bags by feeling them.

In all of the above activities, the expected behavior is made less threatening by adding game elements: a time limit, an elimination aspect, a race, or a game skill, rather than the skill ordinarily associated with the new activity. When, for example, in a scavenger hunt the player must hunt for a square stone or a yellow leaf rather than a piece of granite or a pin oak leaf, the individual is helped to have an experience in handling natural materials without needing to know anything about them except how they look to him. In such an instance the mere altering of the content serves to involve a person in nature pursuits—despite possible resistance to more formalized nature study—because of the excitement of the hunt with its time limit and team competition. Once comfortable in hunting for objects, other ideas about what is found can easily be introduced if the worker wishes.

In this discussion of substituting content and adding gamelike elements to activities in order to motivate individuals or the group as a whole into an unknown area of interest, the implication is that any activity is more readily attempted if it is fun, i.e., if it is not threatening. Or, as discussed in the previous chapter with respect to art and music, certain *structures* are deliberately applied to make these activities effective beginning activities. The beginning, here, is with the content itself and is made more palatable to the suspicious, resistant, or timid participants by its simplicity, achievability, and relationship to what the person already knows something about.

It is not accidental that perhaps the earliest and most popular of children's party games is Musical Chairs. This is simply the combination of the most elementary form of musical activity, of moving to music, and the intense individual competition of obtaining a seat, with all the excitement generated by the gradual narrowing down of the contestants. Its popularity rests in the combination of two basic forms, song and game, plus the least socially demanding behavior. Each child fends for himself. And finally there is the least complicated, or most natural, of skills—walking. Such analysis of the elements within all activities will help the worker select encompassable forms that work for him.

Among the unknowns about group beginnings are just how many will appear at any given meeting and how many will arrive at the same time. The question then becomes when and how to begin? This question is especially accented when the worker is prepared for somewhere around eight people and two or three are his group. Unless he has previously thought through such a possibility and made some advance preparations, he can sit around and wait. Or the worker may be at a loss to provide a meaningful experience for those who do come for the whole meeting. The necessity for of-the-moment adjustments in planning can throw the novice into complete panic. Through experience most workers know to make alternate plans for whatever eventuality presents itself. The beginning worker who has not yet achieved such a flexibility needs to prepare in advance at least two ways to get started at each meeting—one for a piecemeal start and one for the entire group.

A similar kind of preparation is needed to meet the possibility of a larger than expected turnout. This is especially needed for open affairs such as parties and dances. The writer is reminded of one student's experience of making elaborate program plans for a teen-age dance and then on the night of the affair having to discard every one of them because too many people came. The worker who considers and makes allowance for all the possibilities he can think of ahead of time will be able to take the unknown in stride. Preparation is essential for unknowns such as rainy weather, too much noise next door, a traffic tie-up, unexpected visitors, an emergency, or accident.

The eighty case studies in Chapter 9 do not provide the reader with an accurate picture of the frequency of piecemeal beginnings with an activity. In lifting the excerpt from the total record, often the lead-up to the group's engagement has been omitted. What has been highlighted is the moment when everyone is involved in the activity. It must be stressed for a full appreciation of how program develops that frequently the worker will need to start with a small subgroup in order to stimulate the group as a whole, or he may start with the smaller group that has come to the meeting first. The following two excerpts are illustrative of such a process.

> I arrived Saturday night with plans for Casino Night, the theme I had chosen. The night before I had placed a poster where everyone could read it, listing some of the games and asking for their suggestions. Instead of prizes I had planned a special snack, sundaes which they could make. The immediate reaction was that no one wanted to play but they wanted to know about the sundaes. I said only those who participated would get the sundaes . . . M came up to me and asked why I didn't put down such games as rummy and pinochle. I told him I had made provision for any suggestions he might have.
>
> At 6:30 I thought I would try to get the activities started. The first two who were willing to participate were R and E. I brought them into the small living room and taught them how to play Spit. This game was very hard for R to understand or at least he was unwilling to cooperate fully. Finally I had to ask M if he wanted to learn and play with E so that R could watch and learn. We played this game for several rounds—M, C, E, R and myself participating. J was busy building a new box for his turtle and said he would play Blackjack

later on. T stayed upstairs and worked on his models. B and D showed no interest but kept busy in other ways. K and L went off for a while but returned to play a version of two-handed solitaire. This is a game they soon caught on to and were enjoying very much. L enjoyed it so much that he made K come back and play another game.

In this instance the process of getting the group involved in the card game activities was a slowly unfolding one in which the worker capitalized on the little bits of interest that some members showed to involve the others. In the following example, the worker persists in trying to launch his program in the face of direct opposition from one of the group members who eventually becomes involved in the activities also. The choice not to follow the hide and seek game was deliberate by the worker in his desire to offer something different to the group from what they were used to doing.

I arrived Saturday night with my plans for the indoor track meet. I had posters already made so that the boys could see the program planned. At supper we talked a little about the meet and they spoke with a great deal of enthusiasm about the roller skating they had done. Later J and R came out and wanted to know when we would get started. I thought it was about time and went in. C then began a very obvious attempt to get an alternate activity going, a game of hide and seek. I had the nucleus to work with and C could not get enough of the group together to make his activity successful. I then told the boys that the only activity in the recreation room was to be the track meet. Finally, all but D and R wanted to play. By the third event, D began to participate.

Developmental Forms

Developmental activities is a catchall term that is used to refer to the multitude of different things that groups do which are a part of neither the beginning stage nor the ending. Just when the group passes beyond the beginning phase of its group life and moves into this second stage will vary according to each group's timing. However, it is not hard for the worker to sense this movement. Now the awkwardness and clumsiness of the beginning have passed, and the group settles down into what is to be the core of its experience. They know each other and what to expect of each other more or less, although new insights and growth will be obtained through each new group experience.

No attempt is made to discuss what qualities the developmental activities contain since they are varied, unique to each particular group, and lead toward development in many different areas. The reader will see specifically such diverse use of program in the case studies of Chapter 9, Number 18 through 76, where development toward various purposes is illustrated. In the short list of suggested beginning activities previously presented in this chapter the reader can note that many of the same activities introduced as beginners can also be used during the developmental phase of the group's life. Often an activity becomes a favorite with the group and is repeated at its insistence throughout all phases of its life. Close examination of the interaction will reveal that the group uses this ostensibly same activity *differently* according to where it is in its process—beginning, developing, or ending. The familiarity with each other and with the activity will markedly affect how it is experienced.

Developmental activities comprise the bulk of any group's experience just as this phase in its life makes up the predominant part of the group's experience. This category includes the program content that is not specially geared either to launching an activity or to tapering off of a group experience. Since it is so vast in possibilities, the specific examples are left to the reader's imagination.

Reference was made during the discussion of beginning activities to the addition of gamelike incentives to lead into a possibly threatening new content area. This same approach can be applied within the area of developmental activities in order to make any less intrinsically attractive activity appealing to a group. An ordinary activity can be made more palatable by the addition of gamelike incentives. Thus, such simple and often boring routines as washing dishes, cleaning the bunk, or hunting for a lost object can be made appealing by adding elements of competition, game skills, or group cooperation. When a group walks through a field holding hands in a line formation and looks for a lost ring, the chore is easier for all and a bit of fun besides. Among case studies there will be several concrete examples of "gamelike activities" which illustrate other activities made into games by the worker. These of-the-moment improvisations on the part of the worker do much to set a tone for a group and help the members assume a larger amount of responsibility for their own welfare.

By far the most frequently encountered need for of-the-moment adaptation probably is to the situation of encountering two or three when more were expected. In many instances the time will be used in discussion or informal conversations with those who are there. But often the worker also senses the underlying disappointment that "nothing is happening" and the need of those who come to do something. With such situations in mind some concrete suggestions for twos and threes are listed here:

ACTIVITIES FOR TWOS AND THREES

Pencil and Paper games: Connect the Dots, Hangman, Cootie

Games (short duration) with equipment: Chinese Checkers, Checkers, Pick Up Sticks, Blockhead, Anagrams, Scrabble, card games

Puzzles, maze races, Colorforms construction pictures

Magic tricks; mystery games such as The Moon is Round and Tommy, Tommy

Looking at things: pertinent magazines, catalogs, cook book, a map, patterns, rocks or other collections, a camera

Use of equipment: tape recorder, record player and records

All crafts or art activities could lend themselves: simple short-term ones at the beginning such as cutting pictures, folding and cutting, tearing

Gymnastic and physical tests and stunts

Special group chores: arranging the room, collecting equipment

The above list is actually endless and only a few specifics are suggested. They would need to be varied according to whether the group consisted of children or adults, the usual activity and interest of the group, and all the other conditions for effective programming already mentioned. What is most needed is the attitude on the part of the worker that the opportunity for meaningful interactions begins when the first person arrives, not just when all are present. Nor should the above suggestions be considered as only busy work or attention holders and time fillers which are calculated to keep the members' attention away from the small attendance or the opportunity to talk with the worker.

It is even important for the group worker to think ahead and plan differentially what he will do with the particular members who come first. Sometimes patterns are observed wherein certain members regularly come early just for this special chance to have the worker to themselves. The worker might know that he wants to do one thing if a certain person comes and something different if someone else arrives, so that these extra minutes can be best used according to the needs of the particular ones who are there. In certain instances the early comers will need to have an ending built in as soon as the special activity is begun. They will need to be told that this will go only until all the others arrive.

The reader will note that spontaneous planning for twos and threes is discussed here under "developmental forms." The reason for this placement is that a greater number of the meetings fall within this time phase. However, such a need will present itself during any phase of the group's life.

Ending Forms

Appropriate ending activities ought to contain their own particular dynamics. They should not leave the group keyed up, but rather should have a soft spirit—a quiet, reflective quality that suggests closeness and "togetherness." The best ending activities are those that unite, that help the group *to end as a group* and put a period, so to speak, on the experience. Often included in the ending is a look ahead to what is in store for the next meeting. A campfire at the beginning of the camp season should be radically different from the final event of the season, and every piece of the program should lead to the ending. When considering the elements the worker may well ask the question, what do they help the worker and group accomplish? Then it is not difficult to make a selection which supports such aims both in their content and in the mood they create. The last four illustrations in the case studies in Chapter 9 have ending as their focus.

Sometimes an ending activity can be merely a more or less ritualistic use of a very familiar or a favorite activity of the group. Through intuition and experience many workers have come to reserve for the end an activity that the group particularly enjoys. This has grown out of the desire of the worker to help the group end on a happy note and leave with good thoughts about the group experience and the group members. Often a song fulfills this requirement. It is not accidental that "Taps" or "Day is Done" is the means for ending so many scout meetings. And then there is the "friendship circle" in which group members stand in a circle and hold hands. This certainly increases the feeling of belonging during the intermittent days when the group exists only in the minds of its members.

Another kind of ending which can be met through non-verbal activities as well as talking about it applies *when an individual must leave the group*. The individual may be either a group member or a staff person. There is much precedent within all cultures for handling separations—and the ultimate separation, death—through ritualized ways. One need only to consider the practices surrounding funerals to recognize the significance that such activities hold in helping people separate from a meaningful relationship. The wakes, the eating, and other deliberate kinds of doings enable them to pass through a painful experience and look ahead to the future.

The good-bye party for the departing group leader, house parent, or group member is one manifestation of the handling of painful feelings. In such situations the group members are able to express their deep feelings symbolically—with a gift, a song, a poem, some picture taking—and more easily bear the deprivation and imbalance that is certain to occur within the group for a while.

Just as all activity forms can be structured to become beginning ones, so can they be deliberately constructed to convey a quality of ending, for a single meeting or for an ending of the whole group experience. Some content illustrations are suggested in the following list.

ENDING ACTIVITIES

Games: Whisper down the Lane; Indian Chief (guess the leader); Pass the Spark (campfire game).

Crafts: Draw a cartoon of what you'd like to do next week; draw a group mural of the club's achievements; decorate the room with day's products.

Songs: "Good Night, Ladies"; "Good Night, Irene"; "Show Me the Way to Go Home"; Taps; "Each Campfire Lights Anew"; "Friends"; special club song. Both the content itself and the mellow, soft quality of a song would contribute to the spirit of ending.

Dances: Good Night, Ladies; square dances have ending calls (Take Your Lady to a Rocking Chair); Auld Lang Syne; waltz.

Dramatics: The ending of a skit or stunt night with the ensuing applause and curtain calls spells its own ending; special content could be added in some skits such as "what a camper does at night." Continued story.

This discussion has attempted to specify the quality that an activity should convey when it is related dynamically to the time phases in a group's existence. The selected illustrations are merely suggestive and not axiomatic, for there are countless variables that could make any particular choice specified here inappropriate. The author hopes that the reader will catch the flavor of what is being proposed without holding her to exact accountability. The eternal wonder in working with groups is never knowing for sure that any particular content will be used as expected. The magic is not in the content itself, but rather in its use by the worker and the group together!

> I dread the beginning of these large works [the third, fifth, seventh, and ninth symphonies]. Once into the work, and it goes.
>
> —Ludwig van Beethoven *

* J. W. N. Sullivan, *Beethoven, His Spiritual Development* (New York: Vintage Books, 1927), pp. 102-3.

7 A Guide to the Analysis of Non-Verbal Content

Caruso's letters are the letters of a warrior to whom every performance was a battle against the supreme odds of his own previous triumphs. It happened in the wings of the Metropolitan Opera House early in 1916 when Edith Mason was beginning her career as Caruso's was approaching its tragic end. She was singing Oscar the page to his Riccardo in "The Masked Ball," and as they waited for their entrance she was amazed to see that the most idolized of tenors was trembling. "Why, Caruso," she exclaimed incredulously, "are you nervous?" "Mason," he replied, in utter sincerity, "other singers must sing one hundred per cent. Caruso, one hundred and fifty."

—Claudia Cassidy *

The guide to the analysis of non-verbal content was developed by the author for use with her students to enable them to look more critically, week by week, at every activity that was introduced into a group meeting (see Appendix A). Its use has actually served three purposes: (1) It has been a means for showing more specifically just what groups of different ages and purposes actually do. (2) It has forced the student to become intensely aware of far more than the manifest content of an activity. (3) It has helped the student consider the essential helpfulness of his leadership developmentally. In this last regard, the guide has been an impetus toward introspection and self-assessment for the worker as he compares, for example, the long-range view of the "leadership pattern" with his overall assessment of the group's

* Music Critic, *Chicago Tribune.*

development. Or when he considers simply how much of the content he had to introduce and how much came from the initiative of the group itself.

Some of the thinking that preceded the development of the actual analysis form is included here to indicate to the reader some concepts and hunches out of which the form was developed.* Much of this thinking is still at a formative level and needs to be refined and tested to determine just how valid it is. However, since so little writing has been produced to date along these lines, it is included here to serve as a stimulus to others who might wish to devote themselves to similar inquiry as well as to make more clear the thinking out of which the analysis form derived.

Activity Demand of the Non-Verbal Content

All activities, regardless of their specific content form, can be divided into four categories: †

1. *The puzzle.* The individual is pitted against the unknown. For example, pinball games, double crostics, viewing a tray full of objects and trying to recall them; mystery games such as "The Moon is Round" and "Tommy Tommy"; smelling and identifying objects, figure and ground pictures while blindfolded. Much of drawing and painting is of a puzzle order.

2. *Activities of chance.* No skill required, the outcome unknown. For example, Bingo, roulette, fish pond, Hot Potato, Musical Chairs.

3. *Skill, strategy, and endurance activities.* Rules are known, roles are known; outcome in terms of winning or accomplishing the end is unknown. For example, Pick Up Sticks,

* The writer is indebted to Frank Seever for his collaboration in developing the ideas detailed in this discussion. His interest in program has always been deep and his search for better use of it equally insistent.

† For simplicity the game form of activities is used to illustrate conceptualizations. It is assumed that the reader by this time will be able to construct for himself appropriate analogies in such content as crafts, drama, dance, etc.

basketball, relay races, twenty-one, baseball, newcomb, tetherball, quoits, hopscotch, jacks, jump rope, bridge, Ping-Pong, bowling, Coffee Pot, Monopoly.

4. *Aesthetic-creative activities.* Individual or group activities where form, ideas, expression, and style are the most important aspects of successful achievement. For example, Statues, diving, color association game, dancing.[1]

With the above formulations in mind with respect to the game, the following observations are proposed: For a game to be interesting there must be an opportunity for success or failure. The challenge is lost when the pattern is repetitive and one's skill does not improve as in a pure game of chance. Games of chance are boring except for the extrinsic rewards, money or points, that accompany them.

Levels of Worker's Control Within the Content

In games, even when the outcome in terms of achievement is unpredictable, the outcome in terms of its effect upon the group can be predicted. It, therefore, should be possible to select games which progress from the focus upon the worker as INITIATOR-DIRECTOR to the group as DECIDER-PLANNER and the worker as UMPIRE-ADVISOR. Such development, i.e., the diminishing of the worker's control of the group and the emergence of the group's ability to manage itself, is of prime importance in the growth process of a person and contributes to his learning to participate with others in his world and eventually in his future role as responsible citizen in a community. As the worker selects activities which lead to this goal, he places emphasis upon the social, planning, and decision-making aspects of games. He seeks to develop self-propelling individuals and groups.

A specific example of games used sequentially toward the above objective follows:

1. Follow the Leader—worker centered, then member-leader centered.

2. Indian Chief—worker centered, then member-leader centered with a changeable "It" as leader.

3. Individual charades—member-leader with changeable "It" as leader.

4. a. Team charades—two subgroups with member-leader whose qualities for leadership were observed by worker during Indian Chief; subgroups with their member-leader select ideas and control their own activity. Or progression might be to 4b:
   b. Trades (Lemonade)—two subgroups make their idea choices and act these out as a group rather than as individuals.

The role of the worker within the above activities starts out as INITIATOR-DIRECTOR and ends up as UMPIRE-ADVISOR.

The control of activities may be expressed in several ways:

1. Worker (or individual member) in direct control. Game examples: Simon Says, May I, This Is My Ear, Steal the Bacon, Crows and Cranes, Proverbs.

2. Worker (or individual member) in indirect control. Game examples: Mixers such as matching papers or half of playing cards, Human Bingo or Human Tic Tac Toe, scavenger and treasure hunts, Hide and Seek.

3. Group control (leader within). Game examples: Midnight, Red Light, Reuben and Rachel, Spud, Red Rover.

4. Group control with changing "It." Game examples: Tag, Jump the Shot, Dodge Ball with one "It," Cat and Rat, Stinky-Pinky, Concentration.

5. Group control with no leader. Game examples: Buzz, One Hundred, Buck-Buck.

6. Group controls and plans. Game examples: basketball, newcomb, soccer, Trades, charades, Twenty Questions.

Within one given meeting or within consecutive meetings, the worker should enable the group to assume responsibility progressively for its own movement according to his assessment of the amount of self-determination they are capable of carrying. Since the attainment of more responsible behavior for one's self is a prime mark of maturity, striving toward this goal as an important focus of the group worker is certainly in order. Self-direction with respect to behavior and decisions is vital for individuals, and much help can be offered through their participation in group experiences. The group experience itself is a microcosm of the life experience, and the gains made in this one small segment can be carried over to meet other challenges.

The few dimensions of activities that this non-verbal analysis form highlights can help the group worker see more clearly just what is happening in the group within a given activity. The analysis form stresses (1) the demand of the activity upon its members, (2) the pattern of leadership and decision making involved, and (3) the initiative assumed for beginning and ending the activity, the decisions involved in controlling the actual flow of the activity in time. An examination of the possible patterns within Numbers 2 and 3 can help reveal to the worker how much he is the INITIATOR-DIRECTOR and how much the UMPIRE-ADVISOR. This analysis enables him at close range to determine just what the atmosphere in his group is.

Use of the Analysis Form to Spot Patterns

After using the non-verbal analysis form for one semester, a student group worker made the following assessment:

> In reviewing the non-verbal programs of my groups over this last semester I have noted some interesting trends:
>
> 1. *The kind or nature of the activity:* Games of skill, tactics, and chance, mostly involving the group as a whole, proved most popular with the members; eating, second; and arts and crafts, third —with dance, drama, travel, and sight-seeing, each on one occasion. The latter activities have emerged only as the group attained greater bond and I felt that they could be used with some

degree of order and benefit. Organizational activity such as setting up chairs and a projector ranked numerically second in frequency, with eight occasions.

Comment: It would seem from this account that I have felt comfortable in those activities familiar to the boys and toward which they had a preference. I have not felt that they had the capacity or the readiness for new, unfamiliar activity although I was prepared in several areas to introduce and guide activity on the basis of previous experience (dance, drama). I discover that my reluctance to allow varied program, to suggest or introduce it, is based on my lack of confidence in the boys, their ability to achieve something worthwhile in my terms, and their openness to new ideas. I have been afraid of their rejecting my suggestions and, by inference, me. I am slowly developing the professional and personal security to take this risk. Only in this way, by being willing to enthusiastically introduce and recommend new and challenging activities can I enable the members to build on the strengths of their present skills and continue to grow. I intend to use a greater variety of activities to discover and encourage these latent skills.

2. *Activity demand:* The activity demand was by far the great majority in the skill area: chance, 1; skill, 29; aesthetic, 4. Skills include in this case the basic social skills of eating and observing the surroundings.

Comment: The skill category is broad and includes a variety of activities ranging from a low skill order such as sight-seeing to ability in pool and dramatics. The concentration in this area relates to the demands of group games. As there are boys of little athletic skill in the group, I intend to retain group games to strengthen group bond but introduce more chance and "high power It-role games" to involve the latter boys in satisfying game experiences. As bond develops, there is also more potential for growth in the aesthetic-creative area of dance and drama. The skill demand should be gradually increased from simple to complex, from the familiar to the novel.

3. *Leadership evolution:* Worker in direct control, 13; worker (or one member) in indirect control, 7; group in control (leader within), 3; group in control with changing It, 1; group in control with no leader, 9; group controls and plans, 0. These occasions,

spread over seventeen meetings, also indicate shifting leadership: worker (or one member) in direct control moving to group control with no leader, 2; worker (or one member) in indirect control moving to group control (leader within), 1; worker (or one member) in indirect control moving to group control with no leader, 1; and group control with no leader moving to group control (leader within), 1.

Comment: The heavy weighting in the area of "worker in direct control" is reaffirmation of my personal need to have tight control of the group process at all times and the need to risk chaos for the sake of growth. The boys need to be given more leadership initiative and introduced to more activities which allow them increased responsibility. The weighting of the "group control, no leader" pattern second only to "worker control" is an accurate reflection of my tendency to control the activity tightly or to allow free, unstructured activity where control is not so necessary (nothing to hurt in the gym) and the lack of natural or appointed leaders in the group. The shifting leadership patterns indicate, with one exception, a cautious letting go on my part and allowing the boys more autonomy in several instances. I intend to augment this trend by offering games as mentioned under my discussion of "activity demand" and by introducing such individual activities which allow the less athletically skilled to gain some glory by leading the group in their favorite hobby or craft. One of these boys makes and works skillfully with a lariat. If I can interest the group in this skill, I have an able assistant. All of these activity selections must anticipate the differing capacities and skill levels of the members and structure activity so that the maximum number may realize some success from their effort.

4. *Initiative pattern:* Beginning and ending the activity—using the code letters G, group; M, members; W, worker—the total occasions over the seventeen meetings indicated: W-W, 16; W-G, 4; W-M, 1; M-M, 1; M-W, 0; M-G, 0; G-G, 4; G-W, 3; G-M, 0. There were two meetings (6 occasions) when W, G, and M initiated an activity that W terminated; two when W (5 occasions) initiated and terminated all activities.

Comment: This record bears out my penchant for directing the progress and development of activity as mentioned in the other commentaries. Again, more self-starting and self-direction must be introduced through activities which encourage this tendency. It is interesting to note that the members on three occasions and a member on six occasions took initiative to introduce activities, which indicates that the group atmosphere does not wholly discourage member contribution. This summary does not show the relationship of these patterns to the type of activity, but there seems to be no clear correlation.

I am learning to allow the group setting and the evolving dynamics to suggest and support a selection of activity which is a spontaneous product of the group's need and interests. This is more difficult than my totally controlling the flow of activities since I must be prepared in a number of areas simultaneously. This method has the advantage of immediate possibility for the support of positive initiatives. This does not deny that there are many times when the professional must confidently present and "sell" a program to stimulate group growth. And, again, I must be willing to do so at the risk of the program falling flat, at the risk of seeming rejection.

Certainly this student's paper (partly quoted here) speaks eloquently for itself and says all that is necessary to point out what it is possible to learn about the group and about one's leadership from the discipline of submitting the content to a weekly analysis and then pulling together the trends at certain key times. The student worker who made the above summation has a clear picture of where he and his group are and is thus able to project future directions for himself as he attempts to sharpen his skill in using program. Certainly his honesty in viewing his work is apparent in his comments.

While the categories listed for analysis on the non-verbal form are not presented here as exhaustive, nor the best, nor the only possible ones, they do stand as a good illustration of a possible beginning approach toward looking more critically into the nature of the activity and its meaning for both worker and group. Perhaps the reader may be stimulated through these suggestions to extract other dimensions that would yield fruitful insights.

Note to Chapter 7

1. For a discussion in theoretical terms of the conceptualizations of these models of activity, the reader is referred to the writings of psychologist Dr. Omar Khayyam Moore, who has done much to research his notion of "autotelic folk models" and their importance in our culture. Cf. Alan Ross Anderson and Moore, "The Formal Analysis of Normative Concepts," *American Sociological Review,* 22: 9-17, 1957; Anderson and Moore, "Autotelic Folk-Models," *Sociological Quarterly,* I:203-216, 1960; Moore, "Autotelic Responsive Environments and Exceptional Children," Responsive Environments Foundation, Inc., 20 Augur St., Hamden, Conn.

8 Exercises in Analyzing Use of Non-Verbal Content

> *I am a dancer. I believe that we learn by practice. Whether it means to learn to dance by practicing dancing or to learn to live by practicing living, the principles are the same. In each it is the performance of a dedicated precise set of acts, physical or intellectual, from which comes shape of achievement, a sense of one's being, a satisfaction of spirit. . . . There is a vitality, a life-force, an energy, a quickening that is translated through you into action and because there is only one of you in all of time, this expression is unique. And if you block it, it will never exist through any other medium and be lost. The world will not have it . . .*
>
> —Robert Sabin *

The most frequent pitfall confronting the beginning worker who has good intentions about offering non-verbal content fully and generously to his group is that he has not prepared himself sufficiently in advance of the meeting. *Actually, all the creativity, spontaneity, and flexibility in the world will not compensate for a lack of knowledge about particular, concrete things to do and a before-meeting plan of what might be done, including the necessary materials.*

For the beginner, the before-meeting preparation will probably consume as much time as the group meeting itself. This would include the thinking, the assembling of materials and models or concrete examples if needed, and the anticipation of the variety of possibilities that would necessitate on-the-spot changes in plans and directions. At least the worker should approach it this way

* *Martha Graham* (New York: Theater Art Books, 1961).

until he gets the feel of his group and of his capacity to adapt and modify spontaneously. Hopefully, the preparation time is lessened with more experience.

The preparation of the group worker in advance of the meeting can be likened to the preparation of the palette by the painter in advance of the actual putting of the brush to the canvas. The painter goes through a process in placing the paints on his palette. He applies the pure form of the colors he thinks he will want to use and in a relationship to each other that has grown out of his experience with the media and that will facilitate his use of them. He might further wish to intermix some of the colors or lighten or darken them, on the pallete, before he places them on his canvas. Finally, he is ready to apply the paint. He selects a certain size of brush or many different brushes, mixes his colors with the right amount of medium, and then ventures forth—thoughtfully—to get the precise effect he wishes. Perhaps he has made several preliminary sketches of his subject or roughed in some outlines in charcoal, or perhaps he takes off and lets the subject take form from his feeling of the moment. Regardless of how he actually paints, his technical preparations with his materials (in addition to his rigorous previous discipline in learning proportions, form, perspective, use of colors, figures, etc.) are meticulous. When he is finished for the day, he finds he may not have used all the colors he had prepared but he was ready just in case. He then cleans up, salvaging whatever unused materials he can for another time, and takes the old paint out of his brushes. When, as with the group worker, the materials involved include not only the things to be done but human beings, should not the preparations be at least this painstaking?

The group worker will soon learn whether or not he is overprepared. It is better to have more to do than is actually needed rather than the other way around. With adequate preparation by the worker of what he can bring to a meeting, he can more easily be flexible and open to receive what the members bring. He can discard much of what he has planned when it is apparent that the group takes hold in its own way and modifies his plan. He can propose alternate ideas when the group rejects his first suggestion. He can, in short, separate himself from the content enough so that he will not give up and feel personally rejected if the group does not want to go along with him.

The readiness of a group to risk themselves in a new area through their trust in the worker's ability to help them through the difficult spots relates to the spirit the worker radiates as he presents what he brings. And he can *seem* confident only when he *is* confident inside that he knows what he is about to introduce—when he has been willing to learn something new himself, has prepared himself and his materials carefully, when he has internalized the content. While not every session will turn out the way the worker wished it would, his ever ready posture will make success more probable.

If, for example, a worker plans to introduce a series of games, the rules and all conditions surrounding their use should be in his head. The precise order and transition from one game to the next should be figured out in advance according to his purposes for the day, and he might come with a small card listing his selections in sequence. If songs are to be taught, they must be known by the worker and not exist only on a song sheet. When song sheets are used, the attention is focused there and the details of the songs remain there after they are used. If the group worker does not internalize the content, the group never will.

Factors to Consider in Selecting Non-Verbal Activities

The following outline suggests some of the many considerations facing the worker as he attempts to think through in advance what particular things he will do with his group.

1. *Purpose:* In what phase of the group's development is this activity to be introduced? Beginning? Developmental? Ending?

   What particular purpose(s) might this activity serve? Help the individuals express feeling? Build their self-esteem, etc.?

2. *Content:* Should the experience be in games, singing, dancing?

If an overall area of interest is selected, what particular form of the content is best suited? For example, if card playing is the activity, what particular kinds of card games would be better than others? Bridge differs from Rummy, Rummy from Crazy 8's; the simplest is War. The precise selection of the card game will depend upon other factors to be detailed.

To select the precise content form, what is known about the group and individuals concerning such things as their needs, interests, previous experience with the activity, cultural or religious attitudes, intellectual capacity, mores, values, etc.?

Is the activity known or unknown by the group? By how many in the group? If unknown, what is the best and easiest way to teach it? Who should teach it, worker or group member? How can the ones who already know the activity be involved while the novices are taught? In what way can differences in experience be considered so that all have a fairly even chance for success?

Does the worker know about the relation between how many members know or do not know this particular activity? What are the various individuals' general skills in this general area of activity and their acceptance by the rest of the group? Might this activity particularly help a certain member because he is good at this kind of thing? Might it increase a rift already apparent between cliques? Does it tend to further stratify the group in certain ways because it reinforces presently known patterns of meeting certain group problems? How helpful or harmful will the introduction of this content be to enhancing group life?

What materials are needed for the activity? Does the agency have them? Available or in use by others this day?

Will this activity cost any money? How shall it be financed? By agency? By group treasury? By individual contributions?

What special accommodations need to be made of the activity considering the size of the group? Can it be shifted quickly? Is it appropriate for co-ed groups or does it need some modification in such a situation? Is there a difference in content or materials for boys? For girls? For children? For adults? For mental patients? For activities where parents might be present? For a particular racial group?

Is the room appropriate? How should it be set up? How will this activity affect those next door? Across the street?

Is the content something that the agency should sponsor? What if the members want to gamble with money? What if the content pokes fun at a particular group? What if it is against the law?

How will the worker recover if his idea is rejected? Can he move on to another suggestion without being overwhelmed by his own feelings?

3. *Complexity of skill demand:* What is the essential demand of the activity? A chance-like one? A puzzle? Physical or mental skill, strategy, endurance? Aesthetic-creative?

   Is the activity appropriate for the group and its members as is, or does it need modifications? How can the rules and the roles within the activity be modified according to skill of group, age, size, etc.?

   What modification of materials is needed considering the same conditions, the size of room, time of day, weather, etc.?

4. *Conditions surrounding the engagement in the activity:* What is the probable length of time of the involvement? How long should it last? When should the worker move to stop it?

   Does the activity involve elimination of certain members? How will those who are "out" be related to the ongoing activity? How can they be helped to get "in" again?

Are there ways to avoid elimination so that all can participate maximally?

Should the worker rely on the group or members to stop the activity? Should some sense of how long this can go or other similar qualifications be told to the group at the outset?

Does the group need to share space, equipment, time with another group? What is their previous experience in such sharing, possible reactions, possible positives or negatives attending such a demand?

Are there any special leadership roles within the activity which the group members can carry? How much room in this activity is there for group decision making and self-direction? How much experience has the group had in such matters? How much responsibility does the worker think they ought to be able to carry for themselves? How will he offer such opportunities so that they will be supported in their attempts at management?

When and how should the activity be ended?

5. *Transition to the next activity:* What is the overall pattern of the whole day's activities?

How will the room be rearranged most easily according to the flow of the program? Chairs to be rearranged?

Will the worker use patterns that move easily into each other? Circle games following circle games, two teams or several groups?

Will there be a progression leading to more skill demand? More group responsibility for decision making and leadership?

Should there be contrast to the flow of activities? A restful one following a hectic one?

These, then, are some of the considerations in determining what kind of non-verbal content the group should pursue. There may be others as well. At first, such a selection process and such a way of looking at activities will be very deliberate on the part of the worker. Experience will make the selection process easier.

Relating Purpose to Content

In Chapter 6 the lists of Beginning Activities and Ending Activities suggest that many content forms can accomplish a similar purpose. Therefore, to accomplish any given purpose the group worker should try to select the content form that would be most appealing and/or expanding for his group. From the point of view of working toward the underlying purpose, the particular form is of little importance. But from the group members' point of view, it ought to be interesting and not repetitive of what they have done much of the time. In other words, they ought to be offered the opportunity and the incentive through the worker's support and guidance to try new things. To illustrate more concretely the pervasiveness of purpose, the following list suggests a few content forms grouped under a specific purpose.

CONTENT FORMS TO INHIBIT IMPULSIVE BEHAVIOR

Games:	Simon Says, Red Light, Steal the Bacon, jump rope to rhymes; card games—Spit, Double Solitaire; strategy games and team games—baseball, Dog and Bone.
Dances:	Most singing games; Paul Jones Mixer; Dance Freeze; dances that follow calls and patterns—folk and square.
Crafts:	Woodwork, needlepoint, all crafts that need planning, model building, numbered paintings.
Cooking:	Step-by-step recipes, meal planning.
Drama:	Formal play in which lines must be followed as well as cues.

Songs:	Most songs—all rounds; leader-follower, e.g., "The Keeper," "Little Sir Echo."
Holidays and Special Events:	Building up toward a surprise; keeping gifts until the proper day, etc.

Similar specific content selections could be listed under every possible area of interest. Likewise, another list of concrete examples could be formed around such a purpose as *enhancing spontaneous expression and improvisation.* In such a list, the kinds of activities selected would be radically different from the above list. The activities would provide opportunities within their structure for the group and the individuals to add something of their own to the flow of the event. The songs would feature making up a rhyming line; the drama would be creative improvisation; the dance would be rock and roll. While the group's program choice is usually based on content, the worker's includes what purpose the content will serve. He attempts to involve the group in gaining some awareness of the purpose through helping them connect their content choice with why the group is meeting and what kinds of things they have been and will be doing.

It would now be helpful for the reader to practice on his own the approach of looking at activities in terms of what purpose(s) they fulfill. To do this he should make his own list of purposes and after each purpose list a range of non-verbal content forms—games, crafts, etc. He should try to select specific activities within each form which he thinks will enhance the purpose. In order to get started in such an approach, some examples of purpose are listed.*

OTHER PURPOSES

1. To build self-esteem
2. To identify with one's sexual role
3. To accept one's self—as a white Protestant, a Jew, a Negro, a parent, etc.

* The reader is also referred to the categories that organize the case studies in Chapter 9 for a listing of other possible purposes.

4. To accept others in their uniqueness and difference
5. To develop a better relation to authority
6. To express feeling—anger, sadness, appreciation, etc.
7. To build skills in social interactions

It must be emphasized that the mere selection of any content form as it is will not automatically lead to the desired result. After the activity within any content form is chosen, it will need to be structured and adapted so that the desired objective becomes possible. In order for the worker to gear the content form more nearly to his purpose as he considers any particular group's capacities for using the activity, he needs further practice in developing appropriate structures.

The Activity Demand

The reader, first, should review the non-verbal content analysis discussion in Chapter 7 and the sample analysis form, Appendix A. He should then practice listing certain specific activities and try to plot them according to the dimensions of the analysis form. It might be well to illustrate here what is meant by "complexity of activity demand." It should be obvious that the simplest activity demand is the *chance* activity. In the chance-like activity, everyone has more or less an equal opportunity for success. The chance activity is a great leveler. This is why Bingo is so popular with older adults—despite vast differences in physical capacities, sensory acuity, and social skills, the older adult can compete successfully with younger people in this game. He needs, of course, to be able to see and to hear the calls. It would be well to prepare a list of chance activities and think through their appropriateness for various age groups.

A BEGINNING LIST OF CHANCE-LIKE ACTIVITIES

1. Bingo
2. Fish Pond
3. Cards—War

4. Hot Potato
5. In what hand is the button?
6. Hunter-Tiger-Gun or Scissors-Rock-Paper
7. Tilt and blow pictures
8. Paper bag dramatics
9. Dance mixers—picking a shoe, matching cards
10. Carnival games—dropping clothespins in milk bottle, hoops around canes
11. Singing game—Little Sally Water
12. Marbled paper; dyeing Easter eggs
13. Pin the Tail on the Donkey

With this as a start, the worker can review the many activities he knows and extend this list with others that have as their main attraction the chance that anyone might win.

Within each of the other three categories under Activity Demand on the analysis form—the puzzle; the skill, strategy or endurance activity; and the aesthetic-creative activity—there is a range of possible specific activities from simple to complex. The particular skills involved in each of these kinds of activities include (1) skills in handling one's self (body control, thinking and planning ability, emotional control), (2) skills in interacting with others, and (3) skills in handling the content. The reader could now practice by constructing his own lists of simple to complex versions of activities with respect to all three kinds of skills in order to determine how simple or demanding any one activity will be. An illustration of such an approach is given below.

ACTIVITY DEMAND OF STEAL THE BACON

Rules of the Game

To play Steal the Bacon the group is divided into two parts of equal players who form a line facing each other at least ten feet apart. Each player has a number, beginning with 1 and going to the highest number, starting with the player at the extreme left of each line. An object is placed in the center of the area between the two teams. The leader proceeds to call any number and the two players with this number run to the object and try to grab it and get it back to home base without being touched by the opponent. A point is awarded to his team if the player is successful, or to the opposing team if he is tagged.

Skills

A. Handling one's self
   1. Keeping alert to hear your number and get a quick start
   2. Not running when another's number is called
   3. Not losing interest or engaging in distracting activities while waiting
   4. Sizing up your opponent, making judgments about his skills and style of playing

B. Handling the content
   1. Running, shifting directions
   2. Ducking, weaving, outsmarting someone else through actions
   3. Bluffing, feinting
   4. Snatching the object quickly

C. Interaction with others
   1. Cheering for own team members, acknowledging their successes, not undermining others when they lose a point
   2. Good sportsmanship—not taunting or jeering
   3. Timing one's self in relation to opponent, finding the right moment to snatch the object, offensive and defensive motions, not waiting so long that interest of group is lost
   4. Ability to shift directions and reverse objectives quickly in relation to the opponent

A judgment can now be made by the group worker as to the overall complexity of the activity demand as it is viewed against expectations of normal physical, intellectual, emotional, and social development of the group and its members in line with age, life experience, cultural and other factors. Through such a process of looking at the activity demand in various games, the worker could come up with the conclusion that Steal the Bacon has a moderate amount of demand, that it is more complicated than Crows and Cranes (in which the object to be caught is the individual rather than anything else), more complicated than Spud (where the individual is pitted against everyone else rather than one opponent who is trying to do the same thing he is), but less complicated than kick baseball or soccer.

Leadership and Decision-Making Patterns

To gain practice in evaluating the leadership and decision-making patterns in an activity the reader is referred to the discussion of this subject in Chapter 7 in terms of the worker's control within the content. It would be well to review the progression illustrated from Follow the Leader (worker is in direct control) to charades (group controls and plans) as one example of deliberately adding more complex activities, all of which feature the basic skill of following and using various motions. Similar ranges could be plotted now by selecting different skills in *handling the content* and then deliberately trying to vary the activity to lead from the simplest kind of decision making, i.e., where the worker makes the decisions and the group follows them, to the more advanced form in which the group itself controls the decision and plans.

As a reminder to the reader of the several levels of leadership and decision-making patterns considered in the Analysis of Non-Verbal Activities form (Appendix A), this range is repeated here.

LEADERSHIP AND DECISION-MAKING PATTERNS

A. Worker (or one member) in direct control
B. Worker (or one member) in indirect control (for example, worker makes up clues to treasure hunt and gives these to group to follow)
C. Group controls (leader within), leader being either worker or a group member

D. Group controls with changing "It"
E. Group controls with no leader
F. Group controls and plans

Listed below are two columns of related activities that represent the extremes between following the worker and group planning. The reader might try to fill the gap with related activities that would lead toward the ultimate goal, group decision making and planning.

Worker Controls	*Group Controls and Plans*
1. Dribbling relay	1. Basketball game
2. Draw a map, copying worker's sample	2. Makes a group mural, depicting things of the neighborhood
3. Bake a cake, worker assigns jobs	3. Decides supper menu, cooks, decorates table and room, serves
4. Worker teaches a song	4. Group has a sing-down, around topic of songs with a color in the title
5. Worker calls a square dance	5. Group creates a dance to a piece of music to express an idea
6. Worker teaches how to make a puppet from a potato	6. Group creates puppets from various materials, writes skit, makes stage, gives show

Now that these various exercises have helped the reader learn to analyze the components of his non-verbal content more minutely, it will be easier to view content dynamically in terms of what it can do *through the group worker's skilled adjustment* of it to help accomplish various purposes with individuals and groups.

Using the Analysis Form to Analyze Process Records

A final exercise to lead the reader to think in these terms is detailed now in the presentation of three different sessions around the general theme of content of a party. These three parties will be presented through a process record by the group worker in which each incidence of non-verbal content is numbered. The numbered activities will then be plotted according to the dimensions of the Non-Verbal Activities Analysis Form. The records are drawn from three different age groups: (1) boys, 6 to 9 years, (2) boys, 10 through 13 years, and guests, and (3) girls and boys, 12 to 15 years.

Three Examples of Group Parties and the Non-Verbal Content Used

1. A Halloween Party for boys, 6 to 9 years of age *

As the boys were (1) getting dressed in their costumes and I was helping them, it was interesting to watch the transformations taking place among them. Ronnie quickly put on the Frankenstein costume and proceeded (2) to act scarey and monsterous. Jimmy couldn't fit into one costume and finally had to wear Popeye and seemed to like this costume. John's costume was Boy Wonder and when John (3) was wearing his costume he acted very wildly and exuberantly. Karl at first resisted putting on a clown costume and said he didn't want to be a clown. However, when he was presented with a couple other alternatives, he finally decided to become a clown.

The boys very quickly got into their costumes, and once in them (4) all began mimicking each other. The end result was that they were all acting like rough, tough, monster characters no matter what costume they had on. When my group finally joined the other group for the (5) grand march downstairs, the boys were rather subdued.

* Record of Arlene Mazzei, Student Group Worker, Children's Aid Society of Pennsylvania.

When the boys got down to the living room and paraded in front of the three judges, I directed them all back to the stairs and one at a time a boy paraded in front of the judges. Every boy during (6) his individual parade went up to the three judges and acted like he was going to attack them. Not one of them acted at all affectionate with the judges. Following the costume parade, the judges retired to the playroom and decided on the prizes. I had gone over the list of categories with the judges beforehand, and it was worked out that each boy would be receiving a prize and that it would not be done on a best-to-worst basis. When the judges returned with their results, (7) each boy seemed to be very happy receiving his present.

Following the costume part of the program we had a (8) talent show. Again, I handled it the same way as the costumes and the boys sat on the steps and I called one boy at a time to perform. This program was delightful to watch, and the boys all seemed to really show themselves during this program. (9) Herbie began by singing a song. When he got in front of the judges, he immediately became very shy. I gave him a song to sing and he was able to sing it. After he was through singing, he seemed to be very pleased by his performance.

Jimmy (10) followed and did a wild birdcall and jumped around like a bird. (11) Everyone laughed. Jimmy's performance was followed by Ronnie (12) who sang a song he had learned at school. Ronnie did a very good job with this, remembering all the words and singing loudly and clearly. (13) Everyone clapped. (14) Billy followed Ronnie and announced that he would tell a fairy tale. He told the story of The Sleeping Beauty. Billy seemed a little ill at ease, but, nevertheless spoke slowly and relatively clearly. When it was Burt's turn he acted very shy, and it was obvious that he was very uncomfortable being in front of the group. I helped Burt choose a song and (15) he sang one of his favorite songs we had sung this summer at camp. Once he got going with the song he did a very nice job and sat down smiling.

(16) John came next and copied exactly what Jimmy had done and did a birdcall. (17) Karl chose for his act a very appropriate

one for his costume and did a comedy routine jumping around and laughing like a clown. Finally, (18) Evan performed and he very ingeniously portrayed a story about Batman and his grandmother. It was obvious that Evan above anyone else enjoyed being in the limelight and really had a flare for the dramatic. He continued to perform for about five minutes. (19) Burt and a couple of the other boys really enjoyed Evan's performance and laughed a lot.

Following the performances of the boys the judges again gathered to decide on the winners. (20) Every boy received a prize for what he had done, and Evan won the prize for the best performance. Evan seemed to be very happy and proud of his achievements.

Following the talent show, I told the boys to remove their masks and leave them in the house as we would all be going outside (21) for apple bobbing. The boys were becoming a bit more rowdyish with their costumes on and many limits were placed on them. (22) Apple bobbing was a big success and each boy, surprisingly enough, was able to get his apple. Some boys had a little more difficulty than others and especially Herbie had difficulty because he had only one tooth this week. However, with a lot of encouragement he finally was able to pick up an apple with his teeth. The boys all got drenched, their entire heads, but really were having a great time. (23) When we returned to the house, some of the boys were still (24) eating their apples and I suggested that we sit in the playroom and play (25) I Spy while they finished. We played I Spy for about ten minutes and then moved directly into (26) Pin the Candle on the Pumpkin.

I explained to the boys that Pin the Candle on the Pumpkin was the same kind of game as Pin the Tail on the Donkey. I explained that we would be blindfolding each boy and that he would be directed straight ahead of him and he would try to pin the candle on the pumpkin. The winner would be the boy that pinned the candle on the nose of the pumpkin. It was interesting that all the boys were able to propel themselves fairly straight to the target. Ronnie had the most difficulty with this. The first time through the game, Herbie was the winner. The boys liked the game so much they insisted on playing it a second time. The second time went as smoothly as the first.

After this game, we moved readily into (27) a Fish Pond game. The boys all got a lot of fun playing this as they love the mystery of fishing for an (28) unknown prize. Many of the boys, after they got their grab bag, tried to keep it a secret from the other boys (29) and a lot of teasing interaction occurred among the boys. As the boys were engaged in fishing at the fish pond, the housemother was pinning the balloons on the blanket for the next game. They were getting rather wild so I decided that rather than moving quickly into breaking the balloons we would sit again in the playroom and (30) the boys could eat some of their candy and compare prizes that they were receiving. We also (31) sang some songs and the boys seemed to relax a little bit more.

In a little while, we began to play (32) breaking the balloons. As with the pin the candle game, this game proved to be pleasurable. None of the boys remarked about being blindfolded, and all of them seemed to function fairly well under the blindfold. It was amazing that none of the boys began poking each other with a safety pin. It was now about four o'clock and the cook was ready with the refreshments. We had closed the doors to the dining room and the treats that the boys were to receive next were to be a surprise to them. When all the boys (33) gathered in the dining room it was obvious that we had too much food. (34) Because it was the cook's birthday and the boys had been informed of this earlier, they sang her a rousing Happy Birthday. Very few of them (35) ate more than just a little portion of their food, but the housemother was flexible enough to allow them to keep their plates and they could return to them and eat their candy and other things as often as they wanted to.

All in all, the boys seemed to respond well to the amount of structure that I put into the party. I feel that at times they were getting over stimulated and that it was good that I had them rest for a few minutes and involved them in quiet activities. The party was fun, but could have been accomplished with a lot less food.

Analysis of Non-Verbal Activities in Halloween Party

Activity	*Activity Demand*	*Leadership Pattern*	*Initiated*	*Ended*
(1) Dressing in costumes	Skill	Worker, indirect control	Worker	Worker
(2) Ronnie acting	Creative	Group control, changing "It"	Member	Member
(3) John acting	Creative	Group control, changing "It"	Member	Member
(4) Group mimicking	Creative	Group control, leader within	Group	Worker
(5) Grand march	Skill	Worker, direct control	Worker	Worker
(6) Individuals pass judges	Creative	Worker, indirect control	Worker	Worker
(7) Getting prizes	Chance	Worker, direct control	Worker	Worker
(8) Talent Show	Skill, creative	Worker, direct control	Worker	Worker
(9) Herbie sings	Skill	Group control, changing "It"	Worker	Member
(10) Jimmy's birdcall	Creative	Group control, changing "It"	Worker	Member
(11) Group laughed	Strategy	Group control, no leader	Group	Group
(12) Ronnie's song	Skill	Group control, changing "It"	Worker	Member
(13) Group clapped	Skill	Group control, no leader	Group	Group
(14) Billy's story	Skill	Group control, changing "It"	Worker	Member
(15) Burt's song	Skill	Group control, changing "It"	Worker	Member
(16) John's birdcall	Skill	Group control, changing "It"	Worker	Member
(17) Karl's clowning	Creative	Group control, changing "It"	Worker	Member
(18) Evan's story	Creative	Group control, changing "It"	Worker	Member

Analysis of Non-Verbal Activities in Halloween Party (cont'd.)

	Activity	*Activity Demand*	*Leadership Pattern*	*Initiated*	*Ended*
(19)	Group laughs at story	Strategy	Group control, no leader	Group	Group
(20)	Getting prizes	Chance	Worker, direct control	Worker	Worker
(21)	Going outside	Skill	Worker, direct control	Worker	Worker
(22)	Apple bobbing and getting wet	Skill	Worker, indirect control	Worker	Worker
(23)	Returning inside	Skill	Worker, direct control	Worker	Worker
(24)	Eating	Skill	Group control, leader within	Worker	Worker
(25)	I Spy game	Chance	Group control, leader within	Worker	Worker
(26)	Pin Candle on Pumpkin game	Chance/skill	Worker, direct control	Worker	Worker
(27)	Fish Pond game	Chance	Worker, direct control	Worker	Worker
(28)	Getting prize	Chance	Worker, direct control	Worker	Worker
(29)	Keeping prize a secret	Strategy	Group control, no leader	Group	Group
(30)	Eating candy, comparing prizes	Skill	Group control, no leader	Worker	Worker
(31)	Group singing	Skill	Worker, direct control	Worker	Worker
(32)	Breaking balloons	Skill/chance	Worker, indirect control	Worker	Worker
(33)	Went to dining room	Skill	Worker, direct control	Worker	Worker
(34)	Group song	Skill	Worker, direct control	Worker	Worker
(35)	Eating	Skill	Group control, leader within	Worker	Worker

No attempt will be made here to draw a full analysis of the trends that can be observed from the worker's notations of analysis of the non-verbal content, but a few highlights and suggestions will be noted so that the reader can make his own more complete study.

1. When one individual thought up a particular thing to do, it was noted as a "creative" activity demand. When a second child copied him, his performance was judged "skill."

2. Considering the age group involved, i.e., young boys with very little experience in group activities, the following emphases seem consistent with their needs:
   a. Many opportunities for individual activities.
   b. Group activities essentially stressed chance rather than skill.
   c. Prize awards also emphasized chance.
   d. Worker was in direct control of the flow of the activities most of the time.
   e. Worker took much responsibility in starting and stopping and changing activities.
   f. Group was seen to be in control of itself mainly around such group actions as laughing, clapping, listening to one child, eating, and keeping their prizes a secret. It is seen, thus, that the group could exercise some control over itself at certain times when children were engaged in parallel behaviors so that the overall movement of the party could go on.

2. *A Halloween Party for Boys 10 Through 13 Years of Age and Guests* *

In contrast to my usual Sunday afternoon experience, the general atmosphere on this afternoon was one of cooperation and involvement. The committees responsible for the games, the cos-

* Record of John A. York, Student Group Worker, Children's Aid Society of Pennsylvania.

tumes, and the decorations got through their meetings without too much bickering. Notably absent were the proclamations of various boys at various times to the effect that they weren't going to do anything, didn't want to do anything, etc. There were, to be sure, individual squabbles such as that between Mel and Joe and also Robbie's difficulty in relation to his committee. However, these were not of the strong resistant nature of the usual conflicts that arise within this group.

(1) The costume committee put out in the recreation room the various materials we had for costumes, sorted according to pants, shirts, masks, hats, etc. (2) We then drew names out of a hat to determine the order in which boys could pick. (3) The boys then went around the circle picking one item each time they went around. In this way the boys selected costumes which had to be conglomerations of various pieces of clothing rather than selecting any costume that was a ready-made unit. Despite the group-expressed anxiety last week of their fear of being cheated because costumes were not being purchased for them, they were able to take the materials available and make creative use of them. There was a momentary difficulty in imagining what they could do with old clothes, but once the concrete materials were before them, they were able to use their imaginations to create something with these clothes. Thus, there were no comments about the agency being cheap because costume materials were from the Goodwill rather than the 5 & 10. As a matter of fact, (4) the boys seemed to get a big kick out of seeing some of the Goodwill price tags on the clothes they wore.

Of particular note during this time was the difficulty that both Joe and Len had in settling finally upon an idea for costumes. (5) They would get an idea, gather some clothes to carry out that idea, and then change their minds and want to trade it all in and start all over again. It took considerable support from the housefather and myself to enable either boy to gather the materials for a complete costume. For the most part the boys were able to make creative use of the materials at hand. However, with regard to mask materials they (6) resorted to the more conventional types of masks.

The neighborhood children who had been invited to the party this day were outside and expressed considerable interest in what was going on inside the house. The boys were torn between their desire to keep the decorations and costumes a secret and therefore a surprise and their desire to have the neighborhood children see and know what was going on. Thus, the neighborhood children got a smattering of what was going on inside without getting the total picture. The general atmosphere of the afternoon was one of excitement and enthusiasm in planning the party. Much of this, I think, stemmed from the boys' participation in the planning and preparation. They were very much aware that this was their party and its success rested on their shoulders.

After (7) supper the preparation in terms of costumes and makeup began in earnest. Joe, who had finally chosen to be a mummy wrapped up in strips of white sheeting, enlisted the housefather's help in (8) putting together his costume. As is usually the case with Joe, it came down to the housefather's making his costume for him. He displayed considerable anxiety regarding his costume but seemed unable to do much in the way of constructive thinking or actions. When he was finally wrapped up and came downstairs, his costume fell apart a bit and he gave up completely. Despite support from the houseparent and challenges from me, Joe refused to do anything with regard to costuming. When I talked with him about this, he complained that he had given me three ideas of what he wanted to be and I hadn't made any of them. He would not accept any responsibility for making his costume, but rather projected the blame he feared and felt on the workers. I (9) showed Joe various types of costume materials and suggested various ways that these could be used, but he rejected them all because none of them fit in with his idea of what he wanted to be—a woman. However, we had deliberately not made any (10) female attire available as costume material, since we aimed at stressing the male identification of Joe and others; and when he asked for female clothes, we stressed that he was a man and didn't need to be a woman. Finally, at the last moment the housefather (11) shoved a tire into Joe's hand and told him he could go as the Fisk Tire Company ad. Joe accepted this primarily because it was a means for him to get a costume prize.

Ross, who had indicated resistance to the party as a whole last week, had involved himself to the extent of (12) helping with the decorations. However, he still maintained he would not get dressed up in a costume. The housefather and I both accepted this with the expression of our hope that he could be in costume in order to get a prize. We didn't press the matter. About a half hour before the party when the boys were beginning to get involved with the (13) makeup and the final excitement of finishing their costumes, Ross came to me and said that he would like some costume material and (14) proceeded to make himself a fairly decent costume. He then participated fully in the party activities with a much lighter spirit than I had noticed before.

Robbie, who had received a guitar and a wig, had expressed the intention of being a Beatle. However he got so excited and involved with the makeup that I discovered him (15) putting natural pancake makeup on top of the burnt cork sideburns and beard on his face which also had a mixture of white greasepaint here and there. He finally got so much makeup on his face that it began to get into his eyes and he had to (16) go and wash his face and clean off most of what he had on. Dick was able to make the most creative use of his costume material in (17) designing for himself a clown costume. He received considerable (18) support from the other boys in making this costume. The final product was a very creative clown. However, except for a little bit in the initial stages of selecting costume material, Dick did not use his clown suit and makeup as an excuse for his sometimes clownish and clumsy behavior. The total effect was one more of the pathetic kind of clown rather than the jolly, funny kind of clown.

Sam, who had been restricted to the upstairs until party time because of his illness, had put considerable thought into his costume and with some help from me in getting materials (19) made a quite effective beatnik motorcycle rider costume. Despite his restrictions because of illness, he did not display any of his usual whiny, complaining behavior but rather seemed to be excited by the prospect of wearing his costume and having the chance to participate in the (20) preparations of the game committee which met in his room.

Mel used a nightcap, a nightshirt, a white stick and a tube of red lipstick to (21) turn himself into a very convincing case of measles. However some of the other boys accused him of using this as an excuse to suck his thumb and carry a stuffed animal.

There were five neighborhood children and one mother who came to the party. Two of the boys were brothers. The children blended into our group very well. One little six-year-old girl received considerable attention from all the boys who (22) gave her help to get a prize or win a game. The older of the two sisters was treated as another boy from the point of view of the group.

We played several games including (23) Pin the Tail on the Cat, (24) Tug of War, (25) Musical Chairs, and (26) bobbing for apples. For the most part the boys were able to participate in these games for the sake of having a good time. There did not seem to be any real flare of tempers that one might expect in some of the tense competition that went on. The boys seemed to have a particularly good time in (27) misdirecting one another to the target for pinning the tail on the cat. However, none of them expressed resentment in connection with this. In this game Dick and Robbie were the two who managed to hit the bull's-eye. This gave them some status in the group.

(28) Prizes were awarded in each of the games on the basis of increasing value so that each boy got at least a lollypop for his efforts in participating and some boys who won the game got two candy bars. Prizes were also awarded (29) for the costumes. This was set up in such a way that the housefather and I took turns in thinking up awards so that each boy and girl won a prize. In order to distribute the variety of prizes that we had available, the costume committee had (30) blown up balloons putting a number in each one. I had numbered the prizes so that as each winner was announced he would (31) break a balloon and get the prize of the number inside the balloon. The prizes which

included toy trucks, rubber balls, and rubber stamp sets were welcomed by the boys.

The food committee had (32) prepared punch, cider, and cake, as well as taffy apples, candy corn, nuts, and popcorn balls. I called the boys' attention to the fact that there were ladies present and helped them then to choose to have the ladies first in line as all (33) got their refreshments. They were very excited in putting on this party for their friends. The food was served in such a way that the boys (34) ate their cake and drank their cider and then afterwards received the candy, apples, and popcorn balls. They all ended up with bags of candy similar to what they might have had if they had gone Trick or Treating.

With the housefather's help I had prepared a graphic story appropriate to Halloween which (35) I told while the boys (36) passed around in the darkness various items to represent supposed parts of a dead man. This did not go over too well since they were more interested in identifying what the items really were than using their imaginations to become excited by the story.

The particular value of this day seemed to be in (1) the boys' carrying major responsibility for an activity of their own, (2) the boys having an opportunity to do something for others, their neighborhood friends, and (3) the boys having an opportunity for a time to be something they weren't.

The analysis of these activities reflects certain patterns within this group and certain differences by comparison with the group experience of the younger boys at their party.

1. Again there is a balance between activities for the group as a whole and opportunities for individuals.
2. The opportunities for "creative" activities centered around the selecting of costumes and application of makeup.
3. The games stressed primarily "chance" but more skill and strategy than in the younger group.

Analysis of Non-Verbal Activities in Halloween Party

Activity	*Activity Demand*	*Leadership Pattern*	*Initiated*	*Ended*
(1) Costumes sorted and put out	Strategy	Worker, indirect control	Worker	Group
(2) Drawing names from hat	Chance	Worker, indirect control	Worker	Group
(3) Selecting costumes	Creative	Group control, changing "It"	Worker	Group
(4) Boys react to price tags	Skill	Group control, no leader	Group	Group
(5) Joe and Len pick costumes	Creative	Worker, indirect control	Member	Member
(6) Choosing masks	Creative	Worker, indirect control	Group	Group
(7) Eating supper	Skill	Group control, leader within	Worker	Group
(8) Joe puts on costume	Skill	Worker, direct control	Member	Member
(9) Shows Joe other materials	Creative	Worker, direct control	Worker	Member
(10) Withheld female costumes	Skill	Worker, indirect control	Worker	Worker
(11) Gave Joe tire	Creative	Worker, direct control	Worker	Worker
(12) Decorating	Creative	Worker, indirect control	Worker	Worker
(13) Applying makeup	Creative	Worker, indirect control	Worker	Group
(14) Ross makes costume	Creative	Worker, indirect control	Member	Member
(15) Robbie applies makeup	Creative	Worker, indirect control	Member	Worker
(16) Robbie washes	Skill	Worker, direct control	Worker	Member
(17) Dick makes costume	Creative	Worker, indirect control	Member	Member
(18) Group reacts to Dick	Strategy	Group control	Group	Group

Analysis of Non-Verbal Activities in Halloween Party (cont'd.)

Activity	*Activity Demand*	*Leadership Pattern*	*Initiated*	*Ended*
(19) Sam makes costume	Creative	Worker, indirect control	Member	Member
(20) Preparation of games	Creative	Worker, direct control	Worker	Worker
(21) Mel makes costume	Creative	Worker, indirect control	Member	Member
(22) Group helps young girl	Strategy	Group control	Group	Group
(23) Pin Tail on Cat game	Chance	Worker, direct control	Worker	Group
(24) Tug of War game	Skill	Worker, direct control; then group controls and plans	Worker	Group
(25) Musical Chairs game	Chance/ strategy	Worker, direct control	Worker	Group
(26) Bobbing for apples	Chance/ strategy	Group control, changing "It"	Worker	Worker
(27) Misdirecting others	Strategy	Group control	Group	Group
(28) Prizes awarded for games	Skill	Worker, direct control	Worker	Worker
(29) Prizes awarded for costumes	Chance	Worker, direct control	Worker	Worker
(30) Blowing balloons	Skill	Group control, leader within	Worker	Group
(31) Break balloon, get prize	Skill/ chance	Worker, indirect control	Worker	Group
(32) Prepared food	Skill	Group control, worker within	Worker	Worker
(33) Got refreshments	Skill	Worker, direct control	Worker	Group
(34) Ate food	Skill	Group control, leader within	Worker	Group
(35) Halloween story	Skill	Worker, direct control	Worker	Worker
(36) Group passes objects	Skill	Worker, direct control	Worker	Worker

4. The greatest variation from the younger group was in the area of leadership control. At this party there is much more "group control, leader within" and less direct control by the worker. There is equal incidence of worker in direct control and worker in indirect control (13 times each). Indirect control most of the time refers to worker planning in advance, obtaining costume and makeup materials or preparing prize numbers, and the group then acting within these planned structures.

5. The activities of this group were more frequently ended by the group itself than with the younger age group.

It can be seen from these few generalizations that the factor of age and, hence, previous experience in having parties have much to do with the increased ability of the boys to take responsibility for themselves.

3. *A Co-ed Party Given by 12- and 13-Year-Old Girls* *

Preparation for the party included game planning, checking on the refreshments with the girls, talking with them about the list of boys invited, and planning with the three volunteers who were to help with the party. The girls came in after school to check on last-minute details, what they were going to wear, etc., and I talked with them about which boys had accepted invitations.

The evening began with (1) May coming to make cupcakes at the settlement because her oven at home was broken. She brought all the ingredients with her, and Pat and several of the other girls helped her. (2) Sally brought balloons, and she blew them up and tied them together to hang from the ceiling for decorations. The rest of the girls (3) arranged the food, decorated the table, and (4) danced until it was time for the boys to arrive. Elaine, Joan, and Tess were not properly dressed for the party, and Elaine said it was because she had been locked out of her house

* Record of Sylvia Lee, Student Group Worker, Lutheran Social Mission Society, Lutheran Settlement, Philadelphia.

and could not change. I reminded them of the group decision on what they were going to wear, but said that if the other girls did not mind, they could stay. Thinking they must have felt hesitant to come after I had asked them to leave at the last meeting because of their behavior, I was glad that they came. Pat and May had talked with me about Elaine in the kitchen while making the cupcakes, and they said that Sue and Jody were unhappy with the club because of her. I told them that the group was there for all to express their differences and that one girl should not be allowed by the others to run their club. I told both girls that I was pleased that they both had come even though their best friends did not feel they could, and that they were showing Elaine that she could not run them even though they disagreed with her.

Mary, Carry, and Liz were very nervous about the party and kept coming to me and saying that they would stay in the kitchen all night. I said that it would be fine if they would help with the refreshments, but that I hoped they would feel they could participate in some of the games. I mentioned that the boys felt the same way they did, and Liz said that Mary was allowed to come only if she did not sit by any boys. These girls seemed so upset and at the same time excited that all I could do was to reassure them and at least encourage them to come into the party room.

At 7:15, Tess and Barb went downstairs to act as (5) door hostesses, and we talked once more before they left about what they were to do. I also went over with the other girls what they were to do at the party, and everyone was getting very excited. Three of the settlement boys came up then but would not come into the room. Two very well dressed boys came next, and all stayed in the hall. All five, although we encouraged them to come in, decided to go outside and wait for more to come. Soon a large group of boys arrived and they all came up. The three male volunteers helped a great deal in making the boys feel welcome, and some of the girls talked to the boys and made some introductions.

When everyone was in the room, I welcomed all to the party and explained the rules of no smoking and that if anyone left the room, he would not be allowed back in. We moved right into (6) the first game which consisted of collecting autographs in a party booklet with the names of people there who shared their favorite food, song, etc. This got the group moving right away, and even Mary, Carry and Liz participated. The first five to finish (7) received prizes. After the game was called to a halt, those that were not finished still wanted to collect autographs. The (8) next game was a scavenger hunt. When the four groups went to their designated corners to find the articles, group number three had several too many members. Elaine had gotten most of her group together there, but Tess and several others volunteered to go into the other groups. It seemed that all of the members of the groups were being involved, and one group even approached another group to exchange an article that they had for something that another one had two of.

After the scavenger hunt, several of the boys (although they had actively participated in the games) decided that they had had enough and got up and left. No one seemed to be upset by it, and they all got quickly involved in the next game. (9) The boys arranged the chairs in a circle for (10) "Wink 'Em," and since three of the boys refused to play the "silly" game, Mary and I played the boys' parts. After we began, however, Doug joined in since it looked like we were all having a good time. Carry and Liz would not play even though many encouraged them, since this game was more threatening to them because of the closer contact with the boys, but they seemed to enjoy just watching. The other girls thoroughly enjoyed the game since they were winked at by the boys who liked them; and when we reversed the game, they could wink at the boys whom they liked. The three male volunteers were favorites of the girls too.

The (11) final game was a relay with the boys against the girls, and the props involved were hats and umbrellas. They had to put the hat on, run to the end of the room and put up the umbrella, and run back to the next person and put the umbrella down. The girls won and were thrilled with the results. (12) Refreshments were then served, and the girls began to (13) dance by themselves. The boys seemed content at that point by finally (14) getting some food. (They said that was why they came in the first place.) The three volunteers and I mingled with the group then and talked with some of the new boys and girls. Carry kept sending Liz over to me to ask if one of the vounteers liked her. I talked with Carry about it, and she was just shaking while speaking with me. I told her that it was pretty difficult for me to ask him such a question when he had not even talked with her during the evening, so she asked me if I would say something to him before the evening was over. I said that I would. The girls (15) put on slow records then, and more began to dance. The girls seemed to enjoy dancing with the older boys, and the younger boys wanted to dance with me. The volunteer whom Carry liked asked her to dance, and she beamed for the rest of the evening.

At 8:45 I announced that it was time to (16) clean up, so several of the girls began to carry out dishes, sweep the floor, etc. The three volunteers had to leave then. When I walked them down to the door, we met Carry's mother. She walked upstairs with me to get Carry and asked me about the good-looking boys. When she talked with Carry, the boys were all Carry could talk about and her mother seemed very pleased. They both were asking me all kinds of questions about the one that Carry liked. I told Carry that they helped out at the settlement on Friday nights, and Carry said that she would be over every Friday night.

Sally, May, and Pat stayed (17) to wash the dishes, and three of the settlement boys helped. Sally told me that Anne was waiting downstairs to fight her and asked me if I would walk her home. I suggested that the group walk her home, and we began to talk about Sally's situation. Sally said that she knew I would suggest that the two of them get together and talk it out, but she said that she could not do that with Anne. She said that they were to fight over who was the strongest because Anne heard that Sally could beat her up. I told Sally that it took a strong person to walk away from something like that, and she agreed. Doug told her that she must remember that I am only in the neighborhood for a year to two, but that she must live there. Sally said that she realized that, but she wanted to do what I said.

(18) The seven of us walked down together. When we opened the door, a whole gang of kids were waiting. As the group walked across the street, Anne came over to Sally and started knocking her shoulder against Sally's as the rest of the gang egged her on. The girls soon (19) came to blows, and I walked across the street and asked Sally to come home with me and the others. She stopped fighting then and walked away with us. (20) The girls from the club walked her home then.

There are, again, certain differences observable from the analysis of these activities as compared with the previous two parties. Three main factors contribute to these differences: (1) An older age group, more experienced in giving parties and accepting responsibility for them, (2) a party with boys, very acceptable and exciting to some and very frightening to others, and (3) a group of teen-agers who live in the community in primarily intact families and hence have less need for the group experience to provide the central emotional experience in their life situation. The first two groups were boys in residential treatment.

With these differences in mind, the following generalizations can be made:

1. The activities were geared to the group and to cliques, with less provision for distinctly individually-geared ones.

2. The game activities were of a more challenging order, calling for skill and strategy rather than chance.

3. Prizes were awarded in competitive fashion without the concern for random selection and prizes for all.

4. Prizes did not reward every activity nor serve as incentives to motivate the participation.

5. Much of the leadership control rested directly with the group as a whole or various cliques, and there was a greater incidence of the members starting and ending the activities. The group was more responsible for the flow of activities of the evening.

Analysis of Non-Verbal Activities in Co-ed Party

	Activity	*Activity Demand*	*Leadership Pattern*	*Initiated*	*Ended*
(1)	May and others make cupcakes	Skill	Group controls and plans	Member	Clique
(2)	Sally prepares balloons	Skill	Member, direct control	Member	Member
(3)	Arranged food, decorated table	Skill, creative	Group control, worker within	Clique	Clique
(4)	Dancing	Skill	Group control	Clique	Clique
(5)	Tess and Barb hostess at door	Skill	Worker, indirect control	Worker	Clique
(6)	Collecting autographs in booklet game	Skill	Worker, indirect control	Worker	Worker
(7)	Getting prizes	Strategy	Worker, direct control	Worker	Worker
(8)	Scavenger hunt	Strategy	Worker, indirect control	Worker	Worker
(9)	Rearranged chairs	Skill	Group controls and plans	Worker	Group
(10)	Wink 'Em game	Strategy	Group control, changing "It"	Worker	Worker
(11)	Relay	Skill	Worker, indirect control	Worker	Worker
(12)	Refreshments	Skill	Group controls and plans	Clique	Group
(13)	Girls dance alone	Skill	Group control	Group	Clique
(14)	Boys eat	Skill	Group control	Clique	Clique
(15)	Girls put on slow records for dancing	Skill	Group controls and plans	Clique	Worker
(16)	Clean-up	Skill	Worker, indirect control	Worker	Group
(17)	Washing dishes	Skill	Worker, indirect control	Clique	Clique
(18)	Walking downstairs	Skill	Group control	Worker	Clique
(19)	Knocking, fighting	Skill	Member control	Member	Worker
(20)	Walking away from fight and home	Skill	Member control	Member	Clique

6. There was increased group member responsibility for room arrangements and clean-up as well as for the selection of dance content.

7. The worker retained direct control over the game activities; otherwise she gave over much control of the rest of the party to group members.

From the careful consideration of the content of these three parties the reader can now see more clearly some of the elements that contribute to make the tone of each different. The process records themselves would convey the overall impression of the differences in each. But the more minute study of each activity within each party situation shows more clearly why each party was different from the other two.

The overall factor affecting the difference in each party was the capacity of the group members to accept responsibility for themselves. After some assessment of this capacity, each group worker adapted his approach toward helping the group. The individual preferences, skill in activities, and desire "to lead" on the part of each worker were all subsidiary to the needs of the group. No worker was operating out of his own liking of the activity or personal need to control others. By this time, all three workers had become able to curb their own behavior so that the focus of attention was off themselves and on the group. This is what is meant by being professionally related to the group regardless of one's own individual strengths and weaknesses. The main strength illustrated by all three was their ability to use the situation to help the group have a satisfying and growth-producing experience.

* * *

This chapter emphasizes the stringent demands that face the group worker as he attempts to use the huge variety of possible non-verbal content in his work with groups. Many questions were asked, and several schemes for looking at non-verbal content were proposed. These demands can seem overwhelming! But practice in thinking about the content and its use by the worker along the lines suggested will, in time, make the job easier. There is no substitute for the rigorous discipline suggested here—only the promise of self-satisfaction when such skill is developed.

What is being called for now is some mastery of a way of interacting with a group through the non-verbal content in which the group is engaged. This is a new departure, stressing interaction within the group's process. In the past considerable attention has been given to the potentialities which various toys and play materials possess for use by the individual and group. Play therapy, for example, has contributed a valuable body of knowledge of the implications of play and activity choices. Not only is the therapist able to use these findings to appraise the child's psychology dynamically in diagnostic terms, but also he uses the play activities to direct the child into verbal interaction with him so that insight is developed and growth occurs.

This book emphasizes an approach that involves the worker even more actively in the ongoing use of play, game, and all activity materials. In the former instance the non-verbal materials are presented to the participant much like a smorgasbord—an array of tempting selections. He is surrounded by various stimuli and can pick and choose as he wishes. In this second approach of active engagement within the materials, the worker is more like the chef. He selects the ingredients he wishes to use and eliminates other ingredients very directly. He then presents the selected ingredients to the individuals and groups he is involved with, and together they cook up an experience! Often the individuals and groups throw away some of the worker's ingredients and substitute their own preferences—this is all to the good. When the collaboration is successful, the concoction has its own unique aroma and is palatable and satisfying to all.

9 80 Case Studies—Anecdotal Accounts of the Use of Non-Verbal Content With a Special Consideration of the Purpose of the Activity

> *Whatever Matisse's subject matter, representational or symbolic, he aimed at the quintessential and the universal; he reminded us that the great differences of form in the foliage of a tree do not keep us from recognizing its common quality; that "no leaf of a fig tree is identical with any of its other leaves; each has a form of its own, but they all proclaim: Fig tree!"*
>
> —Monroe Wheeler *

The discussion so far has emphasized the interrelatedness of content and structure. Both combine to bring into the realm of possibility the achievement of the basic purpose(s) toward which the worker, the sponsoring agency, and the group members aspire. In the past there has been a tendency when discussing the theory underlying social group work to put "the use of program" off in one special chapter and so to divide it from the worker's central attentions as he attempts to learn and master the method.

Here is a beginning attempt to re-place the doing kinds of activities—the non-verbal actions—in their rightful position as a basic, integral part of the social group work method. If understood and utilized properly, they enhance the purpose which

* *The Last Works of Henri Matisse* (New York: The Museum of Modern Art, 1961).

brings the worker into a relationship with a group. If this part of the methodology is less than precisely and deliberately handled, with the rationalization on the part of the worker that such kinds of involvement "never were my cup of tea," then not only is the group deprived of the fullness of the range of living experiences it ought to have and deserves, but, more important, there is reason to question whether the very achievement of individual and group purpose is really possible!

How often other group work teachers have told this writer that such a spontaneous use of program in such a variety of media with such responsibility and security in the content is "an art" rather than a teachable, transmittable way of working! If this be really so, then the whole future development and refinement of the group work method rests on shaky ground, indeed. While skillful practice is an art in any profession, the components and behaviors that make up the worker's approach ought to be open to logical presentation to the learner.

This writer firmly believes that there *are* transmittable learnings that the practitioner can master. For this reason the theoretical discussion that precedes the following specific actual examples has been detailed. In fact, it has been the teaching of these concepts that has made such anecdotal recordings possible, for the students who wrote them had been engaged in a process of examining analytically what they introduced. There will always be individual differences in style, in creative application of ideas, in imagination, in skill mastery, and in intelligence on the part of the worker in the area of non-verbal content as in every phase of his work with groups. These will combine to reflect differing degrees of worker skill. But at the same time the sheer diversity of the work of many practitioners and students illustrated in the material that follows should show the reader that all workers have a contribution to make in the non-verbal area if only they persist in trying to do so.

In the illustrations that follow (see Appendix C for list of sources) the primary focus in ordering the anecdotes is *worker purpose*. They will now be discussed sequentially with interpretive comments interspersed to make their meaning clearer.

Beginning Activities

1

The following is an excerpt from the record of a co-ed adult group.

There was some informal chatting but this was limited. Therefore, I introduced a paper and pencil game (P's and Q's) which Bill had picked earlier in the week as a game we could play. I arbitrarily divided the group into three teams. As late comers arrived, notably Jane and Nancy who arrived together, I distributed them among existing teams. Bill, again, took the leadership of one team. Robert assumed the leadership of the second, and Jim directed the third. Bill sparked interaction on his team as did Jim. However, Robert decided for his team that they would each make a separate list of words and then put them together. Nancy, when she arrived, hung on the fringes of her team. Ann, on Robert's team, made little effort to participate in a team effort until I removed a vacant chair between her and her team and suggested that she get involved. She then seemed to warm up and take an active part.

When there had been ample time to complete the list of words, I asked each team to choose a spokesman who then read the list they had.

Here the worker deliberately tries to initiate a process of interaction through a pencil-and-paper game and through his adjustment of the environment, i.e., the removal of an extra chair. Physical details such as these, often overlooked, can spell the success of the objective sometimes. In this same sense, a too-large or too-small room has great bearing on the tone of the activity regardless of the content, rules, and the way the worker uses himself.

2

The second game we played was called the Bean Game. Each person was given an envelope with ten beans in it. The object was to keep a conversation going without using the words "yes," "no," or "I." If these words were used, the person using them would give a bean to the person he was speaking to. The one in the end that had acquired the most beans would be considered the winner. Again this took a little time to get started. I began talking to various patients and when they used the words "yes," "no," or "I," I took one of their beans. The patients began to laugh whenever one of them was tricked. Soon they were talking to each other, trying to get more beans for themselves. This was done not in the spirit of fierce competition, but in a friendly, fun manner. The patients seemed to enjoy this game. They seemed relaxed and there was quite a bit of laughter heard among them.

The above activity was a most appropriate icebreaker for the physically disabled young adults in this group. As the excerpt shows, laughter at one's self is practically built into this game.

3

This game involves all the boys in a single activity. Because the boys live some distance from one another, many of them do not see each other outside of the club meeting time. This has resulted in a variety of activities being played by the boys who know each other, but few activities among those boys who do not live close to one another. I made up the following game to help with this problem:

Two players stand directly across from one another with a distance of at least eight feet between them. One player bounces a basketball in the center between himself and his partner. The partner must catch the ball before it bounces a second time. If the ball bounces more than once, or if not caught on the first attempt, or slips from either the hands of the thrower or catcher, then the ball is lost from that team and becomes the possession of the next team.

I asked one of the club members if he would like to play a game and be my partner. He said yes and I explained the above rules to him. There were only the two of us playing for a few minutes, at the end of which, another youngster came over and asked if he could play. I told him yes, but that he would have to find himself a partner with whom to play. He asked another boy and the two of them formed a second team. The ball was lost by the first team and this generated a great deal of enthusiasm among the two fellows on the second team. This enthusiasm was picked up by others in the room, and four other boys expressed an interest in playing and formed two other teams, making a total of seven boys involved in a single activity. With the addition of more teams, more rules (limits) had to be introduced. An imaginary circle was drawn and no one was permitted to step within the circle—which frequently happened and which added to the excitement of the game. The ball had to be bounced in the center of the circle and with as much power as a boy could muster. As each boy was throwing the ball, his teammates would holler the word "harder," thus adding to the involvement of those not directly playing.

The two factors which were emphasized in this game were involvement of each boy in the group and the necessity for working cooperatively with a teammate. This, I feel, has added to the boys' sense of belonging and of being able to contribute to the success of the group.

Just as individuals sometimes need help in their beginnings in a group, so sometimes the group as a whole is constituted in such a way that the worker is required to deliberately construct experiences that force interaction. The above example is one of many similar kinds of attempts in such a direction. Likewise, in the next episode the worker deliberately tries to affect a group situation to enable a shy, new member to make a beginning with the others.

4

I remember that when discussing elements involved in a beginning activity we outlined two general points: (1) the activity has to fit the setting, and (2) the activity has to be appropriate. Along these lines we discussed, too, the fact that cooperation and interaction could be encouraged by limiting the supplies needed in a particular craft project. The individual will then be helped by sheer necessity to work with others or bear the consequences (no craft product, possible group ostracism).

In one of my groups at the residence for older persons is a very wealthy, independent widow who has never participated or showed interest in any activity at the agency. One day quite by accident she passed our meeting room with her daughter who was anxious about the possibility of her mother joining this group for the primary purpose of giving her something to do. To satisfy her daughter Mrs.

Jones came to the group the next week and has been coming since. She is highly skilled in the work we have been doing and had kept largely to herself for a number of weeks. I let this go for a while, hoping that the setting as well as the presence of the other residents would have an effect. Seeing after a few sessions that this wasn't working, I decided to use the very method I discussed above, limiting supplies and "forcing" her into interaction. My guess and judgment proved correct, for it was very important to this woman that she make friends although she didn't know how to go about doing so. For all her wealth, status, and independence, she was unable to carry on a simple conversation with another woman, let alone initiate one. Not until I structured it so that she and another woman, one of the indigenous leaders of the group, were in the same subgroup, working with the same wool, scissors, and needles, was this woman able to engage in anything resembling friendship. This happened only last week and I have yet to see what goes on hereafter, but I suspect that this was a golden opportunity for her—one she can and will not let pass by.

Although this was only one instance of one of the above conceptualizations, it illustrates that the leader can effect results with just a little alteration and/or initiative. This requires of the leader some knowledge of what operates in a group, of the people constituting the group, and above all, of herself. I couldn't have done this four months ago; I didn't have the self-assurance nor the self-affirmation I do now.

This excerpt speaks for itself in highlighting the problem members often have in seeking out on their own what they might need so desperately. The reader can see the effectiveness of a worker's deliberate structuring of a situation to make a beginning interaction possible.

5

In the next episode another individual is trying to make a beginning with a group. This time it is the group worker. He records his very first contact with a group of ten foster children who live in a group residence for boys.

I arrived at S. House for my first time at 5:30 as the boys were sitting down for dinner. The housemother placed me at a table with

Lenny, Dick, and Bert. When I sat down, I reached for a large jug of Koolade. Lenny told me that it was his, so I apologized and then he said I could have some. During the meal, several of the boys asked if they could have some. Lenny did not respond to them but averted his eyes and put his head down. Halfway through the meal, he began to complain of a stomachache. The housefather suggested that he take his plate to the kitchen and go up to his room and lie down. At this point he suddenly began to pour everyone a glass of Koolade and then sat down and finished his dinner, his stomachache seemingly gone.

Here the worker meets the first of many tests as he tried to make contact with the boys he was there to help. It is no surprise that the worker should encounter a rejection within his first minutes with the group—summed up in the attitude, "you cannot eat my food." As the worker was able to continue to reach out despite such a welcome, in fact acknowledge the individuality of Lenny by apologizing to him for wanting and taking a drink without consulting him, i.e., without learning *how things were* at S. House before acting too much, his eventual acceptance was more assured.

6

Three days later the same worker is still involved in making his beginning, in showing the boys that he has the strength to be their worker, to make rules and hold to them. Testing the worker's ability to be their worker is an exhausting and often vexing experience, but there is little possibility of avoiding this learning about each other—worker and group—and much of it happens, as in the following example, in the course of activities.

When the boys arrived from school and changed, they began to play baseball. I assumed the role of umpire and, in view of the fact that they were using the real ball rather than the Wiffle ball to bat, I announced that any ball going over the fence on the fly would be an out. Bill immediately began to yell that that was no rule, that "we make our own rules around here," and Steve, Roy, and Bert all began to keep this up. I told them that it definitely was a rule and asked if they had money in their allowance to pay for a car window if one were broken. I felt that the rule would probably not be tested in any event, as it would take a very good and lucky hit in order to put it over the fence on a fly. So that game went on.

7

In the following example, the group members all knew each other well enough as they were a formed group who lived together. But the bond in this group was not strong, and the boys tended to select their moments of involvement in the group activity according to the merits of the activity as well as their mood at the moment rather than through much feeling for the group. In addition, the boys had markedly varying abilities in baseball and little sympathy on the part of the better players for those who might make their team lose. In this game the reader can see how deliberately the worker shifted his own place from team player to umpire, to catcher, to umpire again, and finally to both umpire and catcher. Through such flexibility and sensitivity the worker moved to enable the sensitive, the hurt, the shy, the inadequate to find their way onto a side in some position. Surely this worker was motivated throughout by purposes other than simply winning or losing a game, or even being fair and objective to both sides. His focus was on the individual and how he could help each make the best possible use of the baseball opportunity.

The weather was lovely, warm and balmy, and the boys were all out in the back yard playing ball or throwing sticks tied to ropes when I arrived. I had brought paints, brushes, and other equipment with which to paint the puppets the boys had made two weeks before. As I came out into the yard to greet the boys, Joe asked what we were going to do today. I suggested that we play ball, as they had been doing, since it was a lovely day and we could enjoy the out-of-doors. Perhaps we could make a baseball game out of it if we chose up teams, I suggested.

The boys seemed to be ready to give up their stick-ball game, and I suggested again that we choose up teams. Bud and Ed rose as the accepted captains, the other boys seeming to concur in their self-appointments. Ed chose Peter and Joe, and Bud chose Ray and me. Steve had gone into the house and apparently wasn't planning to come out immediately. I suggested to Robbie and Lew that they join us, but they preferred, they said, to play by themselves. We began playing three-base ball, and soon Steve joined us as umpire. I asked if he wanted to join the game and he declined. A little later on, I asked him again if he wanted to take my place since I was not helping my team very much, and he agreed. I took the catcher's role and, seeing Robbie hanging around and looking wistfully at us, I asked if he could be umpire. He reluctantly accepted the role and did quite well at it. To help Robbie get more in the game, I suggested he catch while I "ump," and the switch was made.

After the second inning, Joe left the game, complaining that he had a cold. (At one point he had missed catching a ball at first base and Ed had called him "girl." This was the probable reason for his "cold.") I suggested to the boys that Lew take Joe's place, but Ed and Pete would not accept him on their team and were willing to play with only two men. I put Lew in the catcher's position, but he was not very effective and the boys picked on him, far beyond what his inability to catch warranted. I took over the umpiring and catching jobs as the game began to break up. By 3:00 most of the boys had wandered off to watch TV, with only Ray, Ed, Steve, Pete, and myself playing. At one point, toward the end of the game, Bud came out to tell the boys that Command Premiere was on the air, but the boys wouldn't stop until the game was over.

8

Case Study 4 highlighted the particular use of program to help an individual member find her way into the group. The following example also focuses on the use of program to help an individual in his relationships. This time it is the worker who wants to build a relationship with a certain inaccessible group member. The setting is a home for the aged.

For some time I had been trying to make contact with Mr. Strong. Each time I attempted to have a personal interview, I was unable to keep Mr. Strong's attention. He seemed to be afraid of me because I represented administration.

I was aware of the fact that Mr. Strong was in charge of the table shuffleboard area of the Day Room and had often observed him playing the game. I asked the aide to have Mr. Strong do some minor work on the table so that I might approach him while he was near the table.

I asked Mr. Strong if he would teach me how to play the game. He responded eagerly and I received quite an education in "hooks," "hangers," and "rafes." Because he was concentrating on teaching me, I was able to beat him. This led to quite a bond between us because it seems that I am one of the few who has beaten the "champ."

The next day I returned to the Day Room to find that Mr. Strong had seen me coming and was at the table. This time I was able to concentrate on asking him the questions that I had never been able to ask before.

It is now somewhat of a ritual that I play at least one game with him whenever I am in his area. Large groups gather as we battle it out. (At this moment he is ahead two games.)

Out of this experience, I have learned to make better use of program material. I have repeated this type of thing with two men at the pool table and with several others at the checkerboard. I am also able to take men with feelings of not being wanted to these men, Mr. Strong in particular, and ask them to teach the game. So far, three wheelchair cases have learned shuffleboard, and one of them is presently working on pool. Each of these three is showing signs of improvement.

One can speculate that Mr. Strong felt more able to take on a new relationship around a content area in which he felt considerable adequacy. If the new staff member and his expectations were unknown, at least there was comfort in getting to know him on the shuffleboard court as well as emerging respect for a worker who was good at this game. The bond that developed through shuffleboard was able to carry over to new connections with the worker, even that of helping others join the game when the worker requested this. Group workers seem to learn quite early the concept of "starting where the group is." It is equally important to start where the individual is, although, as this excerpt reveals, the carry-over between these two concepts has to be learned by a beginning worker and is not automatic. One can almost sense the worker's feeling of revelation when he discovered that a game can be deliberately used as a beginning with a fearful group member and as a means to help other group members find a connection with higher status members.

9

In the following episode, the same worker reaches out again to an individual through the medium of an activity in which the resident felt most adequate. That his focus is dual in nature will be apparent. He is concerned here with one man who sits in his corner and also equally interested in helping this man make more of a connection with other men in the residence through their mutual interests. This record also shows how terribly difficult it often is for people to ask for the very things they so desperately want in human relationships and yet how they manage, in their own particular ways, to do so because the hunger for human connection is so powerful.

> When I began my work at the city's home for the aged, one of the first men I came in contact with was Frank Burns. He sits in his wheelchair at the corner table in Cherry Cottage working crossword puzzles. If you approached him and he yelled out less than fifteen four-letter words telling you to get away, you figured he was sick. I had tried to make contact with him several times, only to be told to get away. After three futile attempts, I directed my energies toward other men.
>
> After seven months in the institution, I was talking to another man and mentioned that I played chess. Frank hollered out, "Hey, come over here!" As I approached him, I felt it best to be just as rough as he was. "What do you want?" He went on to tell me that he was once a chess champion and that he would beat me so badly that I would quit the game. I told him I would accept the challenge and show him what chess playing was all about. He was roaring with laughter as I left.
>
> The next Monday I entered his Day Room from the side door and walked straight to his table. I put the checkerboard and the chess men down hard on the table and in his tone of voice told him to set them up while I hung up my coat.

I returned to find a small gallery gathered around. As we began, he warned me that if I let him win without really trying because he was a "cripple or something," he could tell. I told him I was there to win and made my first move. What followed was in his words and mine "one hell of a game." He had, indeed, been a champion.

The spectators at first cheered for me until Mr. Burns informed them that gentlemen did not cheer at chess games. I agreed and we continued as our audience stared in amazement. As the game ended, I found myself a winner who was exhausted. Mr. Burns shook my hand and asked for another game. I agreed.

As we set up the pieces, the gallery began to question Frank about his past. He answered with a noticeable amount of pride. One of the other men said he could play chess also. After Frank and I finished, this man sat down to play.

Since that day, Frank and I have enjoyed many good games. He has also started playing chess with two other men and is enjoying the prestige the other men have given him. He still yells a lot, but much of the sting is gone. This week he asked for a "church suit" and some crutches so he could move around better.

Mr. Burns' surge toward life as he experienced the adequate part of himself come to the fore is apparent. That all this happened before an appreciative audience of his peers was reason for added affirmation. That he was much more than an old, crippled, solitary man while he was the center of interest during the chess game must have had great impact on his self-esteem. Moving out of his chair to stand with crutches in new clothing is dramatic—perhaps miraculous!

Beginning an Unfamiliar Activity

10

In my teen-age girls' group, all Negro in membership, at the settlement I had them form a circle with half facing east and half west, and from the center of the circle I demonstrated the dance steps. Every girl caught on quickly. Marian, who recently joined and seems to relate only to Diane, was able to form a relationship with Justine, her partner, and share an experience which seemed enjoyable.

From February 12-19 the agency was observing Negro History Week. I decided that my group might well benefit from a few African dances. Unable to locate a dance syllabus of African dances, I viewed a film entitled "Rhythms of Africa" and from observation originated my own.

I explained that the people of Equatorial French Africa used dance in many parts of their lives and were known to be very skillful dancers. I explained that the first dance was a religious dance into which the people put a great deal of feeling and therefore made gestures which seemed wild. Using African ethnic drum music, I demonstrated the movements. Forming two lines facing each other, the group began. Jeanie said that this was the way her mother shouted in church. I said that that might be true because both were ways of releasing tensions. Dancing along with the group, I demonstrated when there was to be a variation in movement. Every girl seemed to enjoy this . . . Jeanie and Brenda asked to stay after the meeting to do more dancing.

In leading both of the dances mentioned I felt under no pressure because I liked the activity and, more important, because I had carefully structured it. Though my purpose in programming with dance had been initially singular in helping the girls to feel pride in their Negro heritage, I discovered that folk dancing could be adapted to serve many of their needs.

If the group is left to its own program choices entirely, they will most often stick to things they already know. In an effort to expand horizons as well as offer new avenues of self-expression through which new constellations of leadership and achievement can be revealed, the worker often deliberately leads the group into unknown experiences. He is enabled to do so by the strength of his relationship with the group and the trust they put in him in behalf of their own general welfare. Naturally, in any area of risk to the individual the worker must be keenly aware of the existing threat and the courage demanded of the group members, and he must proceed cautiously. The above excerpt shows how close to the group the worker was as she introduced them to completely new kinds of dancing. The aspect of group pride and attitude toward themselves is also contained here.

11

The following experience is drawn from a teen-age boys' group in a correctional institution for delinquents:

I shifted the conversation to the type of program we should have next week. How many of you guys can dance? All of them raised their hands and I asked them what dances they knew. All the ones they named were popular rock and roll dances, so I asked them if there might be some others they would like to learn. Ham suggested the polka and the others agreed with this. Holding this thought for a moment, I asked them if there were a dance that they could teach me. One of the boys said that they could probably teach me the "Slide." I then said that if they could teach me their dance I would try to find out how to do the polka and we could trade dances next week. They agreed to this enthusiastically and on this note the meeting came to a close.

Next week at the meeting there were two new members, Gordon and John, present. Although these two have been known to the rest of the group as cottage mates for some time, it is to be noted that this was the first meeting they had attended. Gordon had attended earlier in the year but dropped out shortly after the group began.

As the boys followed me into the room, they sat down automatically in the circle of chairs. Since there was very little pending from the last meeting, I suggested that we get started with the activity right away. The boys agreed with this and I asked them which they wanted to do first—learn the polka or teach those of us who didn't know it, the "Slide"? After some argument I suggested that we start with the "Slide," as it was more familiar, and the boys agreed. I said OK and asked those who knew it to show the rest of us how it was done. John, Ira, Ham, Richard, and Corny formed a line and started going through the steps while John did most of the explaining.

As we practiced there was one step that I found particularly difficult, and I noticed Tom was also having trouble with it. The center of attention was on me, however, and as I struggled with it the boys encouraged me to keep trying. I started to become discouraged with my attempts and told the group that I didn't think I would ever be able to pick it up. With their encouragement, though,

I tried again and this time was able to pick it up. With their encouragement, "Hey! You're doing it!" I was practicing it a little more to make sure I could explain it when my attention was caught by Ham criticizing Tom's attempts. I stopped what I was doing and asked Ham why he didn't try to help Tom instead of making fun of him. Ham looked a little guilty and went back to practicing his own step. One of the other boys started doing the step beside Tom but did not actually verbally explain the step. Finally, I moved over to Tom and showed him the way that I had picked it up. Tom, however, still had difficulty with it, so I acknowledged that it was a hard step and that he would probably have to practice it for a while. I added that he shouldn't worry about it as it was hard for anyone. He looked relieved . . . Later in the dancing session Tom said he thought he would ask his sister to teach him more about dancing when he got out. I encouraged him to do this so that he would be more at ease with girls.

With dancing again as a focus, a boys' worker also reveals his own courage as he dares to move in unfamiliar territory and use his own status as a novice to encourage group experimentation in a new medium. It goes without saying that a worker must possess a measure of inner security concerning his relationship with the group before he will be free to reveal to them that he does not know all. Sometimes, in face of the worker's own imperfections, the group in reaching out to help him develops new strength as well as a new appreciation of everyone's search for new achievements.

12

I had come to my senior citizens group with them being very set in their old routine, which had been repetitiously followed for the past six years. This consisted of drinking tea, discussing weather, and signing sympathy, birthday, or get-well cards, as the occasion arose. In preparation for a farewell to be held for the former worker, the subject came up of giving her a card. The members proposed following their usual routine of buying a good-bye card from the store and having each member sign it individually.

There didn't seem to me to be any real growth potential in just doing once more this oft-repeated act. I suggested, instead, making a card themselves which would say what they felt more accurately than a store-bought card which would only express what some card manufacturer felt. After some effort at convincing on the part of the worker, one of the members was able to print a very attractive *auf Wiedersehen* on a large piece of oak tag. All the other members signed their messages underneath, some of them being quite creative both in what they said and the designs that some chose to put next to their names.

This routine giving of a card had been structured so as to present opportunities for expression of a higher-level skill and creativity. The card looked quite attractive when finished, and each member felt quite proud of his contribution to the group. This activity had also moved the group away from their usual complete dependence upon the worker to a situation where the group itself was responsible for the plans and their execution.

It is often hardest for older persons to take on new patterns of group life and try out new things. In the above excerpt the sensitivity of the worker to this fact and her gentle way of leading them to something new through a basically old and accepted tradition is apparent.

13

Again, the writer presents a case study of an older adult group to illustrate the risk for both the members and the worker when venturing into new areas of self-expression at a period of life when most people expect merely a gradual diminution of already known powers. The reader can see in the following example the exhilaration possible for worker and group when the "impossible" is attempted. That all people can develop and change as long as they live is well illustrated in this excerpt from a young student's work with senior citizens living in a housing project.

I was very reluctant to try this program with the senior citizens as there are a few who cannot see well, two who have poor use of the hands, and almost all say, "I can't paint." I tried to structure it so no great skill demand was required. I had many large brushes and tilt paintings for those who might be afraid of the brush. There is a paraplegic in the group and there were sponges for her, as I knew she could not grasp a brush or hold the paper to tilt. Their initial response on seeing the paints was, "Are those for your children's group?" My stating that they were for them was met with the denial of knowing how to paint.

I gave a brief demonstration of tilt painting, showing how you simply appy colors to the paper and then jiggle the paper up and down so that the colors run together in interesting patterns, and they started in. I was surprised at the pride they took in their work! Such involvement within the group I had never seen. One lady, nearly blind and able only to distinguish between light and dark, painted a picture which will be exhibited during Senior Citizen Month. Requests came that we do arts and crafts again. Each liked his work enough to take it home.

The experience has taught me to be a little quicker in risking myself, in this instance through program. I may fail, but when there is success, the response of the group is enough to warrant another risk in hopes that they might experience another expanding experience.

14

A different, subtle way of introducing teen-age girls to an area of activity they thought they would not like is illustrated below:

In working with one teen-age girls' group that does not like to do non-verbal activities, I felt that some successful program experiences as a group would be helpful since they have had difficulties with relationships among members. The girls were not interested in planning this kind of program and could not be persuaded to do so.

Before Christmas, I had some samples of Christmas candles and some of the supplies available on one of the evenings when the girls were in the building to make plans for a co-ed program they were taking part in. This group had told me earlier in the year that they did not want any part of arts and crafts program. However, I said that I would be making a candle for myself next Monday night and if they wanted to join me I would have enough supplies.

They liked the candle and wanted to make one. On the next Monday night they were back, and we had an evening of candle-making. The method was interesting enough to hold their attention, and yet not too difficult for them to give up. I also think that the selection of the project was interesting to them. They had a successful experience. I think they had to experience and feel a success before they could plan for one.

Part of the success of such an approach rested with linking up a craft activity with an idea of great interest to the group, Christmas. Another aspect was the selection of a kind of candle-making that was mysterious in its process and results, the pouring of the hot wax into milk cartons filled with ice. The finished candle had a Swiss cheese quality, holes in variegated pattern formed by the melting of the ice. A project such as this was hard to resist.

15

Children as well as adults frequently back off from an art or craft activity because they have learned somewhere that they have no talent for such things. In these instances the approach of the group worker has to be most cautious and related to the underlying fears of the group members. The following example illustrates how one worker led up to an art experience in such a sensitive way that the boys were involved almost before they realized what they were doing. The use of the familiar as well as the exciting and mysterious in materials and the worker's way of suggesting what was expected by doing it himself made the experience possible.

I had wondered for some time how to introduce painting as a creative activity to the boys. I decided that the spontaneous unstructured method would be the most suitable or they would certainly avoid getting involved. The materials to be used should be different and should offer the opportunity to experiment. For this reason I chose a spray paint, natural materials found around the camp site, and paper. I got three cans of spray paint—green, red, and blue—and took a quantity of paper.

After dinner I picked up the materials and went out onto the grass. I then collected leaves, pine cones, pine needles, and a few rocks, and placed these materials on a piece of paper. I opened a spray can, shook it up, and began to paint. The boys quickly gathered around wanting to know what I was going to do and I explained, "I am going to experiment." After I had begun, several indicated they would like to try it as well, and I told them to get a piece of paper and they could try. Several did so immediately and gathered materials, placed them in creative order on the paper, and used the spray paint.

Roy was rather upset by what was going on and took all the paper and began to walk around with it and hang onto it. He wouldn't give it to anyone, but eventually began to drop it piece by piece. In the meantime, Ken, Mickey, and Bert were anxiously trying to get a piece of paper. As soon as Roy began dropping them, Ken ran out and picked up several sheets as quickly as he could.

Soon all of the boys were painting and experimenting except Lonny and Roy. Lonny looked very much as if he wanted to take part, but when encouraged to do so initially had said no. He then got himself into such a position that he couldn't change his mind. I pointed this out to him, saying that here was a case where he had got himself into such a hole and that even though he was dying to try it out, he just couldn't back down. This had some effect. Although it served to point out his behavior to him, he still denied that he really wanted to paint. Roy also came over, and as the cans became empty picked them up and tried to do something with them.

During the whole activity, the boys showed a lot of eagerness and effort in their creative productions. They were quite proud of them and held them up for all to see. Several took home their products and were genuinely pleased with what they had made. They asked to have the activity again, and I told them that I would try to do so as soon as we could.

At no time during painting did I tell the boys that they were engaged in arts and crafts, but rather let it seem that the activity was as natural a part of their daily life as baseball and Capture the Flag.

16

Sometimes progression into new areas of interest in program develops directly out of the creative adaptation of the area of interest in which the group is ready to be involved. The following comments of one worker show how she was able to see the possible connection between cooking and craft experiences.

I am using cooking as my basic program skill. I have discovered that cooking and baking are the most effective tools in communicating to the members at this time. This type of activity offers them the most security and sense of achievement. They were not responding to the other types of programming when they were first presented, such as arts and crafts and games.

I am continuing to add other types of program to the activity while the food is in the oven. This gives me the opportunity to do additional programming. Even within the activity itself, I can introduce things to extend the group's experience. For instance, I can introduce dough for the members to cut out and decorate. This will give them an opportunity to have some artistic experience.

17

The following discussion, again of cooking, illustrates how very diverse a group experience can become even when the group happens to form around one major area of interest. Similar illustrations could be cited with other kinds of interest groups where the skill of the worker led the group into much more than they imagined when they first joined.

I wondered how I was ever going to learn how to make use of program in cooking groups. I had no idea of the potential of program and specifically of cooking. I soon learned. First, cooking was not just standing at the stove, or mixing batter. It could, and has for my groups, involve serving, cleaning up, decorating, party foods, planning, shopping, attempts at budgeting, even the planning of a large-scale dinner party. This all has been in addition to the so-called "regular" cooking projects and holiday dishes.

Nor was I limited to activities related to cooking. The groups have welcomed other activities. Cooking has been a base, a unifying factor, for the groups. Sometimes the meetings were devoted to activities such as crafts. At other times the meetings consisted of a varied type of program including painting, crafts, games, singing, dramatics, etc.

I have so far mentioned only the activities themselves. Much else has gone on. The activities, even the cooking projects, have brought on various group interactions. To mention a few: the projects have purposefully necessitated various groupings and subgroupings, a use of utensils, creativity, individuality, cooperation.

Developmental Activities

As mentioned previously, most of the activities engaged in by workers and groups can be considered *developmental activities.* That is, the group has begun to meet, has passed through its beginning stages, and has not moved into its ending phase. It is going somewhere. The group members and the worker are using the group experience to pursue their separate and combined purposes. Despite the particular form of program choices—whether the manifest content is a trip or a game or a party—certain growth objectives are in the back of the worker's mind as desirable aspects of the group experience. The excerpts that follow are arbitrarily grouped under one of several growth objectives, though any one excerpt might conceivably lead to several objectives at the same time. For purposes of analysis, the writer has decided to highlight only one main objective for each example to illustrate the connection between various content forms and particular objectives.

The Use of Rules

Playing according to the rule is often an area through which the worker helps individuals modify their own impulsive behavior in order to move harmoniously in an outside reality. As the gap is shortened between plunging immediately into what they want to do and accomplishing their objective in a planful way, group members often develop inner rules of conduct that have a carryover value to other life situations.

18

In the following example, the reader follows a group of nine- and ten-year-old boys from some of the most crowded and dilapidated of city slums who go to a city square to feed the animals. They are not only ignorant of the habits of wildlife and of grass and trees, but they are also self-centered, anxious, impulsive, active, and without a concept of other people and things that are different.

As the boys appeared one by one, I reminded them of our decision last week—that we were going on a walking trip to a square downtown and feed the pigeons and squirrels. When Pete heard this, he shouted and screamed with excitement. (This intensified my own excitement about the possibilities which this trip offered.) . . . When we arrived, the boys at first in their enthusiasm scared the squirrels up the trees as they chased after them to give them crackers. I explained that the squirrels first had to feel enough security to trust that the person meant them no harm and taught the boys how to approach a squirrel slowly and with less movement.

The fellows stood rigid, but were still talking a great deal. I made a noise and taught them how you call a squirrel, and they began to imitate this. The group broke up into subgroups and went off in separate directions looking for other squirrels. With repeated cautions from me, the fellows began to realize that you can't run up to the animals and expect them to remain there to be fed. Several of the boys were experiencing success in feeding the pigeons and squirrels and were very much excited by this. They accepted the limit of not walking on the grass. I urged them to sit down on the benches, or at least stand still on the cement walkway, and then call the animals. With the exception of Paul, who continued to run through the park, and Karl, who was straggling along behind the others and not participating in the activity, they were intensely involved in what they were doing.

Pete had given each boy his amount of the group's crackers and bread, which John and Paul partly ate themselves. The boys distributed their food differently. John, a rather impulsive, impatient, and very aggressive youngster, did not break the crackers into edible sizes but simply threw the whole thing at the animals despite my urging him to do otherwise. Willie, the group's leader, who has been regularly attending the meetings and helpful in directing some of the group's behavior, crumbled his supplies into good-sized pieces after being shown what size was best for their mouths. Paul, one of the youngest members of the group, crumbled his crackers into such tiny pieces that even the birds couldn't eat them. Kevin was not involved in the activity but rather watched the others. He threw all of his bread into the pond.

On our way back home we talked about our trip. Several of the boys said they were going to come back again on Sunday with their parents.

It is interesting to see the boys slow down, sit on a bench, watch and hear different sounds, make different sounds. Through such an experience they became aware of something other than themselves. How satisfying this was to them is reflected in their desire to bring their parents along in a few days. It is also striking to see the boys reveal their individual differences in the way they apportion their supply of animal food. The main learning in this experience for these boys, however, was that you can't simply rush up to the first squirrel you meet, however hungry he might be, and expect him to want the cracker you have. You have to conduct yourself in a certain way (follow a strict code of behavior) or he will be scared away. Because the rewards of such behavioral control were so important to these boys, they modified their usual way of acting. Hence, the incentives for change, however short and temporary, were strong enough that behavior was modified. And a start was made that can be referred to with these same boys in other situations when the worker wants them to change other behavior.

19

In the following excerpt of a Halloween Party of teen-age girls, a similar kind of impulsive behavior is operating which the worker had to help the group change before the game could be enjoyed. The rules of the game had to be followed or there would be no game.

The next game we were to play was called "Witch Hunt," and because of my hoarse voice and the excitement of the girls at this point in the evening, no one heard the rules but began to play anyway. The game consisted of the girls walking around in a circle to music; when the music stopped, they were to dash around the room and hunt for witches, pumpkins, and owls. As it happened, several of the girls found some of the hidden things while I was giving directions. I told them that they were spoiling the fun of the game by finding them now, and they responded by saying they would like to play it correctly. They all went out of the room then, and I hid the articles again. When the girls returned, they followed the rules and played the game well.

20

Sometimes an individual shows his immaturity graphically through his relation to rules. For example, he might deliberately break a rule or misconstrue the purpose of a game because the resulting attention he obtains from the group through such conduct, even though negative, is more satisfying than no attention. It is well known that in children's games the younger children enjoy being "It," as in Cat and Rat, and eventually the games shift into those where it is not desirable to be "It," e.g., Three Deep. Yet, there are often those children whose needs are so great that they will deliberately try to be caught and be "It" for the attention this brings even when such action is inappropriate.

In the following example something similar is operating in the case of eleven-year-old David, and the worker carefully tries to help him substitute appropriate behavior as a means of gaining recognition.

> David is learning to cope with the limits of group living. The most significant movement that I have observed in David's behavior is connected with the way in which he attracts attention to himself. During my first few weeks, I found that David would compensate for his lack of skill by turning any performance into a "comedy of errors." For example, if the boys were jumping over a hedge and David (believing he couldn't clear it) took his turn, he would awkwardly plough right into the midst of the hedge and elicit the howls of the others. If he had to climb a rocky trail on a hike, he would deliberately be clumsy and bring laughter upon himself. I believe David realized that the others were laughing at him rather than with him, but I would guess that he found even this reaction more acceptable than having to face the reality of his low skill. The others began to call him "Goofy," and he smilingly played the part.

> In the course of program, I have frequently made David aware of my expectations about performance; that is, doing one's best. He has internalized this expectation to some extent as demonstrated by a more conscientious approach to program tasks. His successes in program are probably increasing a positive self-image. In short, David seems to have reached a point where he is deriving more satisfaction from doing his best as opposed to his previous pattern of playing the clown. In a ball-game series just completed, he maintained the ability to continue the game despite a great deal of hostility thrown his way by other members of his team.

In this instance, sticking to the rule is equated with following the appropriate behavioral demand of the activity. In holding the child to following the spirit of the activity, the worker is really teaching him a most important life rule, that winning (or getting a positive reaction from others) is meaningless unless it grows out of correctly perceiving and following the actions appropriate to the situation. How the world does laugh at the gauche, but not in approval!

21

In the following example one main rule-of-the-game is emphasized, "that you don't quit when you feel like it, but stick it out to the conclusion of the game." Contained in this simple rule are many social and ethical values: you care about others; you know others might not be ready to quit just because you are; do unto others as you would have others do unto you; once you start a task, stick to it; don't be a fair-weather friend.

> Roy asked me after supper if I would play Chinese Checkers with him and I agreed, getting out the board. Jerry was there and I asked him if he wanted to play with us. He said no, and Jay asked if he could play. Roy made a face, and Jay said he knew how to play. I said I thought it would be okay and Jay then agreed. Jerry then said that he would like to play, and so the four of us began. After a few moves Jay quit, and so I removed his marbles. Roy said to him that he always quits. I told Jay that I thought he'd only been "psyching" and wanted to continue, but I told him that quit is quit and he'd have to wait.

In the next game Jay said he wanted to play again, and I asked him if he was going to quit this time. He said no and I added that I hoped not. We played our game, but by the end Jerry was losing interest, although he had been very keen at the beginning, and also was running between turns to clean the tables in the dining room.

We were all set to play a third game, and the housemother, who had been watching, took Jerry's place when he left. This game went well, with Roy winning. He took a lot of pride in winning and said that it was the first time he had ever won. The game had been close, and I commented that Jerry's strategy had proven to be what was needed to win.

One more game and then everyone had had enough, and I asked who wanted to go to the park to play a game of Capture the Flag. All wanted to. After the checkers Jay asked me if he'd done well, saying, "I played OK, didn't I, Mr. B.?" I assured him that he had, adding, "Finishing second both times is pretty good." I believe he learned that it wasn't right to start something and then quit in the middle.

The main point to emphasize here is that following through with a commitment you make is not only an important rule to observe in a Chinese Checkers game, but an extraordinarily important precept to follow generally.

22

The importance of sticking to the rules, whatever these may be, has been stressed. It is equally important for the worker to be able to modify the rules of an activity spontaneously if this will give needed support to the group to accomplish the objective. Through the application of simpler or more complicated rules the worker shows his assessment of the group's capacity at the time. In the following excerpt a worker tries out a game in a rehabilitation center with a group of reticent, self-conscious young adults. This particular age group, so suddenly traumatized through loss of part of the body or of the functioning of part of the body, is plunged into a whole new psychology of life. Whereas they were recently young and full of strength and ambition, now everything they do must be a chore, deliberately thought out to be accomplished. The worker finds them hard to motivate in games, but wisely is quick to change rules in the process of introducing the following game so that it will succeed in doing what he wishes it to do—help them do something with one another.

> I gathered the patients who were in the lounge into one corner and explained how the first game was to be played. We began with the game, "Who Am I?" This is a game in which pictures, cut out of magazines or newspapers, are pinned on the back of each person present. The object is to guess the name on your back by asking questions of others in the group. These questions are supposed to be answered with only yes or no. Although I explained the game quite clearly and gave several examples of the types of questions that could be asked, the patients seemed to have trouble starting. They didn't know what to ask each other, so I went around to individual members and suggested various questions they might ask the person next to them. This seemed to work out quite well. Soon patients began to question each other.
>
> The patients did not stick to the exact rules of the game. Soon they began to give clues to each other, but I felt that this was not important. The important thing was that they were interacting. Soon they were laughing quite freely. I encouraged this interaction by going over to the more reticent patients, or those who were having difficulty thinking of questions, and giving them clues myself. As the patients began to discover who they were, there were exclamations of delight and laughter.

23

This excerpt is from a record of a group of five- and six-year-old boys. The group is a formed one and is all-purpose in nature. The majority of these games are not competition-oriented, such as Spud or Follow the Leader, because they would have little meaning for this age group. Team sports, while participated in, hold no real meaning for the boys since at this age level they are oriented mainly to themselves.

> After tag we played dodgeball, and then I told them we would play some baseball down by the back step. There was a mad dash

for it. I had a Wiffle bat and ball so they could play. The twins started yelling they wanted to be the Phillies and the Dodgers. John told Mitch to shoot fingers, and so I told these boys to be the captains and to choose teams. The other boys paired off and started shooting fingers also. Mitch won first pick and the sides were chosen. John, Joe, and Ron were against Jim, Al, Mitch, and Jack. Since Mitch's team had first pick, the other team would bat first. The boys scrambled to the field and then I noticed Jim was crying. The boys continued to play while I went over to Jim. He was crying because he wanted to bat. I comforted him by telling him his team would be up next and by talking with him for a few minutes. It came time for Jim's team to bat and the boys argued to see who would bat first. I settled it by going eenie-meenie and Jack went first. Al came after Jack, then Jim, and then Mitch. A few of the boys had had looks of compassion on their faces when Jim cried, and they accepted the way I chose the order.

The problem is that every time we play a game or start an activity, everyone wants to be first. This causes confusion and arguments and it is hard for me to settle them. If someone is not chosen first, hard feelings and tears are likely to be demonstrated. I'm going to have the boys limit themselves as to who goes first, because I haven't been able to choose them.

In this example the very choice of activity with its complicated structures and rules is inappropriate for five- and six-year-olds and creates frustrations. While the worker seems to realize that team games hold little meaning for his group, he continues to use the most complicated of team games—baseball—which demands not only teamwork in the field but ordinal batting positions and waiting for others to perform while at bat. Young children do best when they are all involved at once and do not have to wait very long. The matter of taking turns has to be learned, and there are games containing much less time interval between turns. The proliferation of Little League Baseball is a good example of adult projection of its values too early upon the young. This stems, in great part, from the good intentions of volunteer adult male leaders to share their interests with children, but it reveals a lack of imagination and knowledge about appropriate children's activities.

24

Baseball, in all its complexity, is America's national game, and boys learn quite young to understand its rules and to select their heroes. As soon as boys are able to hold a bat, there is a great desire to play this game. As the next excerpt shows, the worker who knows other activities that would be more appropriate and satisfying for the age group will have to search carefully for the appropriate introduction of a different game.

We had been playing baseball when it started to rain and so everyone gathered under the shelter. I asked generally who would like to play Concentration, and Roy and Jay wanted to know how it was played . . . Jay wanted to play Simon Says and I told him after we finished Concentration we would certainly do so. We played several times with the boys seeming to enjoy the game, and then Jay asked again for Simon Says. Everyone seemed agreeable and so we started with Roy doing the leadership. Stan won the first game and so led the second. By this time all the boys were involved, and Stan took quite a while to eliminate everyone. The boys were beginning to lose interest, and so I helped Stan to move his calls a little faster.

When this game was over, I asked the boys if they would like to have a sing-song with "My Bonnie Lies Over the Ocean," and I explained this song-game. Everyone took a seat and we went through the song twice, with Martin particularly enjoying it and all the boys getting quite involved in standing up and sitting down. Roy asked me not to sing so fast and I complied, giving them more opportunity to stand up and sit down each time the letter B began a word. I then asked the boys if they would like to play Lemonade and explained the game. As it was still raining lightly we tried playing under the shelter, but there was not enough room, and so we encouraged the boys to come outside into the drizzle. We played Lemonade until Don slipped and tore a scab off his elbow and we had to give him first aid.

This was the first time that I had introduced structured low organization games for the boys and this came about as a use of the moment because we were sitting about waiting for the rain to stop. Part of the timing was due to the increase in trust the boys have of me. This has taken some six weeks to develop and will possibly regress occasionally. However, I will have many more opportunities to institute games of this kind, including dodgeball and other low organization games that the boys seem to like. Lenny commented during the games that there were several others he would like to play and named them. I was glad we were able to introduce these structured low organization games which before I had felt would not be accepted nor have obtained the involvement that was achieved tonight.

Probably in this situation these games which the boys really enjoyed and liked were tolerated only because it had begun to rain and the boys couldn't stay out on the baseball field. The watchful worker seized the opportunity to inject other games which he had been wanting to use rather than just wait out the rain. Perhaps the next time he mentions the games, the boys will remember their good time with them and baseball may have competition.

However, even if the only game the boys will consider is baseball, it does not automatically follow that this game cannot be used to convey many underlying values that group workers want to develop. All too often workers confine themselves to the popular model of the game—stressing only skill in executing the positions and in batting, and competition and winning.

25

In the following report on George, who lived in a residence for emotionally disturbed boys, one can see the vital place of baseball in helping him to learn to control his anger. Furthermore, the worker begins to help him understand why he is in S. House, removed from his mother and father who could not control him, and how he can begin to help himself out of this placement and back into his family.

The first thing I noticed about George in the course of program contact was his almost total inability to handle frustrations. If there was a close call in a baseball game, George would slam his glove onto the ground, holler that I was a cheater, and curse at me and leave the game. I accepted this kind of behavior for a relatively short period of time.

About four weeks ago I began to set an expectation for George in terms of his behavior during the course of games. I made it very clear to him that I would not tolerate profane language and that he would have to learn how to handle a negative decision in a more mature and responsible way. On several occasions I had to eject George from games. Each time he reacted with great anger and hostility.

I began to notice a change in George during our first week at the day camp site. During the first or second day there we were all playing baseball, and George was called out at first base by me. He immediately began to shout that I was a cheater and he walked around kicking the ground in great anger. I told him that he was not handling this in the right way and he continued to call me a cheater and walk around the field. I told him to get off the field and get back with his team. He turned his back and began to walk away, and in a voice just barely audible said, "Fuck you." I told him that I had heard what he said and he was out of the game.

Strangely enough George was able to handle this ejection in a much better way. He left the field quietly and sat by the back stop, not speaking to anyone and not shouting at me as was his custom in the past. About half an hour later another game began, and one of the team captains picked George. George said that he could not play because Mr. F. had thrown him out of the game. I told George that I had thrown him out of the previous game and that this one was a new start and if he was able to control himself he could play.

Throughout the course of this particular activity, George was able to handle a number of very frustrating situations in a responsible way. After our conversation I had the feeling that George was quite proud of the way in which he had handled himself. He is now taking great pride in his growing ability to control his emotions. On several occasions he has asked me to tell his caseworker about the progress he has made. I have done this. George is extremely anxious to leave the S. House and return to his family, and he has a growing understanding that a good deal of his future lies in his own hands.

And so it is seen how much more baseball playing can mean for George than simply who won the game. In helping George become responsible for his own control of himself as he plays baseball, the game of supreme importance to him, we help George be in control of himself altogether.

In a children's institution a team of two group workers used baseball to enforce the following rules of behavior:

1. Although no one is forced to play, those who choose to do so must follow the rules.

2. No foul language or the player is out of the game.

3. There must be an inning limit determined in advance. You just don't play until it's dinner time and those who are ahead then win. You know at the outset how many innings you are going to play. And if, in the last inning the first team at bat is still behind after its batting, you don't play out the last half inning. There is already a winner. You stick to the rules.

4. If one member of the team quits, he is out for the whole game.

5. A limit of a seven-inning game, or a three-game series, is used to draw out the attention span of the boys as well as the frustration tolerance.

6. All balls and strikes are called. No extra chances. Batting order must be followed.

7. The boys must follow the direction of their own captains and the rulings of the umpire (group worker), however unfair they may seem.

8. The pitcher must stay in his box. There are no running leads from first base. Wild pitches bring a walk to the batter.

The boys have learned to adhere to all the real rules of baseball although they started out quite differently.

Because the game is so popular, the writer has detailed the multiple uses of baseball to teach underlying values that can be termed "living values." If it is not too complicated in skill demand, there can be much development through playing it.

26

In the following example, the worker uses his imagination to downgrade the skill demand and the rules of basketball to the level of his group in a game he calls Towerball.

> My purpose was to make up a game for these eleven- and twelve-year-old boys that would lead up to basketball skills and team play in general. The equipment consisted of two tripods made of poles four-to-six-feet tall, placed in the basketball key circles at each end of the gym floor, and a volleyball.
>
> *Rules*
>
> 1. No one, either offender or defender, is allowed in either circle.
> 2. No running or dribbling with the ball.
> 3. No bodily contact, as in basketball.
>
> *Penalties*
>
> 1. Offensive player in either circle means loss of ball.
> 2. Defensive player in either circle means free shot from center.
> 3. Running or dribbling with the ball means loss of ball to the other team.
> 4. Bodily contact means free shot from center.
>
> The object of the game is for the team on offense to pass the ball from man to man, until they get close enough to the defenders' goal to throw the ball at the tower and knock it over. Positional and team play become important if this objective is to be reached.

Through such an experience this group is learning the behavior appropriate to basketball. While the essence of the competition is preserved, the equipment is radically altered. The rules are drawn from regular basketball play and will be easily carried over when the boys are moved to regular shooting with a regulation size ball. The less difficult game of Towerball is better for these boys now, offering the possibility of success as well as a pattern of uninterrupted action.

27

> We then played baseball with a Ping-Pong ball and wiffle bat. I said we would use chairs for bases and that the runner must be

sitting in the chair in order to be safe. I said the ball must be in the pitcher's hands in the middle of the room for the runner to be called out, in order to avoid collisions at the bases. Except for a discussion as to whether they had to pitch underhand or not, the play proceeded well, and the boys enjoyed their game of "ping ball."

By now the reader must be aware of a pervasive theme of this book, that the basic activity which the worker can read in a game book must be modified and altered by him in order to suit his particular situation. He can take elements from certain games (or other activities) and create his own new games, as the account of Towerball, Number 26, and of Battleship and Submarine, Number 28, illustrate so well. Further game and activity *constructs* will appear on pages to come. Number 32 is an example of keeping a familiar game title but completely changing the rules so that the nature of group activity involved by the game is altered.

In the above example the modification of baseball, through the equipment, was due not to age demands but to the need to adapt it to indoor use.

Competition and Cooperation

28

A Game Construct

Given Situation: A group of boys nine to twelve years old with the older boys taller, heavier, and more skilled in large-muscle sports; one small boy who resists all athletic competition; one isolated boy who is short and heavy and avoids all sports but swimming.

Object of Game: To place the small boy and the heavy boy in a game role which compensates for their handicaps and attitudes and gives them status and the possibility of success through "winning" by playing their part well according to individual capacity.

A game of the nature of "Follow the Leader," "Blind Man's Buff," or "Giant Steps" would place the two boys in powerful "It" positions where they could control the behavior of the bigger boys and prevent their winning by virtue of size or athletic skill.

> The boys line up according to height from the smallest to the largest. Two teams are picked by the worker who chooses two each time for the same team from both ends of the line. This would result in one short, one tall at each choice. The teams line up at opposite ends of a large room. All have blindfolds. A team picks a *battleship* to lie down in outstretched fashion but as small as possible (heels, calves and knuckles touching floor); and the opposing team picks a *sub*, blindfolds him, turns him around thrice, and launches him at the *battleship*. In a count of ten, slowly by the leader, he must try to contact the ship or reach the opposite shore where he becomes a member of the other team. Obviously it is of advantage to be a short ship, and the skill of the *sub* is not a matter of size or age. Hopefully the teams will see the advantage of the small boy and pick him to bring them victory, and he will feel that his size and build can be an asset.

This example shows just how far a worker can go in creating his own games to meet the requirements of his group situation and to accomplish certain purposes. One can admire the ingenuity of this worker as he devised ways to equalize the diverse physical capacities of his group members, while at the same time he maintained in his game an element of competition and suspense. Workers are often disturbed by the overemphasis upon competition in children's games. The real problem is not the competition *per se*, but rather the diversity of capacity on the part of developing individuals to meet it with some semblance of equality of opportunity. The urge to compete or to test one's self against others can sometimes be modified by directing some of this drive toward competing against one's self, e.g., performance this week as compared to last week, working out appropriate handicaps, or, as in the above case, constructing activities that take differences into account.

29

In this episode the worker is trying to direct the boys' attention away from competition to self-improvement. Since this is a rather new concept for most children to accommodate, such a direction will probably need repeated emphasis in order to take hold. And yet, competition with one's self as a goal toward realization of one's greatest potential is one of the basic life goals confronting all people.

I am trying to emphasize through my program things which the boys know little about. One of my goals is to emphasize and utilize cooperation even in essentially competitive activity. This has involved using compromise with them in program: "You can do what you want, but I am adding some of my ways of doing it." In other words, I am beginning to be able to turn all kinds of program, whether it is the most appropriate or not, toward my purposes.

I had a physical fitness chart and we began by doing sit-ups with partners. Ray held Alan's feet and Carl held John's as they did sit-ups. John was very intense about his score and was constantly watching to see that others didn't cheat. It meant a lot to him that he did better than the rest of them in this activity . . . I tried to emphasize that the idea was not fighting or competing against each other, but rather to see that their own bodies were at or above the level that President Kennedy's physical fitness program specified as being fit.

In order to tone down the competitive demand within games, workers often attempt to modify goals and attitudes by verbal interpretations: "It's not so much whether you win or lose but how you play the game," or, "But did you have fun? That's what we're here for, not just to see who is the winner." While these are well intended, they often miss the mark entirely and only serve to say to the group members that their worker really doesn't understand how things go in their world. It separates the worker further from the group in their appreciation of his capacity to understand them and help them with their problems.

In meeting the intense drive to win, or to succeed, or to look good in the eyes of one's fellows, the worker may build in other values with some compensatory reward and gain for the individuals. One such approach is illustrated in the case study which follows.

30

This group of foster children live in a group residence. They range in age from seven through twelve, and when they engage in athletic events their drive toward achievement is fiercely competitive. Because of the wide diversity of physical development, the same boys usually win and some always lose. In making up teams, the boys know this all too well. Patterns of acceptance and rejection on the basis of physical skill operate, and the less adequate boys have their doubts about themselves reinforced whenever sides are chosen. In this sense their egos are constantly taking quite a beating.

At Olympics Night no one ever wanted Bernie, the youngest, on their side because it would be a sure lose. To partially overcome this, we kept the races and relays more individual than team, i.e., we would have play-offs between two fairly equally matched boys, and the winner would get one point every time he won. At the end of the evening the huge total of points achieved through many different activities were added into a grand total, and three top winners were selected. Bernie was sometimes given a point for extraneous activities such as finding additional Ping-Pong balls for use in the races. Where he dug them up nobody knows, but he was thrilled with his extra points and the others didn't object to such awards.

In the three-legged race four contestants raced in pairs with their two inside legs tied together with a bandana. No one wanted to be Bernie's partner because it was a sure lose. Finally, George shrugged a bit and said to Bernie, "Come on." In the race George tried hard to keep in step with little Bernie, but of course they had to lose.

At the end of Olympics Night the winners were announced. In addition, we made a speech about a special award (and followed it up with an extra prize) for the "Best Sport of the Evening, George." We said that at several times during the evening George was interested not only in winning but in helping others to have a good time, too. We hoped all of the boys would take on this attitude at our next Olympics Night. George came out with two prizes that night, one for being second and one for being a good sport. The others were very impressed with his haul.

It is the contention here that children can be encouraged to take on helping values if these are recognized through incentives and rewards that have meaning in the eyes of the group. The results of cooperating and helping have to be made just as tangible as the results of winning.

31

In the following episode at the same group home one can see how the goals for the treasure hunt were radically modified from the usual game to meet the particular circumstances and needs of these boys.

Bernie got the treasure for me, and Mr. Lee and I laid it out with many of the boys sneaking out of the living-room area to try to spot where some of the treasures were. This did not in any way give them an advantage eventually and so I permitted a lot of the good-natured exploration and teasing that this elicited. Joe, Bernie, Lou, and others of the younger boys came frequently to me during the TV time and told me that I really should not have had TV on at all because they wanted the party more than TV. I reminded them that the group had decided that there would be TV (I too decided that a whole evening of activity was too much and valued the quiet period that TV made possible), and though they kept calling for the Hunt to begin, I held them to their hour of TV and sat with the younger boys playing the accordion and talking until the older ones had finished their second show. Bernie found it especially hard to wait, and Mrs. Kay asked if he wanted to suck on a piece of candy. She got a purse full of little candies and distributed these to a few of the boys and this seemed to make their wait easier. I explained that the Treasure Hunt involved running about, not into any boys' rooms, and counting how many candy canes were hidden throughout the house. The fellow who came closest to the right answer would be the winner. The big treasure was wrapped and hidden in an obvious place and there would be a winner who spotted it. I explained that in seeing it and in counting the boys should keep their own scores and not let on either the number or where the treasure was, but to run to Mr. Lee and tell him where the treasure was.

They were surprised that it wasn't a run and grab situation. In fact this worked out well, equalizing the skill and control of each boy since, in effect, each was competing against himself. They stuck with the rules quite well, and the treasure was better hidden than we imagined so that every two or three minutes we had to narrow down the range for them by giving them an additional clue. They whooped it up and dashed about with great abandon. Finally when we pinned it down to the laundry room, Sam dashed back with the first right answer and was quite thrilled with his success. Because he was a winner I permitted him to go and get the treasure, and he was able to distribute nine large chocolate Santa Clauses to the boys. Robbie (Negro) said happily when he looked at the brown Santa, "Boy, I never saw a chocolate Santa before!"

They then also talked about what number they had of the candy canes and Sam again was the winner, guessing 82. Throughout the evening there was a lot of feeling of competition and getting the prizes. I promised the boys that I would keep a tally of who got the most points and when I returned I would bring something for the winners. This seemed to satisfy their urge to get special prizes and they didn't complain too much.

I then sent them to get 8 candy canes each and this created some minor confusion, some bringing back more and some not finding enough. George was particularly worried that there were 8 extra ones. When I played this down and everyone finally wound up with 8, there was squabbling and bartering and exchanges of Santa Claus for extra canes. The candy seemed to make a great hit.

One can immediately note the emphasis upon concrete rewards —in this case, candies—as a vital element in *giving* to these children who have suffered grave emotional deprivations in their formative years. As with the concept of helping others in Number 30, so is the concept of "caring" in this episode conveyed in specific forms that are meaningful to the child. The additional meaning of the brown Santa Claus to the Negroes in the group is noteworthy.

The structuring of the treasure hunt is in line with the needs of the boys: away from a survival-of-the-fittest orientation toward a race against one's self, with emphasis upon accurately recording observations and not adding to the numbers of seen candy canes in order to have the highest score. Additionally, the problem of small, familiar quarters where the normal hiding places are almost too well-known to the boys as well as the possibly unfair advantage gained by those who would peek ahead of time were eliminated because of the rules devised for winning. Mainly, fighting and grabbing and ensuing frustrations and tears were avoided by the directive to leave the candies where they were until all could collect their fair number at the end. The candies were also placed so that they could be easily seen; there was no attempt to make matters tough for the boys, and they were all successful in enjoying the rushing about and in coming up with some number of seen objects at the end. All of these considerations played a part in enabling this activity to succeed. It can be seen from this analysis that it is not enough to select exciting content and offer it to a group. The crucial aspect to make it work is the careful way in which the activity is offered—through advance planning, with the needs and characteristics of the group in mind.

It is noteworthy, too, that the worker decentralized the leadership of this activity by having the boys report their calculations to the housefather who was in the room at the time. In this way, a collaborative working relationship between the group worker and the caretaking staff, who carry so much in the life of the child in residence and whose support to the activity program is vital, can be strengthened.

When the boys had trouble spotting the big treasure, the worker quickly modified the rules, again considering the frustration tolerance of the group. With additional clues at spaced intervals, the boys' drive toward achievement was supported. One reward for the winner was the status he gained from the distribution of the treasure.

32

The problem in this case was one of getting the boys in the Jewish Center together to achieve an objective. It involved planning and cooperation.

The boys were busy chasing each other as I placed this small mat in the middle of the room. John asked me what it was for, and I told him we were going to play King of the Mat and asked if anyone knew how to play. Sam said he thought the idea was for one person to keep everyone off the mat. I replied that he was close, but the idea I had was that everyone would get on the mat and try to throw everyone else off. We played this several times, and then

I took off my jacket and got on the mat, too. Practically in unison they said, "Are you going to play?" To which I replied, "Sure," and added that if they did it right, it wouldn't make much difference. Bill suggested that if they were going to stand a chance they would have to get together first and try to throw me off. This was exactly the reasoning I had been hoping to get, and the four of them made careful plans for the best way of getting me off. After several successful tries at this . . .

In this instance, the worker deliberately pitted himself against the whole group in order to encourage cooperative planning. Again it is suggested, as with the treasure hunt, that the use of the mat as an activity is only one aspect of the emphasis of the experience. Whether the use is for competitive or cooperative purposes depends upon the structures the worker puts in to affect the content. It can thus be seen, with these specific illustrations in mind, that the "prescriptiveness" of mat play—or to put it another way, an analysis of the potentialities of mat play—is in and of itself meaningless. What has to be analyzed is the *use* that the worker makes of the mat to meet his objectives.

33

In the following example the worker injects a specific game into a group experience, knowing in advance what he can expect of the activity because of the rules of the game. To achieve other ends, it would be possible for him to change the rules accordingly.

An outing for an eleven- and twelve-year-old boys' group necessitated a lengthy bus ride. Two boys were playfully throwing cookie crumbs at each other and then hitting one another. They didn't respond to requests to stop, so I decided to involve them in a game which required the use of the mind as well as the hands in minor clapping and finger-snapping movements.

Concentration may be played in a number of ways, but always makes use of a rhythmic pattern, usually to a count of four—two hand claps followed by two finger snaps. Each participant takes a number, and everyone picks up the rhythm. At the first finger snap the leader calls his own number, and follows this on the second

> finger snap by calling the number of another player. The player whose number is called must on the next finger snap call his own number and then the number of another player. The game goes on, with everyone clapping and snapping in rhythm, while those whose numbers are called respond accordingly. When a player loses the rhythm because of trying to say a number, then he may be either eliminated or given a letter in the word "Ghost." Elimination is not too bad in this game, as the hand movements continue and the game goes quickly. It adds to the interest of all as well, since those remaining must remember not to call the number of someone who is out.

A rather simple judgment accounts for the change in tone of this group's experience from distracting to constructive action: you can only do one thing at a time with your hands!

34

In the game that follows an elementary form of decision making is part of the action. Each team has to make a choice on what they will enact at the signal. The basic outcome is chance-like and therefore the skill demand is minimal. However, the boys have to act in unison and submit to group pressure for conformity.

> I shifted to a line team-game, Tiger–Man–Gun. This one involved a little bit of plotting and deciding as a team, and I was glad to see that they were up to it. The teams as they developed became all the boys against Joe and all of the staff. Joe had a great time plotting who his team would be, and the staff let him take this on. The two teams would figure out whether they would be a tiger, man, or gun and then assume the appropriate position when we counted three. Then according to what they chose the tiger could win over the man, the man over the gun, and the gun over the tiger. We then added up the score. After this we had our soda to calm down.

A secondary value of this activity was that the smallest, least accepted group member could align himself with the staff and become the decision maker for his team. This leadership and controlling position is very rare for him in his group life experiences and encouraged his feelings of self-worth. At the same time, since there was no special advantage to the others of the individual capacities of each team member, the group permitted this small boy his few minutes of glory. The success of this activity, aside from the cooperative behavior it demanded, was because the winner each time depended on chance alone.

35

I then taught them how to play Indian Chief, a circle game of little demand, and this was quite a hit. The game involved and put premium on the group's cooperating with one another against the "It" and I was surprised to see how much teamwork the boys were actually capable of. We played this game for fifteen or twenty minutes. When they seemed to be wearing down, I got them to bring chairs into the circle and taught them Upset the Fruit Basket. This was riotous and at the outset we had the usual question about whether they should or should not do it, but as soon as it got started everyone was in there in the spirit. Each boy had his own fruit name, and there was one less chair than boys. When the fruit was called, they all had to change places. Again this involved body contact and horseplay in a legitimate way, and for these reasons suited the bill for the moment. With enthusiasm still pretty high I called a halt.

The progression from one circle game in which cooperation was essential to one in which each fended for himself is noteworthy. Also, the expression of aggression in an acceptable, diluted form made the second game popular and beneficial for the group. This kind of expression of aggression, the bumping of bodies in a race for a chair, is useful in a game because it can be considered indirect rather than direct assault to the person. The boys are so busy getting the chair that there is no time for deliberate bucking against one another. Later examples will show how self-defeating direct aggression games can be.

36

A completely different expectation is set by a game in which the objectives are accomplished more easily when the group remains quiet. In the game recorded below two persons participated at one time while all the others were simultaneously involved by remaining quiet and assisting in the action.

In order to quiet the group a little more, I shifted to a game which I called Popeye and Donald Duck, in which the two central people are blindfolded and have to hunt each other by quacking a call and answering in a Popeye voice. The group had to exhibit some measure of cooperation by not giving their own catcalls, but keeping quiet and by preventing the boys from stumbling over the furniture. This was great fun for all and particularly successful, since it involved the group as well as the participants. There was a little squabbling about who wanted to be Popeye and who Donald, but by assuring all that they would have turns at everything, we got through that part. This also quieted the group, and they laughed as people came close to each other and passed each other by or as people got tangled up in the furniture.

Worker's Role Within the Activity

37

The next illustration is from a meeting with a formed group of late teen-age and college-age girls with great diversity of post high school education. At a crucial point in the action, the worker spontaneously created for herself a special role, "consultant." This action enabled the activity to succeed instead of showing up the deficiencies of some of the girls and the possible sabotaging of the whole experience for all.

At an agreed-upon time, Jill started the program. She asked Joan to start off Charades. Joan described the game and illustrated very cleverly with "Confucious say, wash face in morning, neck at night." This started the game off gaily; but when Bea, a college graduate, guessed the saying and was told she was next, she clammed up and said she couldn't think of a thing. I urged her to try and announced that I would serve as a "consultant" to any girl needing help with her thoughts. This served to help Bea to get on her feet, and with me as a sounding board she was able to think up a good idea. I noticed that each person in turn seemed almost overwhelmed at the challenge of making a creative thought, but would respond when I arose to confer with her. In this way, almost everyone took a turn and the game was very much enjoyed until Jill, in charge of program, called time.

38

In this next excerpt, the reader finds a worker with a purpose similar to that of the last worker: to enable group members to gain enough belief in their capacities to try an activity full of risk.

> At the Rehabilitation Center, I met with a group of physically disabled men. At the beginning of this month we had a party and it was decided at the planning meeting that among the activities would be singing. Several songs were suggested, among them "The Bear Went Over the Mountain."
>
> When I introduced this song, I attempted to make a singing game out of it. I varied the words when I led it to be "The Bear Went Around the Table" and also arranged the room so that there were tables for the participants to go around. To make this activity as non-anxiety producing as possible, I introduced the song and the movements at almost the same time. Both the song and the movements were relatively uncomplicated. I also put this activity in at a moment when I felt the group wanted to move around. As they sang they moved around the room in a form similar to "Follow the Leader."
>
> The group enjoyed the game so much that they not only went around the tables, but out the door, around the hall, and back into the room. The activity seemed to engender some kind of group feeling which probably came about because they were all doing an activity which was physically as difficult for one as for the others. I also felt they were pleased with themselves in that they were able to participate in a program that called upon some strengths which they were not sure they had. I had both of these goals, development of group feeling and realization of strength, in mind when I started the activity. I felt some degree of apprehension about trying something of this sort. Since it did not seem to create any overt stress for the participants, I feel a little freer to attempt a more complicated activity such as square dancing.

In this instance, the worker's special role was one of using his own strength as an impetus and point of identification for the disabled men to unite with as they all tried to follow an activity he had set in motion. To inject one's self with force against accumulated, reality-based resistance demands great presence on the part of the worker. Perhaps, the risk for all, followed by the exhilaration that accompanies success, was reward enough to make a future attempt easier.

In every excerpt in this book the reader may follow the particular role of the worker. The two foregoing excerpts are placed here because the impact of the worker was the especially dramatic force that helped the group move.

Feelings About One's Self and Others

39

I have begun to use crafts to encourage the members who are working with their hands to bring out their feelings. With the support of the craft activity they can participate or not as they like without embarrassment. They do not need to run away if a discussion gets too close to home, since they can become unobtrusive by immersing themselves in their work.

I showed them how to start on their popsicle stick boxes . . . The topic of conversation was due to Tom's singing about macaroni, and we started talking about what we would like to eat. I asked them if they would like to cook pizza sometime, and they all very enthusiastically replied, "Yes." Then Frank poured refreshments so that they could drink while they worked. One of the boys mentioned the word "Spic." I asked what "Spic" meant, and Tim said, "Oh, it means something bad." I said, "Does it? It means South American, doesn't it?" Frank got up just glowering and almost to the point of tears. (He is Puerto Rican.) He clammed up and walked to the other side of the room saying, "Gail, get me my coat. I'm going." Then Tim looked up at me and said, "Shh, don't talk about it; don't say anything." I replied, "Well, what is it? Is it something bad?" Then followed a long, halting discussion in which they eventually came to a sexual connotation of the word "Spic."

While in this meeting one boy almost *did* walk out, it was interesting that the others, who were interested but also uncomfortable with this subject, would lapse into periods of silence as they worked on their popsicle stick boxes. They never would have sustained a discussion for so long, I am sure, without the prop of the craft to occupy their hands.

In the above example, as well as the one that follows, one can notice that program activities offer the opportunity for the expression of attitudes and feelings because of the vast range of free association possible while group members are off-guard, so to speak, and involved primarily in something else. The alert worker can pick up these leads as they occur and turn them toward his purpose.

40

Each of the girls had brought in some food for a party. After unsuccessfully trying to generate enthusiasm and interest in games, I asked them what they wanted to do with the food. Toby started to give out pieces of her cake in a discriminating manner (she gave her friends the biggest pieces in an obvious manner). She offered me a piece of cake, and I refused because I didn't particularly want any cake. She took this as a personal offense, and refused to listen to any response that I offered her . . . Later on in the meeting Joyce started to cut her cake in an arbitrary way. When I accepted a piece of her chocolate cake, Toby said that I like "niggers" better. I was able to respond to her on my preference of flavor of cake which got some support from one of the members who also liked chocolate.

41

During the Christmas vacation, I took both of my B'nai B'rith girls' groups on a trip to New York. We had chartered a bus and representatives of both groups had met and mapped out an itinerary.

During the bus ride, while touring New York and on the trip home, a number of the girls were engaged in yelling out of windows at every boy they saw, or trying to pick up boys that they met along the way. This behavior bothered a large number of girls from one chapter in particular. I did all I could to restrain this subgroup, but under the existing conditions my attempts did very little. The girls that were bothered expressed their feelings to me. I recognized their feelings and calmed them down by telling them that we would take this incident up at our next meeting. I did not feel that I could handle a group discussion on the bus in relation to the matter.

At the next chapter meeting I planned to discuss the incident with the group. I gave a great deal of thought to how to approach the subject without alienating those few girls that were directly involved. I also was aware that many of the girls that were bothered had strong negative feelings about these girls, and I wanted to avoid personality clashes within the group as this was irrelevant to the incident.

After much thought I decided to use role playing to lead into the discussion. I prepared a number of situations that I felt girls were familiar with—all having to do with one or two girls in a group of girls who are out together breaking from the group and flirting, trying to pick up boys, etc. I explained the idea and broke the group into three subgroups. I gave each group the situation written out, and then I went around going over each situation with the individual group.

I gave the entire group some limits as to how much time they would have to prepare a skit around the situation and how long their presentation should be. I also told the girls that I did not expect them to come up with many answers, but to raise questions that could be discussed afterward.

The groups prepared skits and presented them. After each presentation there was a discussion which let all of the girls express their feelings. The majority of the girls were very verbal, and the girls that were bothered by the initial incident related it to one of the situations presented.

The program accomplished two things. First, it provided a legitimate means for the members who were bothered by the behavior of other members in the group to criticize and discuss the incidents. Second, it was an introduction to other types of activities that could occur at chapter meetings.

In this instance two of the most serious tasks confronting the adolescent girl are highlighted: (1) learning appropriate ways to express their newly-felt, overpowering interest in sex and boys, and (2) developing a conduct for themselves that makes them attractive and acceptable to other girls. There is probably nothing of greater importance to the developing individual than achieving success in these two areas. The worker, here, did not attempt a direct discussion when the incident happened because of the technical problems involved during a bus ride—seating, noise, mood and purpose of the group at the time. However, even if this had been possible, it might well have been a less effective approach to the problem. By using role playing the situation is depersonalized, in time as well as in the portrayal of the problem. Within the intimacy of the meeting room, at some distance from the disturbing incident, and with others enacting the problem behavior, all the girls were free to evaluate the behavior and to approach less defensively a standard of more acceptable behavior.

42

This study tells about a Halloween Party for seventeen unmarried pregnant girls in residence.

Perhaps the whole first half of the party was spent reacting to the fine decorations, taking in each other's costumes, and showing off one's own work. Many of the entrances seemed well timed and prompted by a sense of the dramatic. I had brought a book showing how to make some crepe paper costumes and found later that this had provided a stimulus to the girls, but they far exceeded the examples pictured in the book. Their work was especially remarkable because many were complete surprises to one another. Because of close living arrangements, it is hard to keep anything a secret. And yet, some of the costumes were secrets even from roommates. Others were frankly combined efforts and showed the results of the cooperative work.

After all had appeared, the room was a beehive of excitement. I had the accordion and, as planned with the committee, played a grand march while the nurse and group chairman picked out six winners in the costumes. After these were awarded, there followed about fifteen minutes of picture taking. Three girls had their cameras and meticulously posed the pictures. Involved in the posing of the pictures were elaborate precautions to get the girls sitting in such a way that you couldn't notice the pregnant bellies. This was extremely interesting. In fact, now that I look back on the whole party, part of the enjoyment of it all, I believe, came from the fact that the gaudy, floppy costumes did much to conceal and at least obscure for a little while the fact of pregnancy for the girls themselves. They *were* other people for the moment, and this contributed to the hilarity and abandon of the evening.

In this example, the main feeling to be worked with is that of lack of value in one's self, particularly present in the attitude of the unmarried mother-to-be. Release from the oppressive reality through an evening of fantasy is shown above. Neither the desire to take a picture of one's self nor the abandonment in spirit is characteristic of the serious daily living situation of these girls.

43

The patients encountered at a rehabilitation center for the physically handicapped are among the most difficult challenges to the group worker. Often they are the victims of some sudden traumatic experience—accident, paralysis—that almost annihilates their sense of who they are as persons. They are shocked by their new limitations, by their dependence on others for the simple activities of living. Their whole future life will be affected by adjustment in these areas. On top of all this, they are plunged into a new environment with all the expectations of different relationships to others, to living routines, and to re-education activity that the Center demands. What they are physically able to do, what they are motivated to do, and what they dare to risk are all unknowns.

Young and old alike must learn to find that part of themselves that is salvageable and with the patient help of the staff take the slow, uncertain steps toward the outside world again. Often the young are the most depressed, since the contrast between previous and present life styles is so great. Among their great needs is the finding of some way to communicate with others and become a valued person again. This is the point of focus for the group worker. The movement is painstaking and slow, the growth sometimes imperceptible. The resourcefulness and patience demanded of the worker is a sobering fact. Every possible incentive and support are employed to help the patient find the courage to try new ways to accomplish what he formerly could do so easily.

As the following excerpt will show, the tape recorder is such a lure.

I brought the tape recorder to the fourth floor recreation room and set it at the table where Mr. A and Mr. M were. Mr. M was a patient who never came to any group activity because he was so afraid of groups of people. But he took an interest in the tape recorder and not only stayed but participated during the entire program. At my urging, both Mr. M and Mr. A said a few words into the recorder and I then played back the tape so that they could hear their voices. As other patients appeared, they came over to see what was going on. Mr. R began to speak into the microphone and got Mr. M to talk. They were glad to hear their voices played back to them.

I had prepared several games. The first was having each patient read from a little slip of paper (drawn from a jar) part of a well-known commercial, fairy tale, or familiar saying. When read by each in turn, the result was a funny story. Before I tried another activity, Mr. R asked if he could sing into the recorder. After he did, several patients suggested that Mr. K sing. When I asked if others wished to, there was no response so I went on with the next activity.

I read a story with certain missing words which the patients were to fill in. At first I stopped at each missing word and suggested the type of word needed, i.e., noun, verb, type of building. However, the patients soon didn't need this help and began to shout out the missing word without my having to give a clue. After I had read one story, we had the playback. Several funny words and phrases had been given by the patients. Everyone was now participating and the atmosphere was relaxed, comfortable, and happy.

Before reading another story, I asked if anyone else would like to try something. When no one responded, I did the same thing with another story. Then Mr. R asked again if he could sing something. He sang a rousing spiritual. I began to clap. Soon several patients joined me in clapping their hands to the beat. After Mr. R had finished, I asked Mr. K if he would like to sing one more song to end the activity for tonight since it was getting late. Mr. K sang "Swing Low, Sweet Chariot." When he had finished, everyone clapped. I replayed these two songs. The patients commented on how much fun they thought this had been and wanted to use the tape recorder in the future.

It is obvious here that the worker is affecting directly the most vital feelings about one's self as she helped these physically handicapped adults test out and hear back an adequate side of themselves. That they possessed humor, imagination, initiative, and courage could be known by all about each other. The direction, encouragement, and support of the worker here is stronger than in situations where the group members' handicaps are less burdening. The amount of direction in this situation for this purpose is a necessity in order to help the individuals and the group assert themselves.

44

The following excerpt is really not a non-verbal one. It relates the discussion of two different play ideas to determine the vehicle for a dramatics experience for several future meetings. It is included here because it highlights the care and precision that must attend the selection of the particular content in order that the play will enhance the feelings the group members have about themselves. In this instance the girls are teen-agers in foster care who meet weekly as a group downtown at the agency.

During the course of the discussion that followed, I suggested to the girls that they summarize for Rita what we talked about last week. Phyllis began, and the others helped her out. When it was mentioned that the girls want to put on "Snow White and the Seven Dwarfs," Rita made a grimace and said, "I don't want to put that on; I always act like a dwarf. I don't want to be a dwarf." I picked up Rita's statement, suggesting that they may want to stage a play that would involve more equal participation of the girls. This initiated a very lively, joking discussion about the types of performances the girls could stage. They joked about various television commercials.

Finally, I interjected my feeling that the girls have always demonstrated to me a desire to do a lot of dancing and singing and that maybe they should think about putting on something that could use both of these media. Rita readily agreed with this, and she asked the others what kind of musical or something like that we could put on. I finally suggested that maybe the "Wizard of Oz" would be fun. This erupted a very positive reaction from the entire group.

Dorothy said she wanted to be Judy Garland, and everyone laughed. Others picked out other parts . . .

It is of prime significance that these girls' efforts be directed toward something that makes them feel of greater importance, something through which they can test out and show off some of their natural talents to others. An experience that would project them as dwarfs would actually minimize them, make them feel infantile. They already possess an overabundance of feelings of powerlessness. Through the *Wizard of Oz* the worker will be able to create several starring roles.

45

In the following example, taken from work in a residence for emotionally disturbed boys, one boy is helped to verbalize the concern he felt about his illegitimacy. It was important at this time for the agency to know whether Robert actually knew he was illegitimate. His caseworker knew from his work with the mother that she had been wanting to discuss this with Robert but had not found an appropriate opening. They both thought it was time such a conversation took place. So far Robert had not responded to his caseworker's attempts to feel him out on this matter. The sequence of the afternoon is presented at some length because of the belief that the boy's revelation of intimate information to the group worker, in the presence of one other boy, was due to the specific program content involved. The reality demands inhering in a group living situation and the worker's ability to use existing conditions *for her purpose* set the stage for the verbal exchange.

It was a nice day and the boys were late in returning from school. I sat waiting in the sitting room for them, along with some of the rest of the staff who were waiting for certain boys for their casework appointments. Robert, Roy, and Bob were home and were in and out of this room . . . I brought, as I had promised in my conversation with the boys last Sunday, my emu egg—a huge, dark green thing that I had obtained from the zoo. There was much curiosity and discussion and a little testing of me with it. Roy, for example, a couple of times menacingly made as if to throw it in a football pass, and Bob made a big jump for it. I was unsure of Bob's intentions and kept him from having it. But Robert was fascinated by it and we had quite a discussion about why the shell was so hard, the fifty-two day incubation period, whether there were emus at the zoo, what they looked like, why this shell was empty. In the course of all this, I told him of the beak of the baby emu pecking its way out of the egg, of the zoo curator's interest in whether or not it was a fertile egg and why not. Robert took it all in with great interest.

I was here especially to take a first group of interested boys over to the music school for the director to give them a little test to determine which boys would be possible students and on what instruments . . . At the music school, Jerry was taken first, and I walked through the building with the other two, Robert and Murray, explaining what was going on. The building was teaming with other children, a beehive of activity and musical noises, and a well-appointed place. Robert had said in anticipation that he imagined it would be a drab place, but now he was very impressed with the whole thing. After Robert was tested, Mr. Kay had a short conference with me in which he said Jerry was "a hopeless case," but Robert could follow whatever instrument he wished as he had great potentiality.

On the way home Robert begged me to take him to Sears where he could buy a record he had saved for. He had his money with him and I agreed to do so. We discussed what he could be doing with a musical instrument, and I let him feel my enthusiasm about his ability. He wanted to get started, and I outlined how I would help him get a teacher. Robert seemed very pleased with himself.

After buying the record and meeting his math teacher, I started to drive back to S. House with Robert and Jerry. When we were nearing the house, I said I'd like them to roll up the windows for me after we parked and please go into the lobby and bring out the bassinet I had taken out of the car so that I'd have room to transport them. Jerry began to talk about the bassinet. Why was it in the car? Robert said, "The agency has lots of babies to take care of." Jerry asked why a mother would not keep her baby, how could she give it up, and didn't she love it? I said that it is very hard for a mother to give up her baby, but sometimes mothers who have a baby are not married. They realize that to give the baby a good chance in life it is best to give the baby up, and then the agency plans for this baby to have a home. Robert said, "My mother had me and she wasn't married yet." I responded, "She must have wanted and loved you very much." There was silence now and a little smile came over Robert's face . . . Then I parked and we were off to the house.

In thinking about this episode, several factors are important. Certainly, the whole discussion about the egg which was introduced earlier had the worker involved with the boys in the matter of mothers and babies. Then there was the concrete experience of the bassinet—sheer accident, but used by both the boys and the worker to discuss the basic purpose of the agency which brought them together and used by Robert to verbalize this anguishing problem in this period of his life. Robert, a culturally and emotionally deprived Negro boy, usually had difficulty communicating with the adult. But when Jerry took the lead in the discussion, he was able to open up with his burning comment. It is probable that he needed this assist from Jerry to be able to get into the subject. Also, the trip to the music school and to Sears played into the atmosphere of the mothering situation that the worker took on that afternoon. Such activities as shopping and pursuing music lessons are roles usually reserved for one's mother in our culture. Perhaps, Robert felt some of this special quality in the relationship that afternoon. He certainly responded to another maternal type request, that he roll up the car windows and carry out a bassinet! Such "program content" is different from that which is ordinarily thought of when the area of program is considered. So is the purpose of this service different from that of the leisure time agencies.

It might seem strange to approach this episode, the main impact of which was a short verbal exchange, from the point of *program*—things like eggs, bassinets, trips, rolling up car windows, and carrying out the bassinet. This is done deliberately here because often the full assessment of these aspects is not considered and worker's attention is focused only on what was said. The attempt here is not to rate the non-verbal as more important than the verbal, but rather to stress the vital interrelatedness of these two parts of the process. With this realization workers can increasingly value and look at the totality of *all they did,* rather than only what they said, to produce a certain result.

46

The following incident took place during a swimming party for a group of teen-age girls.

Polly, a thirteen-year-old member of the group, wanted to show me how she could do somersaults in the water. She put a bobby pin over her nose and proceeded to go around seven or eight times. She had asked me to count them for her, and I praised her for her skill when she came up. She acknowledged this, but then looked disturbed and swam over to the side of the pool. I went over to see if she were all right, thinking that her sinuses might not feel too well at that point. I asked her how she felt, but she would not say anything. Not getting a word from her, I suggested that she grab a towel and rest for a few minutes. She then walked away and went into the dressing room. When she did not return in ten minutes, I went to see if she were all right.

I found Polly sitting in the corner of the dressing room on a bench, and I went over to her and put my towel around her shoulders. I asked her again how she felt, but I got no response from her. Then I noticed that she kept writing something over and over again on her leg with the bobby pin that she had used for her nose while turning the somersaults. She seemed to want me to read as she wrote, and I finally deciphered, "I love Miss L. but she doesn't like me." Realizing the positive feelings that she had had towards me and knowing that my increased strictness in the last few weeks, and especially that night concerning agency rules, was bothering her, I tried to make Polly realize that I could still care for her even though certain activity on her part was not acceptable to me. She then began to write, "I wish that were only true."

Reassuring her again, I cited an example from my own childhood. This seemed to perk her up, but she still sat there writing my name over and over again on her leg. The other girls came in the room then and asked what was wrong. Polly looked at them and then at me, took off my towel and returned it to me, and then joined the group in preparing to leave. She began talking with the girls and then with me, and she seemed relieved of the burden that she had shared with me through the writing on her leg with a bobby pin.

Here is a good example in which the feelings which needed to be expressed, and which blocked completely one member's participation with the group, were so overwhelming that they could not be discussed verbally. And yet, the message came across and the worker deciphered it. Both member and worker were ingenious in their communication through the bobby-pin writing. We can sense the awkwardness and dilemma of the young girl, who cared so deeply about the worker and was not able to understand the limitations of the worker upon certain behavior as something other than rejection of herself. And one can feel the deep caring of the worker as she accepted what the girl felt, stuck to her position about the need for change in certain actions, and yet conveyed an acceptance and warmth for the member through sharing just with her a piece of her own childhood. The worker's focus is not simply on the relationship that the member has with her, but also on the girl's relationship with her peers—apparent from the meticulous account of the resolution of this episode. Thus the group relationship is viewed as an important piece of reality for this member—much like the insistent demand in life of getting along with others—as she leaves the worker, having obtained the needed reassurance, and takes her place again with her friends.

Understanding the Underlying Purpose

47

In my work with young schizophrenic women I did not understand fully the importance of thoughtful selection of activities until a game choice flopped during one of my group meetings.

I suggested a game we had played in program class, never realizing it was a very bad choice. The game was called, "What you would like to give up and why." It involved writing on two separate pieces of paper—What you would like to give up, and why. The object of the game is to jumble the responses and then to read them aloud. The usual reaction is one of laughter. However, sadly enough, these girls interpreted this as an analytical exercise and the game failed miserably as the responses were far from being funny. I asked the girls what they thought the game involved. Elise said she thought I wanted them to tell me their problems.

I hope I will never make this mistake again. I have learned that the kind of games to use depends on the characteristics of the group.

The worker learned all too painfully that what she had intended to be a fun game was interpreted by her group members as some attempt to analyze them and work with their problems. When groups are formed around one primary problem, the members are likely to interpret all activities with this problem in mind. If the worker's emphasis is sometimes fun experiences, the purpose must be obvious. The writer is reminded of an example in planning new kinds of group experiences in a maternity residence. All the girls could think of was more groups to discuss their problems. It was almost like pulling teeth to help them see that they already had enough of that and were being urged to consider other things—purely for fun and self-expression—that they might like to do.

48

In the example below, which comes from working with foster children in residence, a similar confusion in means and ends is seen. Here the worker is using for craft purposes what is really food—toast, peanut butter, and icing. Some of the group would not accept the use of this medium in an expressive way, particularly with their increased need to eat and be fed. The group process breaks down because of the meaning of icing, i.e., sweets, to one member.

I mentioned to the boys two weeks ago the possibility of making toast-and-peanut-butter houses, and at the time they had seemed interested. When I came today, I found the most stiffened resistance I had encountered in many weeks. In the beginning, there was a good bit of discussion by Fred and Bud about the waste of using food to make these houses. I recognized with them that food is not something to be played with or wasted, but in terms of actual cost, using bread and peanut butter was at least as cheap (if not cheaper) than working with clay or wood or similar material.

There were some teasing attempts to eat the toast and peanut butter, which I did not permit, and after a while this kind of teasing stopped. I had brought four colors of icing for making windows, doors, curtains, etc. The use of the icing was an exciting thing for most of the boys. Bernie and Joe had a fight over the icing tube because Bernie preferred eating the icing to using it, and Bernie took a healthy bite of Joe's hand. I sent Bernie to his room and then had to follow Bud upstairs since he was out to become the Lord High Executioner and wreak the House's vengeance on Bernie.

Clearly in the above instance the group worker used materials that were at cross purposes with the intention of the agency. The care-taking staff in the group residence sets symbolically a tone of caring and nourishing through providing much food and frequent sweets for the boys to consume. It is almost too much to expect that these deprived boys could bear to pass up the sweet icing and permit it to be used to construct a centerpiece.

49

In the following example, again with emotionally disturbed boys in a residence, the group worker is much more sensitive to the overall factors involved in doing group work with children in these particular circumstances.

The Housemother arranged for us to obtain sufficient tickets for all to attend the football game at JFK Stadium on this evening. The boys had a long opportunity to build up toward it. When the big day arrived, all were quite excited about going. They wanted to know what kind of seats we would have. Prior to this, they had, because of their previous experience at the baseball game, wanted to know if we would have to stand in line, go as a part of a huge group of about 1,000 foster children as we did at the other event. We told them this time we would be going in just like we had bought tickets, and we would be able to sit wherever we wanted. They were quite pleased at this and indeed, when we did get in, we found box seats. It was very thrilling to them to be sitting in their own private box.

We took a jug of Kool Ade and peanuts and pretzels so that they could have refreshments without spending their allowances on these items. Lenny very cleverly had brought along a box of Ritz crackers, and he was sharing these with the other boys. The interest in the game was not too great and the stadium was crowded with 50,000 people—25,000 of whom, I am sure, were children under the age of fourteen.

Our boys wanted to climb around and explore the stadium as the game itself was not too stimulating, and so we let them, trusting and advising them that they should return to the box when it was time to go home. Indeed, they did return and at this point were taking part in the great activity of throwing things onto the field. There was a danger of hitting someone with a paper cup, and so I asked them to stop heaving. Finally, I had to hand out early bedtimes to those who would not cooperate.

I told them that at the end of the game they could throw all that they wanted and this seemed to satisfy the boys. With about five minutes to go on the game, the home team scored a touchdown, and in the ensuing bedlam I nodded that it would be OK for them to throw various items as everyone also was doing, feeling that it was quite within the norm of the situation at this point.

We left the game having enjoyed the outing, although I would wonder how much the boys enjoyed the football game *per se* and how much they enjoyed just being out with a bunch of other people, especially with that many other children in such a free type of atmosphere as the football game provided.

The group worker notes first of all how important it is for the boys not to be singled out as foster boys at certain times. The significance of attending a football game in the same capacity as other members of the community rather than in a large group of foster children is acknowledged. Sometimes, the way in which a special treat is offered to institutionalized persons almost completely undermines the pleasure in the event itself. Most important in this episode, probably, is the understanding of the worker of the meaning to these boys of being mixed in with so many other boys of the community and engaging in the same activities as they did.

The record of this trip shows that attendance at a spectator sport can be anything but passive. It is a tremendously active experience including lots of eating, the exploration of the stadium, the cheering, the throwing of paper objects onto the field, as well as the fulfilling of such a responsibility as reporting back to the worker on time and sticking together. Probably the greatest meaning for the boys was the opportunity to be connected with something so much bigger than themselves—to be out in such a huge enclosure, able to yell their heads off without recrimination, and especially, to be able to observe the rest of the people and pattern their behavior after them. There can be no more important goal for institutionalized persons than to learn to be a part of the total community. Such a trip as this football game provided was a step in this direction.

50

A different agency purpose is conveyed in the following example. Here a group-service agency helps some harried adult members relax.

> Working with a group of mothers who need to feel a sense of enjoyment at their one outing during the week and also to feel a belonging to the group, I used the game "Guggenheim." This proved to be one of the most positive game experiences this group of women had ever had. A surge of interaction followed the playing of another game which entailed their writing what they would like to change about themselves on one sheet of paper and the reason on the other. Feeling free in expressing how they felt about themselves through a game was so rewarding for them that they wanted to play another round, and at the end of both they told which sheets were their own.

Here is a tired group of mothers on their night out for fun and recreation engaged by the worker in two pencil-and-paper games. In the second game, the reader can note the complete opposite reaction from what was seen with the group of young schizophrenic women in episode Number 46. These women were able to use the game in its own fun spirit and then go further to identify to each other what each had written about herself. Clearly, the success of the game here was due to the fact that its original purpose was understood and accepted by the group and was consistent with their need at the time, to have a good time. That they, themselves, went further by confiding something personal about themselves was at their own wish and dependent upon their close relationship to and trust of one another.

Accepting Responsibility

51

In the next illustration, the worker solves a problem of one child's lack of participation by creating a special role for him.

> At the beginning of the year, I had trouble getting one boy in my arts and crafts group to participate in the game or two we usually played to end our sessions. Usually he would disappear under one of the tables in the room. Common requesting of him to join us was to no avail. One afternoon, we were to play the group's favorite game, Steal the Bacon. The boy quickly scurried under the table. The situation was handled anew in the following manner.
>
> I divided them into two teams; while helping move the tables, I realized Tony was missing. He had crawled under a table. When I asked him to join us, he replied he did not want to play. I then asked him if he would like the important job of calling out the members' numbers. He agreed and heartily performed.

It would seem that perhaps one way of inducing the hesitant to participate would be to give them, or share with them, the leadership role if the leader does not have to perform directly himself. This is especially true if the hesitancy stems from a fear of possible failure.

52

In the following episode, a frequently occurring situation in group work is encountered. Here one boy wants to try an activity new to him but is afraid of failure. As he asks the worker to do the work for him, he is giving up on his responsibility and placing more value on the end result than on his part in making the end possible.

> During the afternoon Jack had frequently come to me to call my attention to the puppet theatre he was constructing. I was quite impressed and indicated to him that I was. At one point, he asked me for help in making a scalloped fringe for the stage opening. I agreed to help him, but soon discovered that what Jack wanted me to do was to do it for him. I repeatedly reminded him that I was there to help him, not to make it for him. Thus, I helped him to find a way of making a pattern for scallops and then helped him to cut it out and put it up. Jack wanted me to make scenery and the puppets. I said it would be a good idea to consider what his play would be like before we could make scenery and puppets. I promised to bring some materials next week with which we could construct the puppets he wanted. He was quite excited about this, but was unable to include in his planning the nature of the play he wanted to put on.

In this instance, the worker does not fall into the trap of taking over for Jack, but offers him enough support (the promise of concrete ideas and help in the future) that Jack can venture to try some new experiences himself. The worker, here, is valuing the experience of puppet making for Jack more than the production of the best possible puppet and play. In this subtle way, Jack can learn to take responsibility for learning, hard and trying as this might be.

53

In the next account, another boy is helped to take responsibility. This time the responsibility is for how he will act in relation to the other members of the group.

> The boys discussed card games they knew; it became apparent that they all knew how to play Knuckles. They wanted to play. I expressed my own feelings about Knuckles, explaining that my fingers were still sore from last week's game. I wondered if we couldn't find some other punishment to inflict or at least set some limits on the punishment so that it wasn't quite so brutal. With some hesitancy

or reluctance Mel accepted limits on the playing of Knuckles, and we played a couple of hands. Mel won the first hand and with some pleasure worked out the punishment for each player.

There was some confusion because Leon and Al had played a different way in that they had played until one person was left; however, they accepted the rules by which we had played last week. When Mel dished out the punishment he went very soft on everyone, but commented that he wished he could be as rough as he was outside meetings, especially when it came to Carl. What he was referring to was his desire to get back at Carl for the punishment that Carl had administered the week before. In any case, the punch seemed to be gone out of the game and the boys were no longer satisfied with it. Therefore I introduced a new game.

By controlling the extent of the penalty the game became too tame to hold the interest of the boys. In this way the worker is setting a tone for what kind of behavior will be acceptable among the members of this group while he meets with them. A message about responsibility for one's behavior is being conveyed.

54

The following illustration highlights another kind of responsibility. This time it is responsibility toward the agency and its meeting room.

This group of AFDC mothers was very small, and the members showed some apprehensiveness as they came for their second meeting. During the long walk down the corridor to the meeting room, conversation was light and a little forced. As we entered the meeting room, I saw that the table and chairs were arranged as we had them during the previous meeting a week before. There were no ashtrays and since I remembered that all of the members smoked, I suggested that we would have to improvise something.

We stood in the middle of the room looking around for a moment until I suggested that perhaps we could use a flap on one of the cardboard boxes in the corner. Mrs. W picked this up right away, going to the corner, tearing away one section of the thin box. Mrs. V had moved to the other side of the room and was looking behind the cartons. She said "some doctor" must have hidden it there to discourage smoking. She laughed, saying that some of us just won't take care of ourselves.

In the meantime, Mrs. W had taken her seat at the table and was folding and tearing the thin cardboard. I opened the meeting by asking one member to sum up what we had talked about last time. When this had been done, I could see that attention was focused on what Mrs. W was doing. She had folded and fitted the cardboard into the shape of a boat. It was an excellent job and I said so. I thought that it was something she might bring back to her son to play with instead of using it today as an ashtray. "No," she said, "this is for us."

Mrs. V said that it looked like a fancy motorboat and that all it needed was a cabin. I said that it could be a sailboat or a ship. By this time, everyone was smiling, Mrs. W most of all. "You people have to use some imagination," she said. She smiled widely, saying that it wasn't a motorboat and it wasn't a ship or a sailboat. "It's the Ark!" Mrs. V solemnly said that we should be sure to get our ashes into the Ark and not on the table.

As this worker supported the women's desire to leave the meeting room as they found it, he was also supporting their adult sense of responsibility toward all furniture, toward the many material things that surround them in the world. Their wish to present their best selves to the agency is also apparent. The record points up the freedom and spontaneity of the worker to suggest making an ashtray with materials at hand as well as the imagination of a member that can be tapped through such a simple activity. The dual result was self-esteem for the member and a sense of bond for the group.

55

The final example of helping group members accept responsibility is with a group of teen-agers. In this instance, it is the responsibility of every girl to attend the meeting and to bring the food she promised in order for the session to proceed as planned.

At 4:45 it was fairly obvious to everyone that Rita would probably not be coming, and, since she was to bring the apples, that we would not be making taffy apples. No one verbalized this, so I asked the girls if they felt disappointed that they couldn't make taffy apples this week. Dorothy said they were. Phyllis got up and looked through the cupboard and found some sugar cubes. She suggested we use the sugar cubes and also the syrup that was there. None of the girls expressed anger at Rita's not coming today. They began to rationalize their disappointment over the failure of today's program by expressing how hungry they were and saying they were sad we were not having sandwiches this week.

Finally, Dorothy asked if it would be possible to make candy. As we had the cook book there, Anne picked it up and began looking in the candy section. She found a recipe to make clear sugar candy, which consisted of heating sugar until it melted and pouring it into a pan and letting it harden. We decided to make this. I expressed my opinion that they were very disappointed that we couldn't make the taffy apples, and I hoped the making of the candy would help their disappointment. Dorothy took a leading part and was very persistent in making the candy turn out right. Anne and Phyllis both took turns stirring the sugar. The mood of the meeting had been subdued tremendously by the failure of the program. I asked them if this was the first time they had been part of a group that had planned an activity and it had not been carried off. They all said they had never experienced this before, but again no one verbalized disappointment about it. Dorothy said that at some point we could make the apples later and the others agreed.

What a vital way to experience just how important each member is to the group as a whole! Though not much of the disappointment was expressed by the girls themselves, one gets a feeling of the impact of it as the hungry girls wish they had brought sandwiches.

A second aspect of responsibility is illustrated in this excerpt. It is the responsibility of the worker to be prepared just in case someone is absent and the plans must be changed. While the worker should not make everything right no matter who attends, she should have alternative plans in mind so that the program will not completely fail. In this case, circumstances helped the worker recover and be able to offer some substitute kind of cooking. The girls can learn from an experience that all ought to follow through on what they promise to do, but the learning need not be through complete failure.

Relating Ordinary Chores to Gamelike Incentives

56

As in the previous example, here the worker assigns special roles to the children—this time in order to solve a conflict situation. This is an old trick of teachers and an effective way to motivate.

My little girls in Friendship Club were creating a problem with each girl's desire to do something that no one else in the club was doing. It started as soon as we met in the hall to go together to our club room. All at once asked me to let them open the door. It seems at the very first request I had handed my key to one of the girls as we were getting ready for the meeting, and she was so privileged to open the door. The girls all feel that this is a great privilege and I should let them do it. I suggested that we might make a schedule so that each girl would have a chance. Then I remembered "taking the attendance" was also a privileged task. And so we sat down and made up a roster of the seven girls' names and made up a schedule of the tasks that they like to do and continuously fight over. The tasks are opening the door, taking the attendance, and helping to get out the supplies. Each girl takes her turn, rotating the tasks.

57

The following example shows in a powerful way the subtle turning of an ordinary chore, the combing of one's hair, into some sort of a game by offering turns and a time limit to each. This example is all the more interesting because it deals with a white worker and Negro girls.

The following incident took place at a summer camp, and it concerns a group of seven teen-age Negro girls who were beginning their two-week camp session with a four-day outing in the woods. After we reached the campsite and set up camp, it began to rain and the rain continued during the entire four days. Faced with what to do and the possible tensions that could arise under such conditions, I tried to help the girls to have as positive an experience as possible in those beginning days of camp. Besides accepting the challenging tasks of building a fire with damp wood and preparing the food, we spent a good deal of the time sitting in the lean-to, trying to keep dry and warm, and talking.

The girls were very concerned with their personal appearance, especially their hair, and often would tell me how pretty and soft they thought mine was. A pattern gradually developed then, in which they would ask in turn to comb my hair just so they could feel the texture of it. The atmosphere during these times was very relaxed and warm, and a great deal of interaction and free expression followed. Our conversations centered around their home situations with questions relating to how my home life had been, and they also brought up school, racial, and relationship problems. The combing of my hair resulted in a pleasant experience for them and enabled the girls to feel secure enough to freely express their most immediate concerns. This activity began with the request of the girls and the willingness on the part of the worker, and it resulted almost in a game which allotted time for each girl to have a turn.

Much racial feeling is tied up in attitude toward hair. In this case the worker permitted her own hair to be experienced and felt by her group members, knowing full well how different it was from their own hair. It is not surprising that this experience in touching and feeling was very satisfying to them and led to some intimate discussion about race.

58

With my nine- and ten-year-old girls' cooking group, clean-up is not looked forward to. I found a way in which it would be less of a burden and even fun. I made a chart entitled, "How to Keep the Kitchen Spotless." On it I listed and numbered the various jobs that had to be done. I also made up little pieces of paper with the corresponding numbers on them. When the time for clean-up came, each girl selected a piece of paper with a number on it. Then I showed them the chart and read the numbers and the jobs. One of the jobs was inspector who checked on everyone else.

The girls needed a little incentive to get going. But once they got started and the initial complaints were voiced, clean-up went very well. It was necessary for each to do her job so another could do hers. The room was cleaned thoroughly without pushing on my part. No one complained about her job after the first few minutes. Each girl showed me that she had completed her job, and I complimented her.

Again, an ordinary living demand is built into a group's program experience more easily by the way the worker titled and assigned the jobs.

59

A different approach to clean-up, this time in a boys' group, is recorded below. The worker constructed an actual game by creating an indoor snowball fight. That it was a huge success on two levels—the clean-up and the opportunity for a snowball fight—can be seen in this excerpt.

It was about time to clean up since the boys had made quite a mess with their scraps of styrofoam scattered around the room. I said it looked like we had a blizzard here and had the only snow in Philadelphia. We talked about what a disappoinment it was to have no snow, especially around Christmas. I suggested that before we cleaned up we could have a snowball fight. After a little while, I suggested that we see who could toss the most snowballs across the room into the garbage can. In no time at all, the bigger pieces were in the can. The enthusiasm carried over to sweeping up the little bits and leaving the room the cleanest ever. Arnold came up to me and asked if we could have another snowball fight next time.

60

Another approach to clean-up led into a dancing activity in the next illustration. Again, one is struck with just how much fun clean-up can be according to how it is structured. As discussed earlier in this book, these illustrations show the close relationship between activities considered *work* and those considered *play*. It is, after all, simply a matter of attitude to the activity that conditions the meaning to the person.

When the party was finished and the children were leaving, I asked for five volunteers for clean-up. Five hands immediately shot up, and they were all from the older age group. As they began to work, I realized their motives for staying were not just for helping, since the work was not getting done. It was the night before Halloween and there was nothing for them to do. To get them going, I said the two who swept up the most dirt could take home the two pumpkins which were left over. This set them to work rather quickly, and one fellow would not leave when his sister came to pick him up. I happened to have a German polka record with me, so put it on rather loud on the record player. When the competition for the pumpkins was over and they had been awarded to the best sweepers, several of the older fellows grabbed their brooms and danced around the room. It became quite a frenzied activity with all of them dancing then with each other, the Neighborhood Youth Corps worker. myself, or a broom if no partner was available at the time. As a result, the clean-up for these five boys was more fun than the party had been.

61

Following is an account of a gamelike experience which the worker created out of the need to have a group of visitors shown through the building. The quality of this experience is not unlike a scavenger hunt, but at the same time it served another important purpose.

Our settlement house returned a visit to another settlement house. I had ended the mass activity program that I was leading at the other agency. I utilized the groups that were already formed from this previous activity to be the basis of an activity that became a game. The agenda called for a tour of the other agency. I asked that the guests help the visitors to discover all the different things that their building had to offer. I set limits in terms of having the group stay together, where they could go, etc. When the groups were reassembled, each group was given points for different things that they had discovered.

62

The following is another account of how one worker through advance planning turned a problem situation into an experience that provided not only fun but a growth experience in leadership for the boys and an incentive toward music which might not have been possible under ordinary circumstances in the club room.

I am currently working with a club of nine- and ten-year-old boys. Many of our meetings are held in a facility four blocks away from the agency. This necessitates that we meet at the agency and then walk the distance to the gym. Needless to say, getting the boys from one agency to another without incident can be quite a task.

In making use of this reality, however, I did come up with a gamelike activity that provided fun and some basic social work values as a built-in feature. The following activity has helped to make this four-block trip both fun for the children and an opportunity for me to work with them.

The ten boys which make up this group were organized into the following arrowhead formation:

In this position each boy had to keep in step with his comrades while singing a marching song. Since this group has only a temporary leader, each boy gets the opportunity to be in the front of the formation and lead the group.

63

In the situation which follows, the worker's light attitude toward a potential problem situation avoided the necessity of engaging in a struggle with the one child who refused to cooperate at the end of the activity. At the same time, the worker involved the group with this child as he improvised a situation offering great status and caring for the one obstructive boy. Feelings were thus dissipated.

In my nine- and ten-year-old boys' group, the activity for the evening had been gymnastics, and during the putting away of the equipment we experienced some difficulty. The boys had been instructed to carry the mats to the closet. Jack and Jeff started to pick up a mat when Leo came over and stood in the middle of it so they could not pick it up. I saw that Jack and Jeff were beginning to get angry at Leo, so I went over to the mat and asked Leo to lie down across it. I told him we were going to make a mummy out of him. We rolled him up in the mat, and Jack, Jeff, Stan, and myself carried Leo and the mat to the closet—all of us laughing all the way while accomplishing our purpose.

Program and Aggression

64

I have tried to use program with Alan in order to help him accept the limits which games, both active and quiet, and cooperative activity put on his undirected, immature boisterousness. Although I have designed all my programs with the whole group in mind, not just Alan, occasionally I have had opportunities (especially in the free swim time) to work with him intensively on his acceptance of game limits. In the group situation, however, the following incident illustrates his problem and one of the ways I have dealt with it.

We played a game in which one boy stood in the middle and the rest would pass the candy around the circle. When he said stop, he opened his eyes and guessed who had the candy. If he guessed, he not only got the candy but a malted ball. This was going fine, except that Alan began fooling around, playing with the candy and not passing it on. Ray jumped him for it. Alan cowered in the corner crying and said he was leaving. I grabbed his hand and asked him to stay, saying that while Ray shouldn't have hit him, he did have a reason and did Alan know what that reason had been? Alan professed not to know. I explained to him that he had really been messing up the game, and so the others were angry at him. I asked Alan to stay and play right, and see if things wouldn't change. He did a good job. By helping him realize that his unwillingness to stick to the rules of the game was one of the causes of his trouble with the others, Alan was able to turn a troubled situation into a better one.

In the above incident, the worker tries to help an individual become part of the group by holding him to the rules which the others were following. Such a concrete emphasis upon how one behaves in a given situation is often specific enough that the person can work to change that one part of himself. The worker also helps Alan to save face in this situation and to remain in the group. It is far easier for Alan to admit his problem behavior alone with the adult in a momentary aside than to work it out with his angry peers. One would hope that eventually Alan would be able to settle his differences with the group in the group situation. In the meantime, the worker's support of his capacity to do better in a little private conversation was enough incentive to get him back into the mainstream and enable him to show through action that he could do better.

65

Some of the nine- and ten-year-old girls were interested in chicken fights. Dorey was the biggest and the winner most often. When Sally and Beth fought, Sally accidentally poked Beth in the neck with her elbow. Beth began to cry. I went over to her and got some-one to get a wet towel. Beth apparently knew that Sally did not do it on purpose and did not blame Sally, but it hurt and she was crying. I then was careful to make sure the girls were matched according to size.

At a later meeting, I realized that this incident may not have been accidental. Sally voiced her dislike of Beth, and another incident similar to this one occurred. The point is that I should have been aware of the tension at the earlier meeting and not let the two "fight." It was too much of a temptation for Sally.

In this situation, the nature of the activity itself played into existing frictions in the group and made them worse.

66

Once the girls had taken things to eat, some decided to dance. Helen was anxious to dance. Judy complimented her and claimed that she herself didn't know how. Toby asked me to dance. She seemed pleasantly surprised that I accepted. Arlene didn't dance and claimed that she didn't know how. Even after encouragement she wouldn't, whereas Judy started to dance. Dora and Marilyn sat quietly and watched; they claimed that they didn't feel like dancing. Phyllis didn't dance because of her recent appendix operation. Kate danced for a while. I showed them an easy side step which was easy to pick up. Those who were standing and dancing began to do it quickly. The girls seemed interested in learning it, so I showed it to them at that time. Those who were sitting down remained there and could not be encouraged to participate in this activity. I had planned some games that I thought would be appropriate for such a party. I had Toby and her subgroup help me by contributing suggestions and ideas. I didn't think that I could introduce them effectively once the phonograph was on. Toby and her subgroup were those who were doing most of the dancing and whose support I would need to introduce the games effectively.

Sometimes aggression is expressed by passive resistance as in the above example. Sabotaging an activity is an excellent way for a group to get back at a worker.

67

I noticed during a game that they were fairly aggressive toward each other and grabbed and wrestled when they would encounter each other; however, no one got hurt. Next, I lined them up into two lines for Crows and Cranes, and they had a good time running and chasing and catching each other. Since the game hinges upon constantly changing sides, it was easy to balance up the players of less skill by assuring them that the sides would keep changing and that everyone would have a chance to be on all sides. The boys were also excited about getting points for a team, and in general they played this game pretty close to the rules.

The open-endedness of this game, i.e., the ever-changing teams which the worker controls through his selection of the team to be chased, makes it a kind of legitimate free-for-all where chasing, grabbing, and pushing are all accepted. The action is so fast that hard feelings don't get a chance to develop. These features make it a useful game for aggressive boys.

68

The girls, in the following example, tolerated the worker for a brief moment in their group life. One wonders whether the girls' exit had anything to do with the worker's earlier exit while they were engaged in their preparations. Where was the worker's help throughout the dance practice? Certainly, this worker and group were far apart during the whole episode.

> The girls were running wild through the building. They were beginning to fool around and dance on the stage. I suggested that they put together a little dance. I told them what they were doing was nice and that I would like to see more. I told them that I would come back in a few minutes to watch them. When I returned, they put on a coordinated dance number which also included girls who were not in my group but who were present in the room. I complimented them on their performance. In making their exit as part of the dance routine, they began to run and hide again.

69

Not able to compete physically, i.e., to shout louder than all the boys at once, the worker interrupted the process by using his wits—by surprising the group with an unexpected action and injecting what he had to say quickly and effectively. Sometimes action has an advantage over words.

> The boys were hyperactive on this occasion, as there had been an attack on one of their members and they were itching to retaliate. They had heard that boys (enemy gang) from another neighborhood were spreading the word that they were "chicken" and wouldn't meet them. I had tried to get them to discuss the background of the incident, but they all talked and shouted at once and I had despaired of hearing or being heard. I turned to the boy next to me and cupped my hands to his ear, and whispered: "Do you know how to play Rumor? Pass it on!" The boys became interested in the secret and began to listen before their turn came. When the process broke down before all had a turn, it was quiet and I asked, "Do you all want to know what I said? Ask Joe." Joe was player Number 3 and his version was almost totally different. Then I gave

them the original question and commented, "That's what happens to rumors—you can't trust them." From there we went on to discuss the incident.

70

These were nine- and ten-year-old boys, quite hostile and aggressive, always fighting with one another. Kevin and Dougie began fighting with one another over Kevin's kicking Dougie in the knee when the latter boy bent over to tie his shoes. Dougie reached up and slugged Kevin in the chest. I ran over and separated the two boys, telling them that such behavior would not be tolerated in the club room. A basketball was available which the other members were playing with. I asked them to lend me the ball so that Kevin and Dougie could settle this argument. They agreed. I instructed the two youngsters to kick the ball from one side of the room to the other until they had cooled off. They seemed puzzled, and I told them that this is the way we would be settling our fights from now on. The two boys kicked the ball to and fro for a few minutes and then began to work cooperatively in getting it from one side of the room to the other.

By using an external object to project their negative feelings on, both boys were able to work out a successful release of the hostility and anger which each felt for the other. After a short while, Kevin and Dougie were friends again.

Here is the effectiveness of rechannelling aggression onto an object instead of through fists. With the addition of a simple skill demand, energies gradually were shifted from persons to activity. A general guide in dealing with aggressive behavior is to program *away from* aggression.

71

The following two incidents from the same worker's practice show such a change in emphasis.

I am reluctant to reinforce the pent-up aggression of my boys by setting up a game that too closely resembles war and is directed to "killing your opponent." Two excerpts will illustrate past and present:

The boys were tired of my talk and were restlessly moving about the room. I asked them to take their seats, but they rebounded immediately. Several two-party scraps developed, and I separated them before bloodshed. It occurred to me that instead of attempting to suppress the feelings being expressed, I should allow them more complete but controlled catharsis in a game of dodgeball. They responded with enthusiasm to my suggestion. We went to the gym, chose sides, and began. The game became more vicious as it progressed. When we ended the meeting, some unfinished feuds were continued on the street with stones.

72

Three weeks later when the boys were in a fighting mood and shouting at each other loudly, I suggested we use some of the hot air in a fun game. We counted off into two teams and lined up, hands behind back, along the sides of a Ping-Pong table. The ball was placed in the center, and the object was to blow it off the opposite edge. With much laughing and comments about bad breath, the boys gradually became docile and breathless!

73

Here, a sequence of two games helps to move a group from explosive behavior to quietly responsive cooperative behavior. Also, the group moves from participating as individuals to being more related to one another. Blindfold games which stress listening are most useful in developing such a tone.

I started in right after supper since they were so hyperactive anyhow. I thought a bit of organization would calm the group down and made a quick decision to involve them in active group games. At my suggestion, they rolled up the rug, got some chalk, and marked some X's here and there on the wooden floor. For a first game I involved them in a running-around, march-like Musical Chairs in which they all had to end up on an X. This permitted some good-natured shoving, pushing, and rushing, and was quite a hit. Mr. Jay sat and laughingly watched.

To tone them down, I moved right into Dog and Bone which a couple of them remembered from school and the M. Home. Since this game involved being quiet, it changed the tone for the next twenty minutes. Not having a blindfold, we used the sweatshirt of "It" to hide his vision while the Dog tried to steal the bone. There were a few complaints here and there, from Jim and others, that they were hot under the shirt, but in general this added to the fun. I was especially delighted that this game enabled Ray to compete successfully with the older boys. Since he is so tiny, he was able to move quickly and steal the bone without being caught. He got tremendous pleasure from his successes. There was lots of arguing and fighting about the order of the turns, but I assured them all that they would have as many turns as they needed.

We played it through until each boy had two turns of being "It." Bill was very black in spirit but gradually joined in when I did not persuade him deliberately. Lennie was sobbing up in his bedroom, and we could hear the noise even where we were. Jim thought it a little beneath him but despite this joined in and seemed to have fun. The others participated quite well, and all were involved with the exception of Ralph, who sat in the big chair and watched.

74

In this same group there is a progression from the more worker-controlled activity in which three games employ the same expectations of checking behavior to a worker-controlled game where speedy rushing about on command, with a wider expression of energies, is in order.

Our final games then followed in short order. I first played the leader-follower games, starting with On the Bank, In the Brook and then shifted to Do This, Do That, and finally Simon Says—all of which follow the same principle and hinge on inhibition of impulse. That is, the boys do the command only when the leader says it properly. Since they knew these three games, they had fun with them. Everyone was equally able to do them.

I was just about ready to stop because our time was more than up, and I wanted them calmed down before supper, when there was a shout for Upset the Fruit Basket, a game we had done Christmas Eve. I agreed and for the next fifteen minutes we played that game. This has proved to be their most popular activity. They sit in chairs and rush and jump about according to command. They jostle and miss chairs, and in general have a riotous time, all in the nature of the game. I was pleased that there was so little fighting throughout and everyone seemed fairly satisfied. In fact, when I knew it was almost ten minutes before supper and I did not want them so keyed up and said this was it, there was a howl of disapproval but final agreement when I said we would get together this evening and continue other games.

75

In the following illustration, the worker deliberately intervened and turned an activity that he thought would make a problem between his exuberant group and the community into one of a different quality. His approach to the problem of aggressive behavior, that of diverting it through more interesting activity, often proves successful.

I had taken my boys' group to the Federal Building to witness a Superior Court case involving the bribing of a federal employee. The boys (eight ten-to-twelve-year-olds) and I were now headed home after sitting quietly in court for forty minutes. There was new-fallen snow on the ground. Nature took her course, and soon the group was having a fine time throwing snowballs. I knew that there is considerable apprehension in this community whenever any more than three Negroes are seen together "living it up"; the people get suspicious and worried, especially with young boys. Not wishing to reinforce their stereotypes of these boys, nor have cars and passing people pelted, I tried to get the group to stop by asking and then demanding. Nothing worked for more than a few minutes.

It was cold and I suggested that we stop and get some hot chocolate. They wanted everything but that. I offered only hot chocolate, saying that the paper containers would serve to warm their hands. They agreed to this and we left with the containers. I knew that they would have their hands full, too full for the snowballs. But that wouldn't last long, so I thought of a game to prolong the busyness.

I noticed that they had not removed the tops from the containers but were sucking the cocoa through the tiny vent in the top. I gathered them around and proposed that they continue drinking with the tops on until we reached a point several blocks distant (out of the danger zone) to determine the winner. The winner would be the one who could guess how much cocoa was left in his cup, marking the place by pushing a pencil through the side, before he uncovered it.

We had some "messy guesses" with cocoa squirting out and some really "dry wells," but in every case the boys forgot the snow until we were in an open area where it could do no harm.

Here is a worker thinking quickly and adding an experience of great interest for his group. His sense of timing, awareness of the level of his group's interests, and deep caring about the life experiences of his boys come through quite clearly. It goes without saying that his approach, when finally successful, was not "preachy," but acknowledged the fun of snowballs in an appropriate setting.

Some workers seem to think that aggressive children should be allowed to express their feelings through such games as dodgeball and Beater Goes Around. In this writer's experience, these games lead to an accentuation of the problem. The feelings are in no way dissipated, as Case Study Number 71 shows. A better approach than to structure and give form to the angry feelings is to substitute some kind of intense action with a different skill demand through which the feelings can be vented.

A variation of dodgeball may serve this purpose. In crab dodgeball the "It" in the center gets down on the floor with stomach up and supports himself by arms and legs. The circle of players must roll the ball and try to touch a part of his body while he, in crab-like position, tries to avoid the ball. Instead of direct assault, some measure of skill is introduced on both sides. A similar substitution of skill demand operated in the blowing of the Ping-Pong game (Number 72) and changed the tone of the group. It is difficult for this writer to see any merit ever in the circle game in which one person chases another trying to whale him with a belt. Despite the slight structures it is simply too nearly like the very kind of behavior that we are trying to avoid to legitimize through any form of game.

76

After spending a short time in the arts and crafts room, the girls drifted from the room. They went again to the little theatre (this room has a stage and a large sitting area that had no seats out). I attempted to involve them in an activity on the stage or in a game from their running around. This did not prove to be successful. I attempted to get a "catch" going when they discovered some cups and began to throw them around. After beginning the "catch" they began to pass them back and forth. Then they began to toss them all to me. When they began to throw them more forcefully, I reprimanded them for this aspect of their behavior.

I tried to use whatever they were doing to get more relatedness among the members. They preferred to maintain their individual behavior and not become involved in it with someone else.

Here we observe a worker trying unsuccessfully to put some structure into a group's natural expression of aggressive behavior. A deliberate injection by the worker of some different skill demand would be in order.

Ending Activities

Many forms of activities are appropriate for endings. While in most instances it is best that the tone set through the ending be quiet and tapering, in some instances the final activity is an active, exhausting one that hits a high pitch. One consistent ingredient for the final event is that it be a group activity, one that unites those present into one shared experience. Also, the activity should definitely end rather than peter out.

77

The final game was played in total darkness. All were asked to sit in a close circle. Then Jane told a gory story of an accident and here and there passed a supposed entrail about the circle. There were squeals and much excitement in the darkness. Soon Jane announced that she was turning on the light for all to see what had scared them so much—a piece of bacon, insides of a pumpkin, a meat ball, etc. All had a good laugh at themselves.

In this ending activity for pregnant, unmarried residents in a maternity home, the group had a final unifying experience which evoked laughter at themselves, an especially expressive emotional release. Whether an ending activity be tapering off in spirit or high-pitched, the outcome should include increased spirit and morale.

78

The following experience is with a young group of five- and six-year-olds. In this instance an age group which is primarily individually geared is unified around a piece of equipment, the slide.

This game that I made up happened on the spur of the moment with my five- and six-year-olds. They were playing in the Center's back yard on the playground equipment. The boys started to congregate by the slide, and each would go down as quickly as possible. Some of the boys were playing on other things and I wanted to gather them together for a final activity. As the boys started coming down the slide, I stood at the bottom and threw them a ball. If they caught it, they received a certain number of points. The ball was thrown very lightly and easily so that each boy could catch it. The points rose from ten to infinity, and the boys enjoyed the excitement of this activity. I would yell their names as they came down and the points the catch was worth, which added to the excitement and suspense of the game. This catching of the ball while jumping or sliding has become a favorite activity among the boys.

79

The following excerpt is from the final meeting of the Angels, an eight-year-old girls' club in a Jewish Community Center, and employs the medium of a painting experience to unify the group and the year's experience.

I had set up paints for a group mural. Amy had suggested at the end of the previous meeting that we paint, and I had told her at the time that this was a good idea and we would try it.

When the girls arrived, I gave out smocks. Natalie was the first to put on one of these and she remarked on how funny it looked. I mentioned that she looked as if she was wearing wings. Susanne picked this up and began to say, "She's an official Angel." The girls began to repeat this and jumped around the room in smocks.

I said that before we began painting, it would be good to decide what to paint. I said I had thought it might be nice to think of some of the things the Angels had done together, and paint pictures of them. Caroline said, "Playing outside. Jumping rope." Suzanne thought of the Puppet Show. Ronda thought of dancing. I think it was Natalie who thought of the circus we had had the week before. I mentioned the hospital trip, which some of the girls had not gone on. I also mentioned the Purim Carnival and the Passover celebration. Their memory seemed exhausted, so I said, "Why don't we go around the table, and everyone decide on what she wants to paint."

The activity continued with some of the girls working together at different paints. I was conscious of the sharing of the paints, helping one another as each finished with something, cleaning up, working within the limitation of only three basic colors. Here was a kind of activity that came from the group itself, but which I helped to direct in such a way as to promote relationship and help the club as a whole prepare for ending. They did not feel it necessary to have their individual names displayed on the project because this was clearly the club's. It was put up on a wall of the Center with an explanatory sign.

Here, in the course of the final meeting, the girls had the chance to re-experience a whole year's activities and to capture it symbolically in a group mural. How natural that they should avoid signing their names, an act which an eight-year-old normally enjoys doing. One can fairly feel the sense of achievement and group pride that these Angels must have taken with them as they left the Center for the last time that season.

80

The final case study among this book's selections is a fitting ending to the attempt to illustrate the use of non-verbal methods through various concrete examples. This ending includes a series of symbolic and ritualized activities which were used to convey a mood in a dedication ceremony at a residence for boys, eight to twelve years of age. The short program in which the boys, staff, and some guests participated included opening song, speeches from staff and boys, and presentation of a plaque and map. At the end of the ceremony, the performance of three, short gamelike activities by all present produced the essence of closeness, of bond, and of group spirit.

> On the mimeographed program the final event was called "A mystery," and the boys were curious to know what this meant. I asked all present—boys, staff, guests—to get up and move close together in a circle, touching one another. I then explained that what we were going to do was quite simple, but demanded complete cooperation from all if it would succeed. I described how they were to whisper the secret message around the circle without letting others hear, and I started one around. They were quite excited to learn what was said and the final person called out the exact message, "Three cheers for Sunset House!" All were delighted that it came out right.
>
> Then I passed two messages simultaneously, one in each direction, and they had to cross midway around the circle. Bobby was so excited that he jumped up and down for joy in his place on the circle as he awaited his turn. There was much buzzing and touching cupped hand to another's ear as they all tried to get the message around as quickly as possible. I announced the messages as they came back and they made a little jingle.
>
> The final "game" was done in silence. I asked all to hold hands and announced that I was now going to pass the Sunset House Spark of Friendship around the circle in two directions by squeezing my neighbor's hand, but they must be sure to wait to receive the spark before passing it on. Although there was a little bit of hard squeezing going on, the spirit was cooperative and warm. When the sparks all had come back to me, the dedication was over. The boys quietly broke the circle. The mood of the moment was very mellow.

In this illustration all three activities took perhaps three minutes, but their effect in conveying an important message in terms felt by the group was powerful. When during the ceremony one boy made a speech about life in the residence, he rose to the occasion through responsibly reading his prepared speech. He was at this moment straining to reach the adults' world in his method of communicating a message. When, on the other hand, the worker involved the whole group in the final three circle activities, he was conveying a similar message by reaching down to the child's world for the most effective means of communication. Thus, the verbal activities and the non-verbal ones (in the whisper activity there were words used) are shown here in combination to realize a purpose.

10 Art and Form in Group Work

Expressionist art like Van Gogh's by the nature of its intensity and its extremely personal quality, reaches its pitch of achievement at times when the artist is so "inspired" (for want of a better word) that his whole accumulation of knowledge and technical skill is at his command for immediate, as if spontaneous, use. But to think of an artist "inspired" to create a picture without preliminary spadework is as unreasonable as to imagine an actor giving an inspired performance without having learned his lines or a poet creating a master-piece in a language he does not know. The Starry Night *is an inspired painting if ever there was one, but its creation was possible only because Van Gogh worked toward it for so long. He wrote, "I wonder when I'll get my starry sky done, a picture that haunts me always."*

—John Canaday *

The reader may wonder that so many of the quotations used as chapter introductions in this book are drawn from thinking in the field of the arts. This was done deliberately to highlight the inspiration that a study of productivity and creativity in such fields has provided for the author. The aim toward creativity in the use of the social group work method is not unlike the aim toward creativity in any endeavor. Too long has the use of activities by groups suffered from comparison with the lowest form of expression in the doing activities—busy work! An equally valid view, and much more appropriate model, is toward the highest level—that of artistic creativity.

That is to say, the use of non-verbal content by the group

* "*The Starry Night:* Free Expression and Studied Expression" (New York: The Metropolitan Museum, 1958).

worker is, in fact, *an art.* Many of its underlying theories and concepts are derived from the sciences. In this sense then, this book is essentially a study of *form.* Or, as the critic of aesthetics, Clive Bell, would say, the search is for "significant form." By significant form, in a group work context, is meant *a created experience* springing from a logical selection of content and structures introduced sequentially in a planful pattern, with deep awareness of the requirements of the users as well as consciousness of some of the possible outcomes—stripped of all irrelevancies that might obscure its vitality.

In this sense, the created form is an abstraction—of life—developed by the group worker deliberately out of his knowledge and skill, and offered to his members for their use. The group experience, then, is not merely a piece of living, but because of its planful initiation and use by the worker, *it is heightened living.* As such, the resultant interplay of the process—the individuals with each other and with the worker, plus the ever-shifting forces of interaction affecting each individual of his own inner motivations and the pressures of the external world—can be considered a thing of beauty, or an aesthetic experience, or the ever-shifting form. This amalgam, or form, is peculiarly the worker's creation, extended by the impact of the group members upon it. It springs from the worker's grasp of the values of the culture in which he lives, the values selected for emphasis by the social work profession, and the values upon which his particular agency wishes to focus. It takes into consideration the values which motivate the group members as they seek out a meaningful experience.

Creativity

In discussing art, Susanne Langer offers this definition: "Art is the creation of forms symbolic of human feeling." Her following elaboration is pertinent to this present discussion:

> The word "creation" is introduced here with full awareness of its problematical character. There is a definite reason to say a craftsman *produces* goods, but *creates* a thing of beauty; a builder *erects* a house, but *creates* an edifice if the house is a real work of architec-

> ture, however modest. An artifact as such is merely a combination of material parts, or a modification of a natural object to suit human purposes. It is not a creation, but an arrangement of given factors. A work of art, on the other hand, is more than an "arrangement" of given things—even qualitative things. Something emerges from the arrangement of tones or colors, which was not there before, and this, rather than the arranged material, is the symbol of sentience.
>
> The making of this expressive form is the creative process that enlists a man's utmost technical skill in the service of his utmost conceptual power, imagination. Not the invention of new original turns, nor the adoption of novel themes, merits the word "creative," but the making of any work symbolic of feeling, even in the most canonical context and manner. A Greek vase was almost always a creation, although its form was traditional and its decoration deviated but little from that of its numberless forerunners. The creative principle, nonetheless, was probably active in it from the first throw of the clay.[1]

What is suggested for the social group worker's consideration is that the form that he imparts to the group experience must be capable of being termed "a creation"—involving varying degrees of craftsmanship or technique, but arising *first in his head* as a conception. As he conceives the experience-to-be, he knows also what must be its general structure, its content, its focus, its degree of elaboration, and some of its possible consequences. He selects his *form,* which enables the group members to use it to express their own feelings. Thus he works toward a definite purpose or goal. It is foolish to think that the group members can use an experience creatively if it is not offered creatively!

In Japan (as well as many other cultures) every person is an artist, that is, his life view holds aesthetic values. The education of each child, from earliest days, includes education of his aesthetic sense. That is not to say that there are no professional artists in Japan. But everyone is able to take brush in hand unselfconsciously and paint, or execute exacting caligraphy. Even the wrapping of a gift is governed by a sense of tradition and respect for the aesthetic import of the object. The same can be said for the arrangement of flowers, the partaking of tea in the traditional tea ceremony, or the writing of the haiku (the seventeen-syllable verse), an art form deeply related in context to nature.

The characteristic artistic sentiment of the Japanese derives from their deep awareness of and appreciation for nature as a pervasive force in their lives. Such a value is ingrained early in the life experience of each child. The success of the Japanese craftsman is not entirely due to his cleverness with his hands and his neat and intricate skill; it is derived also from his artistic sense which enables him to have command over and mastery of the various materials. This artistic sense springs from a concept that unites man and nature and also life and art.

> Western peoples regard the existence of pure art as separated from human living; that is, they are cognizant of the world of abstract beauty. Japan until about the middle of the nineteenth century was not aware of the possibility of making a distinct separation between life and art. Paintings, for example, were not independent works of art for art's sake . . . They were primarily decorations for utility rather than works for artistic appreciation, closely associated with man's life.[2]

In Japan there is no separation between the decorative and the "pure" art. All art aims at a harmony between beauty and utility, and both are arts of life and of religion. Thus, there is a close blending of life and art and a subsequent beautifying of life through art.

The connection between creative expression and life, itself, is less fortuitous in the American heritage. A dominant value here is that of mechanical and technological achievement. Such a pervasive influence has provided the analogy by which group workers have viewed their use of program content—program is a tool and this tool accomplishes certain results! The mechanical implications of this concept are obvious, and because of them social group work has suffered greatly throughout its development.

Is it not possible now to begin to view program content as *form* and to view content and form as unitary? The form develops out of its relationship, its organic unity, with the content. The form of the content is what the group worker creates that is the reflection of all that he knows, all that he feels, and of attitudes that he does not even know he knows. It is his own subjective creation, springing from both internal forces and their interaction with the social context of which he is a part. It derives from his function, broadly viewed, as he meets his group. In social group work form would include not only the preparations and the offering of the experience—but also the recording of it, the planful relating of it to other subsequent experiences, and the grasping of its meaning as fully as possible.

Professional Purpose and Innovation

This collection of non-verbal examples is suggestive, it is hoped, of the many uses to which such content can be put. Although most of the specific examples in this collection are games, the same approach can be part of whatever medium the worker chooses to use. Probably games do comprise the most frequent program content used with groups, especially in work with children and youth. Regardless of the content of the activity and the precise form of it selected, however, a concern with structure and purpose as they are deeply connected with how the content will be used will provide the group worker with a consistent underlying approach. If the worker concentrates upon which activities are useful for beginning, for introduction to a new content form, for development, for ending, there will develop a thread of continuity permeating all that he does that will enable him to develop content dynamically for use by the group. In addition, the special uses of program are endless: to express attitudes and feelings about self and others, to express aggression, to offer an indirect or direct way to cope with group and individual problems, to present growth opportunities to individuals and groups, to induce verbalization of feelings and attitudes.

Perhaps the reader can be encouraged through the work of the many group workers here recorded, drawn from the records of meetings in a large variety of agencies and settings, to use his imagination in creating his own form within the diverse categories of possible activities. Perhaps he can move with more confidence to create his form to meet more effectively the particular need of the moment. Perhaps he can gain more confidence to risk trying what he is not expert in himself. Perhaps he can see that there are many roads to Rome, that there is always more than one thing that will suit a group's need at a particular time and many forms can accomplish the same basic objective.

In short, it is hoped that this collection of examples will encourage further experimentation in the form and greater direction, precision, deliberateness, and unity in the underlying purpose for which the form is used. When this happens, group workers can then be more accountable for their part in the interaction process and be able to look more squarely to what particular use the group can make of whatever is introduced as the fabric of its experience. It has been said in the past that the worker is "there for the group." Until he is ready and able to move freely and unselfconsciously with the group in whatever medium the group chooses and needs to use, he is subtly diverted from offering his help fully because of his own program biases. To be *truly there* for the group he must possess the know-how, the freedom, and the desire to move out generously in every conceivable program area.

Group Experience as Life Experience

People are known and know themselves through what they do or accomplish in living. The same holds true for what they do not do with their lives. Closely bound up with what a person accomplishes is the way in which he achieves objectives, the way he gets along with others and with himself as he pursues his goals.

The essential message which this book attempts to convey is that a deep connection exists between a person's actions in his small group experiences and how he behaves and learns to behave in the full range of other life experiences. There are two primary means of meeting the challenges of living open to everyone.

The first is learning to cope with the situation that one encounters in the world as he finds it. This has to do with learning "the rules of the game" so to speak. Another way to put it is that each person, in learning to get along in life, must learn to take on appropriate behaviors, must understand the basic expectations of others of himself and give back to others in acceptable ways. He must learn to discipline his impulses and inhibit his desires at certain points so he can get along with others. This process of learning to accommodate one's self to the larger group of which he is a part is what can be called "socialization." Through this process one learns to handle himself with respect to other people, to his environment, and to the ideas in his world which affect him. These learnings, through family living, school experience, and participation in other group experiences dominate the attention of the young child, the adolescent, and the young adult. The first life chore, then, is to find some degree of comfort in how one behaves in his world *vis-à-vis* the others he encounters.

The second kind of learning for living is achieved, most often, after one has some idea of the demands of the first. This second grows out of knowing the rules of the game and has to do with such things as innovating, creating, developing one's own unique style of living. It is only after one has some measure of security in understanding the expected behaviors that one can dare to bolt away at points to develop his own life style. But experience in both kinds of learning situations should be simultaneous from earliest childhood. To learn to follow prescribed procedures, one needs repeated opportunities, beginning with simple forms. The same would hold true for innovative challenges.

Both of these responses to the situation of living are possible avenues for the group worker to pursue as he develops opportunities for group experiences for his members. The power of the peer group in influencing behavior has long been appreciated and demonstrated. Consider the many years of work with second generation nationality groups who have used group experiences to learn to Americanize themselves—to learn behaviors their families could not teach them. Or, the work with antisocial gang groups, whose behavior reflects all too little family influence toward acceptable behavior, illustrates that much has been done through work with groups to help them take on more appropriate rules and roles for living. The same could be said for all work with adolescents. They are in a period of life in which part of their very development toward responsible adulthood includes breaking, for a time, with the strictures of their parents, and drawing support for how they will act from their contemporaries, often in the security of the group.

Implications for Group Work

The implications drawn from these two kinds of learning for the nature of the group experience itself are great. And since, what the group *does* holds such a vital place in the meaning the group experience will have, the implications for the use of program are equally great. It seems important, then, that groups have the chance to be helped to hold themselves to the rules of what is done. This would include all kinds of training to develop necessary skills, unpleasant as the rigors of such training sometimes are. It would also include learning to live by the rules and the discipline involved in such training as well as the capacity to accept an unfavorable decision gracefully.

For such learnings to occur a group can gain much from following the prescribed script in a drama event, sticking to a musical score, accepting certain discussed ground rules for a trip, following the recipe exactly in making a cake, or not running with the ball in basketball. These are all expected behaviors, and the group member must lend himself to the demands of the situation in order to be fair. He also cannot expect to hit the target with consistency unless he learns the correct way to hold the bow and arrow, nor can his copper enameling succeed unless he follows the proper steps in this process. All these disciplines hold important life meanings within them and should not be discarded under the naïve bias of the worker that they lack freedom and creativity.

Once the disciplines are learned, then the matter of innovation is possible; and the group's program needs to have as much of this within it as possible. For certain groups that have been culturally or emotionally deprived, the amount of freedom to innovate might be limited to short periods of time, or introduced around particular areas. On the other hand, the learning experience might be deliberately simplified through the use of the most uncomplicated kinds of materials (as in finger painting) because self-expression without technical worries might seem to be the most important learning experience for those individuals.

What is being suggested here is that the worker value both kinds of experiences—those demanding discipline and mastery of a process and those with little technical demand that emphasize spontaneity, improvisation, creativity, and innovation. The important matter for the worker to be concerned with is *when* to use either, according to his group's need rather than his own preference. While he might, as an adult, place great value on the free and creative opportunities, he needs to balance this aspect with an understanding that his group members can be led toward using freedom and innovative opportunities only after they have accepted some discipline. Through such a balance in approach much mediocrity of achievement will be avoided.

Need for Further Research

In order to pursue such goals as these there is need for much more research into the nature of the demand of various activities as well as the method of using them. In this regard further exploration of the "prescriptiveness" of activities—as has been begun by Gump, Sutton-Smith, Vinter and others (see Note 25, Chapter 2)—will be useful in helping the worker know just what is demanded of the individual as he pursues various activities. The close connection between this behavior and outside living has much within it to pursue. Investigation, such as that undertaken by Omar Khayyam Moore and others, of the various kinds of activities—the game of chance, of strategy, the puzzle, the aesthetic creative experience—would be another fruitful area to pursue.

And finally, as suggested in these program excerpts, further attention needs to be given to the development of *form*, to the modifications the worker must make of any given activity within the everchanging interactional group process for achievement of particular purposes. Through such planful adaptations the worker's effect on what he introduces will be more precise and deliberate, with the goals of social work, or whatever profession he represents, serving as guideposts. Only through more knowledge about what one uses, and how, and for what purpose, will the group worker become able to use program with responsibility and skill.

Notes to Chapter 10

1. Susanne K. Langer, *Feeling and Form* (New York: Scribners, 1953), pp. 40-1.
2. Yuzuru Okada, *Japanese Handicrafts* (Tokyo: Japan Travel Bureau, 1956), pp. 4 and 5.

Nature loves individuality, resists and punishes the loss of it in any field of creation. If our civilization goes contrary to this divinity within the nature of us all, if it does not learn these secrets of behavior, of character, of appropriate changes of form, then what is going to happen to us? Where shall we go? Now is the time for us to say wherein lies salvation for us as human beings.

Is the solution creativity? Yes, that is the element needed now. It alone can prevent us from becoming standardized, from losing our rich and potent sense of life.

—Frank Lloyd Wright

Appendix A

Analysis of Non-Verbal Activities

Name of Worker ____________________

Name of Group ____________________ Date of Meeting __________

Session No. ____ Age ____ Sex ____ No. Present ____ Type of Group ______

(1)	(2)	(3)	(4)	(5)
Activity	*Activity demand*	*Leadership and decision-making patterns*	*At whose initiative*	*How end initiated*
(Game, craft, song, etc.)	(Puzzle, chance, skill, strategy, endurance, aesthetic-creative, other)		(Worker, one member, clique, group, other)	(Worker, one member, clique, group, other)
1.				
2.				
3.				
4.				

1. Code for (3): A. Worker (or one member) direct control; B. Worker (or one member) indirect control; C. Group control (leader within); D. Group control with changing "It"; E. Group control with no leader; F. Group controls and plans (if more than one pattern emerged, include symbol for each in order of occurrence).

How long after meeting was this form completed? __________ Date ______

Appendix B

The Social Group Work Method in Social Work Education *

Marjorie Murphy

CHAPTER IV. Learning Experiences and Curriculum Organization, pp. 50-52

Program Media and Program Skills

There was substantial agreement on the necessity for the social worker using the group work method to know (1) resources for program activities and (2) criteria for selection and assessment of program media in a service group. A degree of skill in use of some program media was often, but not always, thought a necessary accompaniment to learning resources and criteria. There was great disagreement about whether skills in use of media are properly curriculum objectives for which the schools should take responsibility or whether they are rather derived from the "life-learning" experience of the school applicant; whether this learning is better acquired in practice and should therefore be part of in-service training; whether students who are sufficiently stimulated by their understanding of people and of social work goals and methods may be expected to find the resources and develop the skills they need on their own initiative; whether, if content about program media is an appropriate part of curriculum it should be offered in class or field instruction or both. There is uncertainty about whether such content can meet standards for graduate school course or laboratory credit. There were expressions of sensitivity (from faculty, agency staff and students) about emphasis on "activities" in social group work method. In contrast, use of activities as means of nonverbal communication, and of deepening the worker's knowledge about the activity interests and resources of users of service, were emphasized as behaviors desired for all social workers rather than for

* Extract from Volume XI, A Project Report of the Curriculum Study, Werner W. Boehm, Director and Coordinator, 1959 Council on Social Work Education. From Part II, Findings.

group workers alone. Some educators stressed necessity for students to develop attitudes of respect for program media and sufficient ability in using them to encourage group members' initiative, creativity and ability and provide them with opportunities commensurate with their own potential. (As one educator phrased it, "Giving people a pat on the back and telling them anything goes because they are being expressive is selling them down the river.")

The learning experiences offered by the schools consulted ran a gamut from dependence on incidental learning in class and field (without specified inclusion of content on program media) to one instance of a course in program methods continued through four semesters concomitantly with the group work methods course. In some cases, program media were dealt with directly in the group work methods course in order to teach use of media as an integral part of method. In other cases a program media and skills laboratory was thought to require time and structure outside of the methods course. In one school a course on social aspects of children's behavior had been substituted for a previous program laboratory course and was required of all first year students whether their major interest was in group work or casework. The course, planned to parallel the human growth and behavior course, drew on anthropological and social material illustrated with games, arts, crafts, uses of play within different age groups and cultural settings. Assessment of the meaning of expressive activity and use of skills in social work for maintenance of healthy personality and enhancement of social functioning were emphasized. Observation of school age and pre-school children were among learning experiences used. The course attempted to give a "feel for skills" but counted on students' field experience for their own practice of them.

The view that schools have responsibility to teach a specific theoretical approach to use of program media in group work method was rather consistent. Some persons suggested that this is as far as class teaching should go. Others consider an actual trying out and evaluation of program media essential to learning theoretical understanding of them. Some educators thought field instruction in the agency is the effective setting for this learning to take place and were troubled that the schools have not yet worked this out in their curriculum planning nor made other than hazy assignment to field teaching. Agency personnel observed differences in students' individual needs for learning. For students who have had considerable experience as camp counselors, or in work with youth agencies which have rich program resources, comparatively brief classroom treatment in the basic methods course is adequate. For students without experience in work with groups prior to social work school, more concrete learning experiences, including class work, are needed.

One suggestion was made that the school fulfill its responsibility not through formal curriculum but by setting up a yearly, inclusive community workshop, in cooperation with agencies, to be attended by agency personnel in need of this content, as well as by students. The idea was envisioned as a means of securing the best teaching and conceptual content available, and providing students with an enriched learning opportunity in a practical situation with professional workers, with economy of time investment, and without the administrative problems of credit or non-credit courses in the school.

It is the author's impression that schools' experience with this content has been more uneven and has been more handicapped by inadequate instructional facilities than in other parts of group work curriculum. Curiously, only one instance was encountered of the social work school drawing upon other resources of the university campus for curriculum and instruction in program media and skills. Whether this is prevalent elsewhere was not revealed by school catalogues perused. In the case observed, resources of the educational psychology department, art department, education and health departments were drawn on for direct contributions and for consultation with social work faculty.

CHAPTER V. Educational Objectives of the Social Group Work Curriculum, pp. 67 and 68

XIV. Understanding and appreciation of and ability to participate with a range of communications skills used in providing group work services:

Ability to perform responsibly, with appreciation for respective roles of other participants, in interviews and in discussions with groups of various sizes and kinds. Familiarity with, appreciation of and ability to observe, interpret, appropriately stimulate and respond to non-verbal communication. Awareness of the potential of role-playing and at least a minimum degree of skill in its use.

XVI. Familiarity with resources for program media and understanding of criteria for selection of media and evaluation of program experience:

Awareness of the significance to persons of their own performance

—in various kinds of activities

—in making use of media and resources available to them

—in contribution of creative activities to personal development as well as to group participation at different stages of maturation.

XVII. Awareness, appreciation and ability to observe, facilitate and interpret communication through program activities:

Not only ability to help group members involve themselves, but to understand what children, teen-agers and adults are saying through their participation, their interests and their accomplishments and failures to accomplish.

Appendix C

Case Study Source List

Record material is drawn from work in the following agencies:

B'nai B'rith Youth Organization, Philadelphia Region
Children's Aid Society of Pennsylvania, Philadelphia
Delaware Valley Settlement Alliance, School Settlement Program, Philadelpiha
Department of Public Welfare, Public Assistance Division, Baltimore
Ferris School for Boys, Wilmington, Delaware
Florence Crittenton Service, Inc., Philadelphia
Friends Neighborhood Guild, Philadelphia
Horizon House, Philadelphia
Lighthouse, Philadelphia
Lutheran Social Mission Society, Lutheran Settlement, Philadelphia
Magee Memorial Hospital, Philadelphia
Nationalities Service Center, Philadelphia
Neighborhood Center, Philadelphia *
New York City Mission Society, Camp Sharparoon
Peoples Settlement Association, Wilmington, Delaware
Philadelphia Housing Authority
Philadelphia Department of Public Welfare, Riverview Home for the Aged
University Settlements, Philadelphia
Wharton Center, Philadelphia
YM & YWHA, Mt. Vernon, New York
YM & YWHA, Philadelphia *
York House (Home for the Jewish Aged), Philadelphia

* Now known as Jewish Y's and Centers of Greater Philadelphia

A Limited Bibliography of Program Resources

All too often the group worker becomes overwhelmed with the huge amount of program resources he encounters in the library; he assumes he must become familiar with the contents of all the possibilities. Sometimes this very vastness serves to steer him away from program content altogether. The suggestion of this writer is for the group worker to become thoroughly familiar with *one* program resource in each medium—any book will do! Then the worker's primary attention can be saved for where it belongs, for focus on *the use* of the concrete ideas he has. In this spirit we list below several books for each of several categories of activities that groups like to do. These are not by any means put forth as the best available—there is no best one—but are suggestive of what would be required to form a good minimum working knowledge of program content.

Art

D'Amico, Victor. *Art for the Family*. New York: Doubleday, 1954.

———. *Creative Teaching in Art*. Scranton, Pa.: International Textbook Co., 1942.

Ellender, Raphael. *Basic Drawing*. Garden City: Doubleday, 1964.

Lowenfeld, Viktor. *Creative and Mental Growth: A Textbook on Art Education*. New York: The MacMillan Co., 1949.

Mayer, Ralph. *The Artist's Handbook of Materials and Techniques*. New York: The Viking Press, 1957.

Mendelorwitz, Daniel M. *Children Are Artists*. Stanford: Stanford Univ. Press, 1963.

Williams, Hiram. *Notes for a Young Painter*. Englewood Cliffs, N.J.: Prentice-Hall, 1963.

Crafts

Bale, R. O. *Creative Nature Crafts*. Minneapolis: Burgess Publ. Co., 1959.

Exploring the Hand Arts. New York: Girls Scouts, 1955.

Frankel, L. *Creating From Scrap*. New York: Sterling, 1962.

Green, A. S. *Arts and Crafts for Primary Grade Children*. Minneapolis: T. S. Denison, 1962.

Green, M. C. *Gifts, Gadgets and Glamour: Craft Projects for Gift-giving*. Milwaukee: Bruce Publ. Co., 1961.

Hunt, W. Ben. *The Golden Book of Indian Crafts and Lore*. New York: Simon and Schuster, 1954.

Ickis, Marguerite, and Esh, Reba S. *The Book of Arts and Crafts*. New York: Association Press, 1954.

Lewis, Griselda. *Handbook of Crafts*. Newton, Mass.: C. T. Branford, 1960.

Newkirk and Zutter. *Crafts for Everyone*. Princeton: Van Nostrand, 1950.

Winter, Garry. *Crafts and Hobbies*. New York: Arco Publishing Co., 1962.

Camping and Outdoors

Chapman, Margaret; Gaudette, Marie; and Hammett, Catherine. *Outdoor Activities for In-Town Groups*. New York: Girl Scouts.

Hammett, Catherine T. *Your Own Book of Campcraft*. New York: Pocket Book, Inc., 1958.

———, and Horrocks, C. M. *Creative Crafts for Campers*. New York: Association Press, 1957.

Hammett, Catherine T., and Musselman, Virginia. *The Camp Program Book*. New York: Association Press, 1951.

Jaeger, Ellsworth. *Council Fires*. New York: The MacMillan Co., 1949.

Jobe, Mabel L. *The Handbook of Day-Camping*. New York: Association Press, 1949.

Musselman, Virginia. *The Day Camp Program Book: An Activity Manual for Counselors*. New York: Association Press, 1963.

Rubin, Robert. *The Book of Camping*. New York: Association Press, 1949.

Information on public and private camping grounds can usually be obtained by writing to the Department of Conservation of any state capital.

Cooking

Bates, Joseph D., Jr. *The Outdoor Cook's Bible.* New York: Doubleday, 1964.

Berolzheimer, Ruth. *The Candy Book.* Chicago: Consolidated Book Publishers, 1965.

Betty Crocker's New Picture Cook Book. New York: McGraw-Hill, 1961.

Coping with Camp Cooking. Editors, Camping Guide Magazine.

McDonald, Barbara G. *Cooking Fun.* New York: Walck, 1960.

Perkins, Wilma L. *The Fanny Farmer Junior Cookbook.* Boston: Little, Brown, 1957.

Rombauer, Irma S., and Becker, Marion R. *Joy of Cooking.* New York: Bobbs-Merrill Co., 1946.

Dancing

Champion, Marge. *Let's Dance with Marge and Gower.* New York: Grosset and Dunlap, 1954.

Durlacher, Edward. *Honor Your Partner.* New York: Devin-Adair, 1949.

Herman, Michael. *Folk Dances for All.* New York: Barnes and Noble.

Kirkell, Miriam. *Partners All, Places All.* New York: Dutton, 1951.

Mettler, Barbara. *Materials of Dance as a Creative Art Activity.* Boston: Mettler Studios, 1960.

Murray, Arthur. *How to Become a Good Dancer.* New York: Simon & Schuster, 1964.

Shaw, Lloyd. *Cowboy Dances.* Caldwell, Idaho: Caxton Publications, 1940.

Tobitt, Janet E. *Promenade All.* New York: Girl Scouts, 1947.

White, Betty. *Teenage Dance Book.* New York: David McKay, 1958.

Dramatics

Burger, Isabel. *Creative Play Acting,* 2nd ed. New York: The Ronald Press, 1966.

Carlson, Bernice. *Act It Out.* New York: Abingdon Press, 1956.

Durland, Francis Caldwell. *Creative Dramatics for Children: A Practical Manual for Teachers and Leaders.* Yellow Springs, Ohio: Antioch Press, 1952.

Eisenberg, Helen and Larry. *Fun with Skits, Stunts, and Stories.* New York: Association Press, 1955.

Siks, Geraldine Brain. *Creative Dramatics and Art for Children.* New York: Harper, 1958.

Tobitt, Janet E., and White, Alice. *Dramatized Ballads.* New York: Girl Scouts, 1937.

Walker, Pamela P. *Seven Steps to Creative Children's Dramatics.* New York: Hill and Wang, 1957.

Ward, Winifred L. *Drama with and for Children.* Washington: U.S. Dept. of Health, Education and Welfare, Office of Education, 1960.

——. *Playmaking with Children from Kindergarten to Junior High School.* New York: D. Appleton, 1947.

Games and Sports

Anderson, Doris. *Encyclopedia of Games.* Grand Rapids, Michigan: Zonervan Publ. House, 1955.

Empleton, Bernard E.; Fleming, Prudence; and Yates, Leon. *Water Fun for Everyone.* New York: Association Press, 1965.

Fray, Richard L.; Morehead, Albert H.; and Mott-Smith, Geoffrey. *The Complete New Hoyle,* the official rules of all popular games of skill and chance, rev. ed. Garden City, N. Y.: Garden City Books, 1956.

Geri, Frank H. *Games, Rhythms, and Stunts for Children,* Upper Elementary Grades. Englewood Cliffs, N. J.: Prentice-Hall, 1957.

Harbin, E. O. *Games of Many Nations.* New York: Abingdon Press, 1954.

Hunt, Sarah Ethridge. *Games and Sports the World Around.* New York: The Ronald Press, 1964.

Ilg, Frances L.; Ames, Louise B.; Goodenough, Evelyn W.; and Andressen, Irene. *The Gesell Institute Party Book.* Parties for different ages from 3 to 15. New York: Harper & Brothers, 1959.

Johnson, June. *The Outdoor-Indoor Fun Book,* for children 6 to 12. New York: Harper & Brothers, 1961.

Journal of Health, Physical Education, and Recreation. *How We Do It Fun Book.* Selected games. Washington, D.C.: American Association for Health, Physical Education, and Recreation, 1964.

Kraus, Richard. *The Family Book of Games.* New York: McGraw-Hill, 1960.

——. *Recreation Leader s Handbook.* New York: McGraw-Hill, 1955.

Latchaw, Marjorie A. *Pocket Guide of Games and Rhythm.* Englewood Cliffs, N. J.: Prentice-Hall, 1956.

Menke, Frank Grant. *The Encyclopedia of Sports,* 3rd rev. ed. New York: Barnes, 1963.

Pick, John B. *The Phoenix Dictionary of Games,* "How to Play 458 Games." New York: Phoenix House, 1952.

Thomsen, Robert. *Games Anyone?* Adult games. New York: Doubleday, 1964.

U.S. Children's Bureau *Hand Book for Recreation Leaders.* Washington: U.S. Gov't. Printing Office, Publ. #231, 1959.

Hobbies and Puzzles

Bricker, W. P. *The Complete Book of Collecting Hobbies.* New York: Sheridan, 1951.
Malac, Margaret. *Hobbies: the Creative Use of Leisure.* New York: Harper, 1948.
Newgold, Bill. *Guide to Modern Hobbies, Art and Crafts.* New York: McKay, 1960.
Stiere, Emanuele. *The Book of Indoor Hobbies.* New York: McGraw-Hill, 1949.
Wagner, Glen A. *Hobbycraft for Everybody.* New York: Dodd, Mead, 1954.

Music

Ellison, Alfred. *Music with Children.* New York: McGraw-Hill, 1959.
Krone, Beatrice and Max. *Music Participation in the Secondary School.* Chicago: Neil A. Kjos Music Co., 1952.
Landreck, Beatrice. *Children and Music, an Informal Guide for Parents and Teachers.* 1952.
Music Makers. New York: Camp Fire Girls Inc., 1956.
Reever, Grace, and Kurtz, M. V. *Music Fun, A Text-Activity Book.* 1940-46.
Stinson, Ethelny L. *How to Teach Children Music.* New York: Harper, 1941.

Nature and Science

Candy, Robert. *Nature Notebook.* Boston: Houghton Mifflin, 1953.
Conservation. New York: Camp Fire Girls, Inc.
Enjoying Nature. Washington: National Recreation and Park Assn.
Frontiers, Fun with Science for Camp Fire Girls. New York: Camp Fire Girls, Inc., 1949.
Gaudette, Marie. *Leader's Nature Guide.* New York: Girl Scouts, 1942.
Goodrich, Warren. *Science Through Recreation.* Girl Scouts.
Hillcourt, William. *Field Book of Nature Activities and Conservation.* New York: Putman, 1961.
Hubler, Clark. *Working with Children in Science.* Cambridge, Mass.: The Riverside Press, 1957.
Nature Program Guide. 1130 Fifth Ave., N. Y.: National Audubon Society.

Peterson, Roger Tory. *How to Know the Birds.* New York: Girl Scouts, 1949.
Price, Betty. *Adventuring in Nature.* New York: Association Press.
Saunders, John R. *Golden Book of Nature Crafts: Hobbies and Activities for Boys and Girls.* New York: Simon and Schuster.
Swezey, Kenneth W. *Science Magic.* New York: McGraw-Hill, 1952.

Puppets

Arnott, Peter Douglas. *Plays Without People,* puppetry and serious drama. Bloomington: Indiana University Press, 1964.
Baird, Bil. *The Art of the Puppet.* New York: Macmillan, 1965.
Batchelder, Marjorie H., and Comer, Virginia Lee. *Puppets and Plays; a creative approach.* New York: Harper, 1956.
Galdstone, Olive. *Plays with Puppets.* New York: Play Schools Association, 1965.
Hooper, C. H. *Puppet Making: Through the Grades.* Worcester, Mass.: Davis Publications, 1966.

Songs

Boni, Margaret, and Lloyd, Norman. *Fireside Book of Folk Songs.* New York: Simon and Schuster, 1947.
Botsford, Florence. *The Universal Folk Songster.* New York: G. Schirmer, 1937.
Eisenberg, Helen. *How to Lead Group Singing.* New York: Association Press, 1955.
Girl Scouts. *Sing Together.* New York: Girl Scouts, 1949.
Hoffelt, Robert O. *How to Lead Informal Singing.* New York: Abingdon Press, 1963.
Kolb, Sylvia and John. *A Treasury of Folk Songs.* New York: Bantom Books, 1957.
Seeger, Pete. *American Favorite Ballads.* New York: Oak Publications, 1961.
Seeger, Ruth. *American Folk Songs for Children.* New York: Doubleday, 1948.
Zansig, Augustus. *Singing America.* Boston: C. C. Birchard, 1940.

Trips

Akberg, Henry G., ed. *The American Guide—A Source Book and Complete Travel Guide for the United States.* New York: Hastings House, 1949.

Bossemeyre, James L. *Travel U.S.A. Handbook*. Washington: National Association of Travel Organizations, 1965.

Norman, Jane and Theodore. *Wonderful Places to Take Children*, 3 vols. Manhasset, N. Y.: Channel Press, 1962.

Witkovsky and Schrag. *So You're Gonna Ride a Bus*. National Jewish Welfare Board, 145 E. 32nd St., New York.

Miscellaneous

Canter, Irving. *Journalism in the Jewish Center*. National Jewish Welfare Board, 145 E. 32nd St., New York.

Educational Media Index, 1964. Source for films, recordings, television programs in various fields.

Educator's Guide to Free Tapes, Scripts, and Transcriptions, compiled and edited by Walter A. Wittich and Gertie Hanson Halsted, Randolph, Wisc. Revised annually.

For additional listings of specific content resources the reader is referred to the publications lists of such national organizations as Girl Scouts, Young Women's Christian Association, National Jewish Welfare Board, National Federation of Settlements and Neighborhood Centers, National Recreation Association, and Playschools Association.

Index*

* All numbers refer to pages except those in boldface type, which refer to the case studies in Chapter 9 (pages 174–258).